English Grammar Workbook

3rd Edition with Online Practice

by Geraldine Woods
Grammarian

A Wiley Brand

English Grammar Workbook For Dummies®, 3rd Edition with Online Practice

Published by: **John Wiley & Sons, Inc.**, 111 River Street, Hoboken, NJ 07030-5774, www.wiley.com

Copyright © 2018 by John Wiley & Sons, Inc., Hoboken, New Jersey

Published simultaneously in Canada

For general information on our other products and services, please contact our Customer Care Department within the U.S. at 877-762-2974, outside the U.S. at 317-572-3993, or fax 317-572-4002. For technical support, please visit https://hub.wiley.com/community/support/dummies.

Wiley publishes in a variety of print and electronic formats and by print-on-demand. Some material included with standard print versions of this book may not be included in e-books or in print-on-demand. If this book refers to media such as a CD or DVD that is not included in the version you purchased, you may download this material at http://booksupport.wiley.com. For more information about Wiley products, visit www.wiley.com.

Library of Congress Control Number: 2018932103

ISBN 978-1-119-45539-4 (pbk); ISBN 978-1-119-45543-1 (ebk); ISBN 978-1-119-45541-7 (ebk)

Manufactured in the United States of America

10 9 8 7 6 5 4 3 2 1

Contents at a Glance

Table of Contents

Introduction

Does this resemble the inside of your head when you're preparing to talk with an Authority Figure (teacher, boss, mother-in-law, parole officer, whatever)?

> *Glad to have met . . . to be meeting . . . to . . .* Uh oh. Maybe just *Hi! How's it going?* Nope. Too friendly. New direction: *You asked to see whoever. . . um . . . whomever wrote . . . had written . . . the report.*

If you answered yes, you're in the right place. *English Grammar Workbook For Dummies,* 3rd Edition, helps you navigate the sea of grammar without wrecking your grades, your career, or your mind. I mention grades and career because the ability to speak and write according to the rules of Standard English gives you an advantage in school and in the working world. Even if you feel relatively comfortable in everyday situations, you still may benefit from practicing some of the trickier grammar points, especially if you're facing high-stakes exams such as the SAT, ACT, or AP. Some of these tortures (sorry, I mean *tests*) focus entirely on English skills, and some require you to use those skills to answer questions on other subjects. *English Grammar Workbook For Dummies,* 3rd Edition, helps you prepare for both situations.

This book presents the latest guidelines for Standard English. Yes, latest. When an English teacher is pounding them into your head, the rules of Standard English usage seem set in stone. But language isn't static. It moves along just as people do — sometimes quickly and sometimes at the speed of a tired snail. To keep you sharp in every 21st-century situation, *English Grammar Workbook For Dummies,* 3rd Edition, presents information and then practice with the current, commonly accepted language of texts, tweets, emails, and presentation slides, as well as what's proper in more traditional forms of writing.

English Grammar Workbook For Dummies, 3rd Edition, doesn't concentrate on the sort of grammar exercise in which you circle all the nouns and draw little triangles around prepositions. You'll find identification problems in this book, but only a few. A closely guarded English-teacher secret is that you don't need to know too much terminology to master grammar. Instead, most of the practice problems concentrate on how to express meaning in real-life speech and writing.

Each chapter begins with a quick explanation of what's acceptable — and what's not — in Standard English. Next, I provide an example and then hit you with a bunch of questions. After completing the exercises, you can check your answers at the end of the chapter. I also tell you why a particular choice is correct to help you make the right decision the next time a similar issue pops up. Sprinkled liberally throughout the book and online are comprehensive exercises, so you can apply your knowledge to the material in an entire chapter. In the appendix, you find editing exercises that rely on skills you've honed throughout the entire book. The callout numbers pointing to the corrections in the answer key for these exercises correspond with the numbered explanations in the text.

Foolish Assumptions

In writing the *English Grammar Workbook For Dummies*, 3rd Edition, I assume that you . . .

>> know some English but want to improve your skills

>> aspire to at least one of these: a better job, higher grades, and improved scores on standardized tests

>> hope to become more comfortable if you're an English-language learner

>> wish to communicate clearly and effectively

>> prefer to follow the conventions of Standard English or to ignore them with a specific purpose in mind

>> want to write within tight word limits (in tweets or texts, for example) while still expressing exactly what you mean

>> seek information on how to adjust the level of formality so that you are confident and appropriate in every context

The most important assumption I've made is that you have a busy life. Who doesn't? With this fact in mind, I've tried to keep the explanations in this book clear, simple, and short. For more complete explanations, pick up a copy of the companion book, *English Grammar For Dummies*, 3rd Edition, or, if you need to review the fundamentals, *Basic English Grammar For Dummies*, written by yours truly and published by Wiley. In those books, I go into much more detail and provide more examples, accompanied by step-by-step explanations.

Icons Used in This Book

Icons are the cute little drawings that attract your gaze and alert you to key points, pitfalls, and other helpful things. In *English Grammar Workbook For Dummies*, 3rd Edition, you find these four:

TIP

I live in New York City, and I often see tourists staggering around, desperate for a resident to show them the ropes. The Tip icon is the equivalent of a resident whispering in your ear. Psst! Want the inside story that will make your life easier? Here it is!

WARNING

When you're about to walk through a field riddled with land mines, it's nice to have a map. The Warning icon tells you where the traps are so you can avoid them.

EXAMPLE

The Example icon alerts you to (surprise!) an example and a set of exercises so you can practice what I just finished preaching.

TEST ALERT

If you're getting ready to sweat through a standardized test, pay extra attention to this icon, which identifies frequent fliers on those exams. Not a student? No worries. You can still pick up valuable information when you see this icon.

Beyond the Book

As they say on late-night television commercials, "Wait! There's more!" Look online at www.dummies.com to find a cheat sheet for *English Grammar Workbook For Dummies*, 3rd Edition, where you can zero in quickly on crucial information. Competitive? You can also test yourself with online quizzes oriented to a single chapter or to a heftier amount of information.

To gain access to the online practice, all you have to do is register. Just follow these simple steps:

1. **Find your PIN access code:**

   - **Print-book users:** If you purchased a print copy of this book, turn to the inside front cover of the book to find your access code.

   - **E-book users:** If you purchased this book as an e-book, you can get your access code by registering your e-book at www.dummies.com/go/getaccess. Go to this website, find your book and click it, and answer the security questions to verify your purchase. You'll receive an email with your access code.

2. **Go to** Dummies.com **and click** *Activate Now.*

3. **Find your product (***English Grammar Workbook For Dummies***, 3rd Edition) and then follow the on-screen prompts to activate your PIN.**

Now you're ready to go! You can come back to the program as often as you want. Simply log in with the username and password you created during your initial login. No need to enter the access code a second time.

Where to Go from Here

To the refrigerator for a snack. Nope. Just kidding. Now that you know what's where, turn to the section that best meets your needs. If you're not sure what would benefit you most, take a moment to think about the aspects of writing or speaking that make you pause for a lengthy head scratch. Do you have trouble picking the appropriate verb tense? Is finding the right word a snap but placing a comma cause for concern?

After you've done a little grammatical reconnaissance, select the sections of this book that meet your needs. Use the table of contents and the index to find more detail about what's where. If you aren't sure whether a particular topic is a problem, no problem! Try a couple of sentences and check your answers, or whip through an online quiz. If everything comes out okay and you understand the answers, move on. If you stub your toe, go back and do a few more questions in the book or from the online quiz until the grammar rule becomes clear. Or, if you like to start with an overview, hit the exercises in the appendix first. Then zero in on the sections that address the errors you made in those exercises.

1

Building a Firm Foundation: Grammar Basics

Adapt language to suit your situation, audience, and purpose.

Identify the basic elements of a sentence: the subject, verb, and complement.

Sort verbs into "action" and "linking" categories.

Examine the proper format for statements, commands, questions, and negative remarks.

Form noun plurals properly.

Ensure that your sentences are complete.

Chapter 1

Tailoring Language to Suit Your Audience and Purpose

When it comes to language, one size does *not* fit all. The way you tell an Authority Figure (teacher, boss, emperor, whatever) about an app you invented differs from the way you explain your brainchild to a friend. If you're like most people, you probably switch levels of formality automatically, dozens of times a day. But sometimes you may find yourself wondering how to express yourself, especially in emails, texts, and tweets. If you hit the wrong note, your message may not receive the reaction you'd hoped for. Very few investors react positively to someone who writes, "Yo, want in on this?" Nor will you find it easy to get a date if you ask, "Would you consider dining with me at an informal Italian restaurant that offers relatively good pizza?" In this chapter you practice identifying levels of formality and examine situations in which each is appropriate.

Climbing the Ladder of Language Formality

Proper English is important. The only problem with that statement is the definition of "proper." Language has many levels of formality, all of which are "proper" at times and completely unsuitable at others. Many gradations of formality exist, but to make things easier, I divide English into three large categories: what I call "friendspeak" (the most casual), "conversational" (one step up), and "formal" (the equivalent of wearing your best business attire). Take a look at these examples:

> c u in 10 (friendspeak)

> There in ten minutes. (conversational)

> I will arrive in ten minutes. (formal)

All three statements say the same thing in very different ways. Here's the deal:

>> **Friendspeak** breaks some rules of formal English on purpose, to show that people are comfortable with each other. Friendspeak shortens or drops words and often includes slang and references that only close friends understand. (That's why I call it "*friend*speak.") No one has to teach you this level of English. You learn it from your pals, or you create it yourself and teach it to your buddies.

>> **Conversational English** sounds relaxed, but not too relaxed. It's the language equivalent of jeans and a T-shirt. Conversational English is filled with contractions (*I'm* instead of *I am, would've* instead of *would have,* and so forth). Not many abbreviations appear in conversational English, but you may confidently include those that are well established and widely understood (*etc., a.m., p.m.,* and the like). You may also see acronyms, which pluck the first letter from each word of a name (*NATO* for the *North Atlantic Treaty Organization* or *AIDS* for *Acquired Immune Deficiency Syndrome,* for example). Conversational English may drop some words and break a few rules. The example sentence for conversational English at the beginning of this section, for instance, has no subject or verb, a giant no-no in formal writing but perfectly acceptable at this level of language.

>> Formal **English** is the pickiest location in Grammarland. When you speak or write in formal English, you follow every rule (including some you never heard of), avoid slang and abbreviations, and trot out your best vocabulary.

Think about your audience when you're selecting friendspeak, conversational English, or formal English. What impression are you trying to give? Let your goals guide you. Also consider the situation. At work you may rely on conversational English when you run into your boss at the coffee machine, but not when you're submitting a quarterly report. At school, choosing conversational English is okay for a teacher-student chat in the cafeteria, but not for homework. More on situation and language appears in the next section, "Matching Message to Situation."

Can you identify levels of formality? Before you hit the questions, check out this example:

EXAMPLE

Q. Place these expressions in order of formality, from the most formal to the least. Note: Two expressions may tie. For example, your answer may be A, B and C — in which case expression A is the most formal and expressions B and C are on the same, more casual level.

A. sketchy block

B. That is a dangerous neighborhood.

C. Where gangs rule.

A. B, C, A. Expression B is the most formal because it follows all the conventions of English. Every word is in the dictionary, and the sentence is complete. (See Chapter 3 for more practice with complete sentences.) Expression C, on the other hand, is an incomplete sentence and is therefore less formal. Also, in Expression C the verb *rule* has an unusual meaning. Your readers or listeners probably understand that gangs aren't official authorities but instead wield a lot of unofficial power. The statement is more conversational than formal. Expression A employs slang (*sketchy* means "slightly dangerous"), so it's closer to friendspeak than to formal English.

A. regarding your proposal

B. in reference to your proposal

C. about that idea

A. like, earlier

B. heretofore

C. until now

A. Please do not abbreviate.

B. abbreevs not ok

C. I prefer that you write the entire word when you text me.

A. Awkward!!!!

B. Your behavior disturbs me.

C. Calm down, guys!

5

   A. Are you into electronic dance music?

   B. edm 2nite?

   C. Tonight that club features electronic dance music. Would you care to go?

6

   A. M left J's FOMO

   B. Mike left John's house when he got a text from Fran about her party.

   C. M = gone FOMO F's party

7

   A. #newbaby #thanxmom #notkillingmewhenIcriedallnight

   B. Dead tired. Baby cried all night. Feeling grateful to my mom.

   C. Now that I'm caring for my new baby, I am grateful to my mother for tolerating me when I was an infant.

8

   A. In retrospect, jumping into the pool blindfolded was foolish.

   B. broken ankle but YOLO

   C. No water in the pool. Who knew? Broken ankle!

9

   A. 2G2BT

   B. 4real?

   C. u sure?

10

   A. ATM card not working.

   B. My bank card was rejected.

   C. ATM?!?!?

Matching Message to Situation

When you're listening or reading, you probably note the difference between formal and informal language constantly — maybe unconsciously. Knowing levels of language, however, isn't enough. You also need to decide what level of formality to employ when you're speaking and writing. Before you choose, consider these factors:

>> **Your audience.** If your message is going to a person with more power or higher status than you (an employee writing to a boss or a student to a teacher, for example), you should probably be more formal. If you're speaking or writing to someone with less power or lower status than you, conversational English is fine. In a higher-to-lower situation, however, the person with more authority may wish to employ formal English in order to serve as a role model or to establish a professional atmosphere. When you're dealing with peers, conversational English is a good bet. Only your closest friends rate — and understand — friendspeak.

>> **The situation.** At the company picnic or in the cafeteria, most people opt for less formal speech. Similarly, at get-togethers with family and friends, formal language may sound stiff and unfriendly. When you're in an official meeting with a client or teacher, however, formal English is safer.

>> **The format.** When you're speaking you have more leeway than when you're writing. Why? Unless you're reading prepared remarks, you probably can't produce perfect sentences. Not many people can! The writing in texts, tweets, and instant messages tends to be in conversational English or, with your buddies, in friendspeak. Exceptions occur, though. A text to a client should be more formal than one to a friend, and journalists or officials often tweet in formal English. Email can go either way. Because it's fast, the dropped or shortened forms of conversational English are generally acceptable, but if you think the reader expects you to honor tradition (the written equivalent of a curtsy or a hat-tip), go for formal English. Always employ formal English for business letters, school reports, and similar paper-based communication.

Listen to those around you or read others' work that appears in the same context you're navigating. Unless you want to stand out, aim for the same level of formality you hear or see.

Think about the audience, situation, and format. In the following example, decide whether the writing or speech is appropriate or inappropriate.

EXAMPLE

Q. Text from a department head to the CEO requesting a salary increase:

greenlight $20K or I walk

A. **Inappropriate.** Think about the power ladder here. The CEO is on the top rung, and the department head somewhere farther down. Even though texts tend to be informal, this one is about money. When you ask for money, be polite! To be polite in Grammarland is to use formal, correct language. The department head should have written something like "If you cannot raise my salary by $20,000, I will seek employment elsewhere."

11. Email from student to professor about the assigned reading of Shakespeare's *Hamlet*:

Best. Play. Ever.

12. Chat between friends:

There's this prince, he's named Hamlet. He's freaking out about his mother's marriage to his uncle only a couple of months after Hamlet's father died.

13 Portion of an essay about the play, written as a homework assignment:

The Queen's new husband is not a sympathetic character. Dude, he's a murderer!

14 Cover letter from a job applicant to a potential employer, a tech start-up:

Attached please find my resume, pursuant to your advertisement of July 15th.

15 Instant messages between classmates, discussing their grades:

A+!!!

sick

ttyl

ok bfn

16 Portion of a letter to the editor of the town paper from a citizen:

The lack of a stoplight on that corner has led to several car crashes. The city council is right to think about the expense of installing one, but what about the cost of human life and suffering?

17 Comment on social media post about a tax to finance improved traffic flow:

You morons should stop stealing our money. We coulda bought five stoplights made outta gold for the amount of money you spent on office furniture. To conclude, shut up!

18 Email to the mother of a potential tutoring client:

I have an advanced degree in mathematics and many years of experience teaching algebra. My rates are on a par with those of other tutors in the area. Also, I get along well with kids!

19 Tweet from the president to the members of the local garden association:

Meeting tonight at 8 p.m. #springplanting

20 Speech by the class president to fellow students at graduation:

We made it! We're out of this place! But Roger and May are gonna totally ship anyway!

Answers to "Tailoring Language to Suit Your Audience and Purpose"

In this section you find all the answers you're looking for. Well, maybe not the answers to "What is the meaning of life?" or "Why is the sky blue?" but definitely the right responses to the questions in this chapter.

(1) **A and B, C.** Both A and B are formal English expressions. Each employs businesslike vocabulary (*regarding, proposal,* and *in reference to*). Expression C takes the formality level down a notch, substituting *idea* for *proposal* and *about* for *regarding* and *in reference to.*

(2) **B, C, A.** Expression B sounds fancy, and it is. You find *heretofore* in legal documents and in many other types of formal English writing. (It means "before this time," by the way.) Expression C is something you probably hear and say all the time. It's conversational. Expression A might be conversational without *like,* but adding that little word puts this one in the friendspeak category.

(3) **C, A, B.** Expression C hits the top of the formal meter, and B is at the bottom. (You probably already guessed that *abreevs* isn't a real word. Also, B breaks its own rule by including *ok* instead of *okay.*) In between expressions C and B is A, which is grammatically correct without being stuffy.

(4) **B, C, A.** Expression B is a complete sentence, and so is C. But *guys* isn't formal, so C slips into conversational English. Expression A pops up in friendspeak, whenever someone does something impolite or embarrassing. The four exclamation points (three too many in standard, formal English) also situate this one in friendspeak.

(5) **C, A, B.** Expression C features two complete sentences, and every word is in the dictionary. Expression A is also a complete sentence, but asking if someone is *into* this type of music (or anything else) brings slang to the sentence. Slang is never formal. Expression B has an abbreviation (*edm* = electronic dance music) and a "word" (*2nite,* or "tonight") that is okay only when you're texting, and sometimes not even then.

(6) **B, A and C.** Both expressions A and C are written in friendspeak. They use abbreviations and an acronym: *M* and *J's* stand for names — probably *Mike* and *John's* — and *FOMO,* which is "fear of missing out." This usage shows up only in the least formal situations, usually texts between friends. Expression B is a full sentence with all the words written correctly and completely.

(7) **C, B, A.** Expression C explains the speaker's situation in clear, Standard English. Expression B has half-sentences (probably because the speaker is sleep-deprived), so it's less formal, in the category of conversational English. Expression A, with its hashtags (the # sign) is the sort of communication only friends will appreciate. It's written in friendspeak.

(8) **A, C, B.** Expression A is a complete sentence and employs some sophisticated vocabulary (*retrospect*). It's formal English. Expression C has incomplete sentences (*No water in the pool* and *broken ankle*). The one complete sentence is a humorous, short comment (*Who knew?*). For these reasons, C stands for conversational English here. Expression B is friendspeak; *YOLO* is an acronym for "you only live once."

(9) **A and B and C.** Did I catch you here? All three of these texts are in friendspeak. Expression A expresses doubt with an abbreviation for "too good to be true." Expression B asks if something is "for real." Expression C also asks for confirmation, saying, "Are you sure?"

(10) **B, A, C.** Expression B is a complete, correct sentence, so it's formal English. Expression A drops a couple of words, so it's more conversational. Expression C makes sense only if you know that the person who texted this stops for cash often and freaks out when the card doesn't work. It's friendspeak (and maybe a request for a loan!).

(11) **Inappropriate.** Professors and teachers aren't your friends. They're in charge of your education. English teachers in particular — even the ones who show up in class wearing jeans and sneakers — value language. True, the message may appeal, because English teachers tend to think that everything they assign is worthy material. However, the message may fail (and the student also) if the teacher expects formal language.

(12) **Appropriate.** This chat is a good example of conversational English that's perfectly fine. The friends are conversing — your first clue. They break a few rules, such as illegally stringing together two complete sentences: *There's this prince, he's named Hamlet.*

(13) **Inappropriate.** Homework assignments have no room in them for *Dude*, unless you're writing fiction and a character says that word. The first sentence establishes a formal tone; the second sentence should match, not lower, the level of formality.

(14) **Inappropriate.** Surprised? Job applicants should be formal, but they should also avoid outdated expressions and overly stuffy language, especially for a tech start-up where innovation and rule-breaking are valued. "Attached please find" should be "Attached is." "Pursuant to" would be better as "in response to."

(15) **Appropriate.** This one's in friendspeak, entirely proper for two pals sending information quickly via instant messages. Translated for those who need actual words, this exchange reads as follows:

Friend 1: I got an A+.

Friend 2: That's great. (*Sick* is slang for "excellent, wonderful.")

Friend 1: I will talk to you later. (The first letter of each word creates this expression.)

Friend 2: All right (or okay). Bye for now.

(16) **Appropriate.** This paragraph is quite formal, and its purpose is to persuade readers that a stoplight is needed. To convince someone, you want to sound informed, sane, and thoughtful. Formal English fills that slot!

(17) **Inappropriate.** Social media has a reputation as an "anything goes" sort of medium, but before you post, think about your purpose. Who would pay attention to this writer? To persuade someone not to tax, or to persuade someone of anything, you need a real argument, not just a set of insults like *morons, stealing,* and *shut up.* Proper grammar isn't essential, but if your goal is to be taken seriously, mistakes such as *coulda* (instead of *could have*) and *outta* (instead of *out of*) don't help.

(18) **Appropriate.** Job applicants usually want to sound competent, and those seeking teaching roles should be even more formal than others. Why? Because language in academic situations is generally formal. You may have wondered about the last sentence, which includes the informal term *kids.* Here, the writer breaks into conversational English, but with a reason: to show that the writer can relate to and be comfortable with the child to be tutored.

(19) **Appropriate.** Tweets may have no more than 280 characters, so the number of spaces, letters, and symbols can't go above that number. Dropping words is fine in this format, as is directing people who are interested in attending the meeting to other tweets about spring planting.

(20) **Inappropriate.** Unless you're in a school that prizes informality to an extreme degree (and those places do exist), a graduation speech should be something that appeals to the entire audience. Roger, May, and the speaker may know that *ship* means to be in a romantic relationship, but Roger's grandmother probably doesn't.

Chapter 2

Identifying the Major Elements of a Sentence

Cops trying to crack a case often create a line-up. A possible suspect appears with several other people who could not have committed the crime. Behind one-way glass, a witness stares at the group and then chooses — *That's him!* When you crack a sentence, you face a line-up too — the words in the sentence. In this chapter, you practice identifying the major criminals . . . er, I mean *elements* of a sentence: the verb, the subject, and the complement or object. Because subjects are often nouns and you frequently need to determine whether you have a singular or plural subject, I throw in a little practice with noun plurals as well.

Going to the Heart of the Matter: The Verb

Before you do anything to a sentence — write, analyze, or edit — you have to locate its heart, also known as the verb. The words that express action or state of being are verbs; they pump meaning into a sentence, just as a real heart pumps blood into veins and arteries. In this section, you practice identifying verbs, sorting out types of verbs, and examining the role of helping verbs. For information on another important verb characteristic, tense, read Chapter 4.

Treasure hunt: Finding the verb

To find the verb, think about the meaning of the sentence. Ask two questions: What's happening? What is, was, or will be? The first question gives you an *action verb,* and the second question yields a *linking verb.* An action verb expresses action. (How shocking!) Action verbs aren't always energetic, however. *Sleep, dream, realize,* and *meditate* are all action verbs. Think of a linking verb as a giant equal sign. This sort of verb links a person, place, or thing to a description or an identity. In the sentence "Mary is tired," *is* links *Mary* and *tired.* Most linking verbs are forms of the verb *be* or one of its close cousins (*seem* or *remain,* for example). Verbs that express sensation — *taste, feel, sound,* and *smell,* for instance — are also linking verbs if they can be replaced by a form of *be* without completely changing the meaning of the sentence.

TIP

You may find more than one verb in a sentence. For example, this morning I showered and washed my hair. In that last sentence, *showered* and *washed* are both verbs. Sometimes a single verb is formed with two or more words. Keep your eye out for forms of the verb *do* and *have,* as well as the word *will.* They may show up next to the verb or a couple of words away. You have to locate all the parts of a verb in order to understand how the sentence functions. (More on other types of multi-word verbs appears in "Aiding and abetting: Helping verbs" later in this section.)

EXAMPLE

Q. Find the verb(s) in this sentence and indentify each as linking (LV) or action (AV):

Gloria was a tennis fanatic, so she rushed out to buy tickets to the championship match.

A. **was (LV), rushed (AV).** This sentence makes two statements, one about Gloria herself and one about her actions. To locate the verbs, ask your questions:

What's happening? *rushed* This is an action verb because it explains what Gloria did.

What is, was, or will be? *was* This is a linking verb because it explains Gloria's personality, "linking" *Gloria* to *tennis fanatic.*

TIP

Did you stumble over *to buy?* A verb with *to* in front is called an infinitive, the head of a verb family. Oddly, infinitives don't function as verbs in a sentence. If you reread the statement about Gloria, you see that the sentence doesn't say that she bought tickets. She *rushed.* Maybe she was successful, and maybe she wasn't. Either way, *to buy* is an infinitive, not a verb.

EXAMPLE

Q. Identify the verbs in the sentence and label them linking (LV) or action (AV):

My cat sleeps all day because he has always been lazy.

A. **sleeps (AV), has been (LV).** When you ask *What's happening?* the answer is *sleeps,* so you know that *sleeps* is a verb. Even though it doesn't require much energy, *sleep* is something you do, so it's an action verb. When you ask *What is, was, or will be?* the answer is *has been.* That verb, like all forms of *be,* is a linking verb. Did you include *always?* The word gives a time range, not a state of being or an action. It's an adverb, not a verb, even though it's tucked inside the verb *has been.*

1　The fire engine raced down the street.

2　Around the curve, just ahead of the railroad tracks, stood seven donkeys.

3　One of the donkeys, frightened by the noise of the siren, ran away.

4　Another looked worried but did not move.

5　Was he brave or was he determined to defend his herd?

6　Most likely, the animal did not notice the noise or did not care.

7　Did you know that the donkey was eating George's lawn?

8　George's house was not on fire, but several others on his street were burning.

9　George left the donkey alone and went inside for an extra-long lunch.

10　Because of the donkey, George did not mow his lawn.

Choosing the correct verb for negative expressions

Three little letters — *not* — turn a positive comment ("I like your boots") to a negative one ("I do not like your boots"). Apart from the fashion critique, what do you notice about the negative statement? The verb changes from *like* to *do like*. You need that extra part because "I not like" isn't proper English. Negative verbs don't always rely on a form of the verb *do*. Sometimes *have*, *has*, or *had* does the job. Sentences with a *be* verb can turn negative without any help at all. In this section you can try your hand at *not* creating the wrong negative verb.

Q.　Rewrite the sentence as a negative expression.

Mark's acting received an Academy Award.

EXAMPLE

A. **Mark's acting did not receive an Academy Award.** Two things change when the positive verb (*received*) becomes negative (*did not receive*). *Received*, a past-tense form, turns into the basic, no-frills, bare infinitive (*receive*). The helping verb *did* pairs with it. As you probably noticed, *not* is tucked between the two parts of this verb, its usual spot.

11 My phone buzzes like a bee.

_____

12 Sheila is in love with bees.

_____

13 She wanted to be a beekeeper.

_____

14 Looking at bee hives gives her hives.

_____

15 The bee flying near our picnic table left Sheila alone all afternoon.

_____

16 Sheila will ask me to change my ringtone.

_____

Questioning with verbs

In many languages, you say the equivalent of "Ate the cookie?" to find out whether your friend gobbled up a treat. In English, you nearly always need a helping verb and a subject (the person or thing you're talking about) to create a question: "Did you eat the cookie?" (The verbs *to be* and *to have* are the only exceptions.) Notice that the combo form (*did eat*) is different from the straight past tense (*ate*). Other question-creators, italicized in these examples, change the tense: "*Will* you eat my cookie?" or "*Do* you eat cookies?" (This last one suggests an ongoing action.) In nearly all questions, the subject follows the first (or only) verb.

Rewrite the statement so that it becomes a question. Add words or rearrange the sentence as needed.

EXAMPLE

Q. You found a wallet on the ground.

_____

A. **Did you find a wallet on the ground?** The helping verb *did* comes before *you* in this question. The past-tense form, *found*, changes to *find*, the basic, bare infinitive.

17 You took the wallet to the police station.

_____

18 The cops always accept lost items.

_____

19 The wallet was stolen.

_____

20 The detectives seemed interested.

_____

21 They noticed seven credit cards, each with a different name.

_____

22 The photo on the license matches a mug shot.

_____

23 The police will act swiftly.

_____

24 You want the reward for recovering stolen property.

_____

Aiding and abetting: Helping verbs

In addition to _has_, _have_, _had_, and the _be_ verbs (_am_, _is_, _are_, _was_, _were_, and so on) you can attach a few other helpers to a main verb, and in doing so, change the meaning of the sentence slightly. Consider hiring the following helpers:

» _Should_ **and** _must_ **add a sense of duty.** Notice the sense of obligation in these two sentences: "David _should_ put the ice cream away before he eats the whole thing." "David _must_ reduce his cholesterol, according to his doctor."

» _Can_ **and** _could_ **imply ability.** _Could_ is the past tense of _can_. Choose the tense that matches the tense of the main verb or the time period expressed in the sentence, as in these examples, "If Hanna _can_ help, she will." or "Courtney _could_ stray from the beaten path, depending on the weather."

» _May_ **and** _might_ **add possibility to the sentence.** Strictly speaking, _might_ is for past events, and _may_ for present, but these days people interchange the two forms: "I _may_ go to the picnic if I can find a bottle of ant-killer." "I told Courtney that she _might_ want to bring some insect repellent."

>> **Would usually expresses a condition or willingness.** This helper explains under what circumstances something may happen. ("I *would* have brought the cat had I known about the mouse problem.") *Would* may also express willingness. ("He *would* bait the trap.") *Would* sometimes communicates repeated past actions. ("Every Saturday he *would* go to the pet store for more mouse food.") The present tense of *would,* the helping verb *will,* may also indicate a condition in the present or future. ("I *will* go if I *can* find a free ticket.")

EXAMPLE

Add a helper to the main verb. The information in parentheses after the fill-in-the-blank sentence explains what meaning the sentence should have.

Q. Lisa said that she _____ consider running for Parks Commissioner, but she hasn't made up her mind yet. *(possibility)*

A. **might** or **may.** The *might* or *may* shows that Lisa hasn't ruled out a run.

25 The mayor, shy as ever, said that she _____ go to the tree-planting ceremony only if the press agreed to stay outside the forest. *(condition)*

26 Kirk, a reporter for the local radio station, _____ not agree to any conditions, because the station manager insisted on eyewitness coverage. *(ability)*

27 Whenever he met with her, Kirk _____ always urge the mayor to invite the press to special events, without success. *(repeated action)*

28 The mayor _____ make an effort to be more open to the press. *(duty)*

29 Lisa, who writes the popular "Trees-a-Crowd" blog, explained that she _____ rely on her imagination to supply details. *(possibility)*

30 Lisa knows that Kirk _____ leap to fame based on his tree-planting report, and she doesn't want to miss an important scoop. *(ability)*

31 All good reporters _____ know that if a tree falls or is planted in the forest, the sound is heard by a wide audience only if a radio reporter is there. *(duty)*

32 Sound engineers, on the other hand, _____ skip all outdoor events if they _____ do so. *(condition, ability)*

Zeroing in on the Subject

Every sentence needs a subject — the who or what performing the action or existing in the state of being expressed in the sentence. Subjects are usually *nouns* (words that name people, places, things, or ideas) or *pronouns* (words such as *he, it, who,* and so forth that substitute for nouns). Before you search for the subject, find the verb. Then place "Who?" or "What?" before the verb. For example, suppose the verb is *had parked.* Your subject questions are *Who had parked? What had parked?* The answer is the subject.

TIP

The subject often, but not always, appears before the verb. Don't scout location. Use logic and the questions and you'll find what you're looking for — the subject. Also, not every subject appears in the sentence. In commands (*Take out the garbage now,* for example), the subject is *you,* because the listener or reader is the one who is supposed to *take out the garbage.* Lucky you!

Locate the subject(s) of each verb in the sentence.

EXAMPLE

Q. Angelo raided his piggy bank because his car needed a new muffler.

_____

A. **Angelo, needed.** In this sentence you find two verbs, *raided* and *needed.* When you ask *who raided?,* the answer is *Angelo raided. Angelo* is the subject of the verb *raided.* (You can ask *what raided?* also, but that question has no answer.) When you ask *who needed?,* you get no answer. The question *what needed?* gives you *car needed,* so *car* is the subject of the verb *needed.*

33 Ana and Max spend all their free time in the library.

_____

34 Max has grown quite tall, but he has not adjusted to his new size.

_____

35 Once he reached under a library table to pick up a book Ana had dropped.

_____

36 Max stood up too quickly and smashed his head on the bottom of the table.

_____

37 There is a dent in the table now.

_____

38 Did you see a dent in Max's head?

_____

39 Max's thick hair and equally thick skull protect him from most head injuries.

_____

40 When Max hit it, the table fell over and broke Ana's toe.

_____

When one isn't enough: Forming noun plurals

When I was in elementary school, the only spell check was the teacher's ruler. "Don't you know you're supposed to change the *y* to *i* and add *es*?" Miss Hammerhead would inquire just before the ruler landed (*Bam!*) on a pupil's head. Hammerhead (not her real name) was teaching spelling, but she also was explaining how to form the plural of some *nouns,* the grammatical term for words that name people, places, things, or ideas. Here are Miss Hammerhead's lessons, minus the weaponry:

>> **Regular plurals pick up an *s*.** For instance, *one snob/two snobs* and *a dollar/two billion dollars.*

>> **For nouns ending in *s, sh, ch,* and *x*, tack on *es* to form the plural unless the noun has an irregular plural.** For example, *kindness/kindnesses, splash/splashes, catch/catches,* and *hex/hexes.* I tell you more about irregular plurals in a minute.

>> **For nouns ending in *ay, ey, oy*, simply add an *s*.** Monkey becomes *monkeys* and *boy* changes to *boys.*

>> **For nouns ending in *y* preceded by a consonant, change the *y* to *i* and add *es*.** *Butterfly/butterflies* and *mystery/mysteries* are two such examples.

>> **Hyphenated nouns become plural by changing the most important word.** You can have two *mothers-in-law,* but no *mother-in-laws,* because *mother* is the defining characteristic.

>> **When making the plural of a proper name, add *s* or *es*.** Don't change any letters even if the name ends with a consonant-*y* combo (*Smithy,* perhaps). Just add *s* for the *Smiths* and the *Smithys.* If the name already ends in *s, sh, ch,* or *x* (*Woods,* for example), you can add *es* (*Woodses*).

>> **Irregular nouns cancel all bets: Anything goes!** Sometimes the noun doesn't change at all, so the plural and singular forms are exactly the same (*fish/fish deer/deer*); other times the noun does change (*leaf/leaves* and *child/children*). When you're unsure about an irregular plural, you can check the dictionary. The definition lists the plural form for each noun.

EXAMPLE

At the end of each sentence is a noun in parentheses. Write the plural in the blank, as in this example:

Q. When she was angry, Jennifer often sent dinner _____ flying across the room. *(plate)*

A. **plates.** Love those regular plurals! Just add *s*.

41 Jennifer works at one of the local mental-health _____. *(clinic)*

42 Jennifer refers to these establishments as "brain _____." *(house)*

43 The town eccentric, Jennifer has dyed several _____ of her hair light green. *(thatch)*

44 Jennifer sees her unusual hair color as appropriate for all _____. *(woman)*

45 Few people know that Jennifer, an accomplished historian and mathematician, has created a series of _____ on the Hundred Years' War. *(graph)*

46. Jennifer also knows a great deal about the role of _____ in colonial America. *(turkey)*

47. The _____ of envy at Jennifer's scholarship were quite loud. *(sigh)*

48. However, her paper did not impress her _____. *(brother-in-law)*

49. Some _____ in the Sullivan family opt for veterinary school. *(child)*

50. Danny went to dental school so he could work with _____ instead of dogs. *(tooth)*

Adding Meaning: Objects and Complements

Three important elements — direct objects, indirect objects, and subject complements — don't always show up in a sentence, but when they do, they add information to the idea begun by the subject and the verb. To locate objects and subject complements, keep these points in mind:

>> After an action verb, you may find a word — or several words — answering the question *whom?* or *what?* begun by the verb. That's the direct object. For example, in the sentence *Lulu hates sports, hates* is the action verb and *Lulu* is the subject of *hates.* Ask *Lulu hates whom?* and you get no answer. Ask *Lulu hates what?* and the answer is *sports. Sports* is the direct object of the verb *hates.*

>> Action verbs also occasionally appear with a direct object and an indirect object. In the sentence *Lulu gave me an annoyed glance,* the subject-verb combination is *Lulu gave.* The direct object of the verb *gave* is *glance,* which answers the question *Lulu gave what?* The indirect object questions are *to whom? to what?* So now you have *Lulu gave an annoyed glance to whom?* The answer is *to me,* and *me* is the indirect object. (You don't get an answer when you ask *to what.*)

>> After a linking verb, simply ask *who?* or *what?* to find the subject complement. In the sentence *Lulu is a terrible basketball player,* the subject-verb combo is *Lulu is.* Now ask *Lulu is who? Lulu is what?* The answer is *a terrible basketball player.* The most important word in that answer is *player,* and *player* is the subject complement.

TIP

Most of the time the distinction between objects and complements doesn't matter. When a pronoun completes the thought begun by the subject and verb, however, you have to be alert. In formal English, the same type of pronoun that acts as a subject also acts as a subject complement. Subject pronouns and object pronouns don't always match. For more about subject and object pronouns, check out Chapter 6.

EXAMPLE

Locate the objects and subject complements in each sentence. Underline each one and label it as a direct object (DO), an indirect object (IO), or a subject complement (SC).

Q. Lulu hates baseball too even though she is very athletic.

A. **baseball (DO), athletic (SC).** *Hates* is a linking verb. Ask *Lulu hates whom or what?* and *baseball* pops up as the answer. *Baseball* is the direct object. *Is* is a linking verb, so when you ask *she is who or what?* the answer, *athletic,* is a subject complement.

51 Lola, during the annual softball game between two branch offices of our company, swung the bat with all her strength.

52 She is extremely strong because she exercises for 2 hours every day.

53 The bat hit the ball and lifted it over the outfield fence.

54 There was wild joy in our cheering section!

55 The applause always sounds louder when Lola plays.

56 Compared to Lola, the next batter seemed small and weak.

57 He is the president of the company, and he alternates between branch-office teams every year.

58 The pitcher tossed the president a slow ball.

59 Who would challenge him?

60 The president smacked the ball a few feet, but he reached third base anyway.

Answers to Questions about Major Elements of a Sentence

Now that you've identified the major players in the sentence game, it's time to tally up your score. Check your answers to see how you did.

1. **raced (AV).** Ask *what's happening?* The answer is *raced. Raced* is an action verb.

2. **stood (AV).** Even though *stood* sounds like inaction, it's still expressing what happens, so it's an action verb answering the question *What's happening?*

3. **ran (AV).** What's happening? The frightened animal *ran*, that's what's happening! *Ran* is an action verb.

4. **looked (LV), did move (AV).** The sensory verb *looked* is a stand-in for *was*, so it's a linking verb telling you about the donkey's state of being. *Did move*, on the other hand, tells you what's happening, so it's an action verb. Are you wondering why *not* isn't listed here? *Not* is not a verb. It's an adverb. (For more on adverbs, turn to Chapter 8.)

5. **was (LV), was (LV).** Each of these verbs tells you about the donkey's state of being, so they're linking verbs.

6. **did notice (AV), did care (AV).** Negative statements often rely on forms of the verb *to do*. Here you find *did notice* and *did care*, both of which tell you what's happening. They're action verbs.

7. **did know (AV), was eating (AV).** Questions often need a form of the verb *do*, such as *did* in this sentence. Both verbs tell what's happening (even though *know* is not a very energetic activity), so they're action verbs.

8. **was (LV), were burning (AV).** The first part of this sentence describes the house, telling you its state of being, so *was* is a linking verb. The second part of the sentence tells you what the houses were doing (*were burning*), so *were burning* is an action verb.

9. **left (AV), went (AV).** Both verbs tell you what's happening, so both are action verbs.

10. **did mow (AV).** Did you include *not*? Nope. *Not* is an adverb, not a verb. *Did mow*, on the other hand, tells you what's happening, so it's an action verb.

11. **My phone does not buzz like a bee.** The positive verb *buzzes* turns into *does buzz* in the negative, with *not* between the two parts of the verb.

12. **Sheila is not in love with bees.** With your sharp eyes, you probably noticed that no form of the verb *do* appears in this sentence. The verb *be* is special. (See Chapter 4 to find out exactly how special, and annoying, *be* can be.) A simple *not* does the job here.

13. **She did not want to be a beekeeper.** The past-tense verb form *wanted* turns to *did want. Not* completes the negative transformation.

14. **Looking at bee hives does not give her hives.** Here the present-tense form *gives* changes to *does give*, with *not* in between.

(15) **The bee flying near our picnic table did not leave Sheila alone all afternoon.** The past-tense verb form *left* changes to *did leave*, which becomes negative with the addition of *not.* Were you confused by *flying*? Although *flying* expresses action, it isn't the verb in this section. (For more information about this sort of "fake verb," turn to Chapter 17.)

(16) **Sheila will not ask me to change my ringtone.** The positive, future-tense verb form *will ask* needs no other helping verb. The *not* does the job when it's tucked between *will* and *ask.*

(17) **Did you take the wallet to the police station?** Typical question format: the two parts of the verb, *did* and *take,* are separated by the subject, *you.*

(18) **Do the cops always accept lost items?** This one's in present tense because the original statement contains the present-tense verb, *accept.*

(19) **Was the wallet stolen?** Because this sentence is about state of being, expressed by a form of the verb *be,* you don't need a helping verb here. However, the subject *(wallet)* should follow the verb.

(20) **Did the detectives seem interested?** This one's about a state of being, but the verb, *to seem,* needs the helping verb *did* to create a question.

(21) **Did they notice the seven credit cards, each with a different name?** The helper *did* precedes the subject, *they,* in this question.

(22) **Does the photo on the license match a mug shot?** Here you see the same pattern: helping verb *(does),* subject *(photo),* main verb *(match).*

(23) **Will the police act swiftly?** The helper, *will,* changes position to create a question instead of a statement.

(24) **Do you want the reward for recovering stolen property?** In this question, you add *do* to the main verb, *want,* to land in question territory.

(25) **would.** The going is dependent upon the press arrangement. Thus *would* is the best choice.

(26) **could.** The agreement wasn't possible, so *could* wins the prize.

(27) **would.** This helping verb expresses repeated actions in the past.

(28) **should.** Once you imply duty, *should* is the helper you want.

(29) **may** or **might.** Lisa, if she's in the mood, will cover the tree-cutting without seeing it. This possibility is expressed by the helpers *may* or *might.*

(30) **can.** You need to express ability in the present tense, which *can* can do.

(31) **should.** Gotta get that duty in, and *should* does the job.

(32) **would, could.** *Would* expresses a condition, and *could* adds ability to the sentence.

(33) **Ana, Max.** The verb in this sentence is *spend.* When you ask *who* before that verb, the answer is *Ana and Max. Ana* and *Max* are both subjects of the verb *spend.*

(34) **Max, he.** *Who has grown? Max has grown. Max* is the subject of the verb *has grown. Who has adjusted? He has adjusted. He* is the subject of the verb *has adjusted.* (*Not* isn't part of the verb.)

(35) **he, Ana.** *Who reached? He reached. He* is the subject of the verb reached. *Who had dropped? Ana had dropped. Ana* is the subject of the verb *had dropped.*

(36) **Max.** This sentence has two verbs, *stood* and *smashed*. When you ask *who stood?* the answer is *Max.* You get the same answer for *who smashed? Max* is the subject of both verbs.

(37) **dent.** Did I catch you with this one? *There* is never a subject. (Neither is *here*, which often appears in similar sentences.) The real subject, which you find with the usual questions, appears after the verb. *What is? A dent is. Dent* is the subject of the verb *is.*

(38) **you.** The verb in this sentence is *did see*. Ignore the fact that the sentence asks a question and ask the usual subject questions. *Who did see? You did see. You* is the subject of *did see.*

(39) **hair, skull.** When you ask *What?* before the verb *protect*, the answer is *hair* and *skull*, both of which are subjects of the verb *protect.*

(40) **Max, table.** *Who hit? Max hit. Max* is the subject of the verb *hit. What fell and broke? The table,* which is the subject of the verbs *fell* and *broke.*

(41) **clinics.** For a regular plural, just add *s*.

(42) **houses.** Regular plural here: Add an *s*.

(43) **thatches.** For a noun ending in *ch*, add *es*.

(44) **women.** This is an irregular plural.

(45) **graphs.** Did I fool you? The *h* at the end of the noun doesn't, all by itself, call for *es*. Only words ending in *sh* or *ch* require an added *es* in the plural form. For *graph*, a plain *s* will do.

(46) **turkeys.** For nouns ending in *ay, ey,* and *oy*, add *s* to form a plural.

(47) **sighs.** Regular plurals are fun; just add *s*.

(48) **brothers-in-law.** To create the plural of a hyphenated word, add *s* to the most important word, which in this case is *brother*.

(49) **children.** No *s* in sight, but *children* really is plural.

(50) **teeth.** Irregular plurals wander all over the map. This one changes the vowels.

(51) **bat (DO).** This sentence is long, but only one direct object shows up when you ask, *Lola swung what? Lola swung the bat.* Because *swung* is an action verb, *bat* is the direct object.

(52) **strong (SC).** *Is* is a linking verb. Ask *she is who or what?* and the answer is *she is strong. Strong* is a subject complement.

(53) **ball (DO), it (DO).** This sentence has two verbs, *hit* and *lifted*, both paired with the subject *bat. Bat* is an action verb. When you ask, *bat hit whom or what?* the answer is *ball.* When you ask *bat lifted whom or what?* the answer is *it.* Both are direct objects.

(54) **No objects or complements.** Yes, this is a trick question. *There* is never a subject. In this sentence, *joy* is the subject. If you ask *joy is who or what?* you get no answer. No answer, so no complement or object.

(55) **louder (SC).** *Sounds* is a linking verb, connecting the subject *applause* with *louder*, the subject complement.

56) **small (SC), weak (SC).** *Seemed* is a linking verb, a close relative of *was*, a member of the *be* verb family. When you ask *batter seemed who or what?* the answer is *small* and *weak*. They're both subject complements.

57) **president (SC).** After the linking verb *is* you find the subject complement *president*. No complement or object follows the second verb, *alternates*.

58) **president (IO), ball (DO).** First ask *the pitcher tossed whom or what?* You may have been tempted to answer *president*, but the pitcher didn't throw a person. The direct object is *ball*. Now ask *the president tossed the ball to whom or what?* The answer, *president*, is an indirect object.

59) **him (DO).** The verb is *would challenge* and the subject is *who*. When you ask *who would challenge whom or what?* the answer is *him*, a direct object.

60) **ball (DO), base (DO).** Ask *the president smacked whom or what?* The answer is *ball*, a direct object. *He reached whom or what?* The answer is *base*, a direct object.

Chapter **3**

Having It All: Writing Complete Sentences

D id you hear the story about the child who said nothing for the first five years of life and then began to speak in perfect, complete sentences? Supposedly the kid grew up to be something important, like a Supreme Court justice or a CEO. I question the story's accuracy, but I don't doubt that Supreme Court justices, CEOs, or anyone else with a good job knows how to write a complete sentence.

You need to know how to do so, too, and in this chapter I give you a complete (pardon the pun) guide to sentence completeness, including how to punctuate and how to combine thoughts using proper grammar. (For more on how to make your combinations stylish, check out Chapter 17.)

TEST ALERT

The evil geniuses who write standardized tests want to know whether you can write a proper, complete sentence. Because testing companies seldom willing to pay teachers to read your writing, this topic often turns up on those exams in a "choose the best" multiple-choice for-mat. Test takers, stay alert. Business people, this chapter is also important for you, because incomplete sentences seriously mar your writing.

To write a proper, complete sentence, follow these rules:

> » **Every sentence needs a subject/verb pair.** More than one pair is okay, but at least one is essential. Just to be clear about the grammar terms: A verb expresses action or state of being; a subject tells you who or what is acting or being. (See Chapter 2 for more on this topic.)
>
> » **A grammatically correct sentence contains a complete thought.** Don't leave the reader hanging with only half an idea. (*If it rains* is an incomplete thought, but *If it rains, my paper dress will dissolve* is a complete and truly bizarre thought.)
>
> » **Two or more ideas in a sentence must be joined correctly.** You can't just jam everything together. If you do, you end up with a run-on or "fused" sentence, which is a grammatical felony. Certain punctuation marks and what grammarians call *conjunctions* — joining words — glue ideas together legally.
>
> » **Every sentence finishes with an endmark.** Endmarks include periods, question marks, and exclamation points.

Just four little rules. Piece of cake, right? In theory, yes. But sometimes applying the rules gets a little complicated. In the following sections I take you through each rule, one at a time, so you can practice every step.

Finding Subjects and Verbs that Match

The subject/verb pair is the core of the sentence. First, zero in on the verb, the word (or words) expressing action or a state of being. Next, look for the subject, a word (or words) expressing who or what is doing that action or is in that state of being. Now check to see that the subject and verb make sense together (*Mike has been singing, Lindsay suffered,* and so forth). More on locating subjects and verbs appears in Chapter 2.

 WARNING

Some words that look like verbs don't function as verbs. Checking for a match between a subject and a verb eliminates these false verbs from consideration, because false-verb pairs sound incomplete. A couple of mismatches illustrate my point: *Lindsay watching* and *Mike's message having been scrambled.*

 EXAMPLE

Q. In the blank, write the subject (S)/verb (V) pair. If you find no true pair, write "incomplete."

Mike, tomato plants wilting, gave up and ordered a salad online.

A. **Mike (S)/gave (V), ordered (V).** Did I catch you with *wilting?* In the preceding sentence, *wilting* isn't a verb. One clue: *tomato plants wilting* sounds incomplete. Just for comparison, *tomato plants are wilting* makes a subject/verb match. Hear the difference?

1 Duke, sighing repeatedly because of her inability to score more than ten points at the dog show. _____

2 Charlie fed a steak to Truffle, his favorite entrant in the Dog of the Century contest.

_____

3 Duke, my favorite entrant, gobbled a bowl of liver treats and woofed for about an hour afterward. _____

4 Entered in the Toy breed category, Duke is sure to win the "Most Likely to Fall Asleep Standing Up" contest. _____

5 Having been tired out by a heavy schedule of eating, chewing, and pooping.

_____

6 Duke sleeps profoundly. _____

7 Once, having eaten through the dog-food bag and increased the size of her stomach by at least 50 percent. _____

8 One of the other dogs, biting the vet gently just to make a point about needles and her preference not to have them. _____

9 Who would be surprised by a runoff between Truffle and Duke?

_____

10 Not surprised by anything, especially by liver treats.

_____

Checking for Complete Thoughts

Some subject/verb pairs form a closed circle: The thought they express is complete. You want this quality in your sentences, because otherwise your reader echoes the outlaw who, with his head in the noose, said, "Don't leave me hanging!"

Some expressions are incomplete when they're statements but complete when they're questions. To illustrate my point: "Who won the game?" makes sense, but "Who won the game" doesn't.

EXAMPLE

Q. If the sentence has a complete thought, write "complete." If the reader is left in suspense, write "incomplete."

Whenever the cow jumps over the moon. _____

A. **Incomplete.** Aren't you wondering, "What happens *whenever the cow jumps over the moon?*" The thought is not complete.

Remember, the number of words doesn't indicate completeness. The content does.

TIP

11. The cow, who used to work for NASA until she got fed up with the bureaucracy. _____

12. On long-term training flights, the milking machine malfunctioned. _____ _____

13. Why didn't the astronauts assume responsibility for milking procedures? _____ _____

14. For one thing, milking, which wasn't in the manual but should have been, thus avoiding the problem and increasing the comfort level of the cow assigned to the jump. _____

15. The cow protested. _____

16. She mooed. _____

17. Because she couldn't change NASA's manual. _____

18. The author of the manual, fairly well known in the field of astrophysics, having also grown up on a farm, though that experience was a long time ago. _____

19. NASA has reached out to the cow community and promised to review milking procedures. _____

20. Applying to NASA, her mother, when only a calf. _____

21. Quitting was not a bad decision, however. _____

22. Twenty years of moon jumping is enough for any cow. _____

23. Unless NASA comes up with a better way to combine moon jumping and milk producing, the administration will have to recruit other species. _____

24. Will NASA send a flock of sheep to the moon someday? _____

25. Perhaps someday, having heard "the sheep jumped over the moon," set to the same music. _____

Improving Flow with Properly Joined Sentences

Some sentences are short. Some are long. Joining them is good. Combined sentences make a narrative more interesting. Have I convinced you yet? The choppiness of the preceding sentences makes a good case for gluing sentences together. Just be sure to do so legally, so you won't end up with a run-on sentence.

TEST ALERT

Test writers sometimes throw improperly joined sentences at you to see whether you recognize this sort of error. Read this section of the workbook carefully to ace those questions.

To join sentences correctly, you need one of the following:

>> **A conjunction:** A *conjunction* is a word that unites parts of a sentence. To connect two complete sentences more or less equally, use *and, or, but, nor,* and *for.* Be sure to put a comma before the conjunction. To highlight one thought and make the other less important, use such conjunctions as *because, since, when, where, if, although, who, which,* and *that* — among others. These conjunctions are sometimes preceded by commas and sometimes not. (For more information on comma use, check out Chapter 11.)

>> **A semicolon:** A *semicolon* (a little dot over a comma) pops up between two complete sentences and glues them together nicely. The two complete thoughts need to be related in some way.

WARNING

Some words look like conjunctions but aren't. Don't use *nevertheless, consequently, therefore, however,* or *then* to join complete thoughts. If you want to place one of these "false conjunctions" between two complete thoughts, add a semicolon and place a comma after the "false conjunction." For more information on commas, see Chapter 11. Also, most writers of formal English don't use a dash (a long, straight, horizontal line) to link two complete sentences one after the other. A semicolon is better for that job. However, a single dash can tack words to the end of a complete sentence, so long as the addition is less than a complete sentence. Two dashes may also be used to tuck a complete sentence *inside* another complete sentence.

EXAMPLE

Q. Circle the letters next to the legally combined, correct sentences. You may find one, more than one, or none.

   a. Kathy broke out of jail, five years for illegal sentence-joining was just too much for her.

   b. Kathy broke out of jail; five years for illegal sentence-joining was too much for her.

   c. Kathy broke out of jail because five years for illegal sentence-joining was just too much for her.

A. **b, c.** The problem with choice a is that a comma can't unite two complete thoughts. In choice b, the comma has correctly changed to a semicolon. Choice c works because the conjunction *because* connects the two ideas correctly.

26

a. The grammarian-in-chief used to work for the Supreme Court, therefore his word was law.

b. The grammarian-in-chief used to work for the Supreme Court, and therefore his word was law.

c. The grammarian-in-chief used to work for the Supreme Court, consequently, his word was law.

27

a. His nickname, "Mr. Grammar," which had been given to him by the court clerks, was not a source of pride for him.

b. His nickname, "Mr. Grammar," had been given to him by the court clerks, and it was not a source of pride for him.

c. His nickname, "Mr. Grammar," had been given to him by the court clerks, it was not a source of pride for him.

28

a. Nevertheless, he did not criticize those who used the term, as long as they did so politely.

b. Nevertheless, he did not criticize those who used the term; as long as they did so politely.

c. Nevertheless, he did not criticize those who used the term, and as long as they did so politely.

29

a. He often wore a lab coat embroidered with parts of speech, for he was truly devoted to the field of grammar.

b. He often wore a lab coat embroidered with parts of speech, he was truly devoted to the field of grammar.

c. He often wore a lab coat embroidered with parts of speech because he was truly devoted to the field of grammar.

30

a. Kathy's escape wounded him deeply; he ordered the grammar cops to arrest her as soon as possible.

b. Kathy's escape wounded him deeply, and he ordered the grammar cops to arrest her as soon as possible.

c. Kathy's escape wounded him deeply, consequently he ordered the grammar cops to arrest her as soon as possible.

31

   a. Kathy hid in a basket of dirty laundry; then she held her breath as the truck passed the border.

   b. Kathy hid in a basket of dirty laundry, and then she held her breath as the truck passed the border.

   c. Kathy hid in a basket of dirty laundry, then she held her breath as the truck passed the border.

32

   a. Kathy passed the border of sanity some time ago, although she is able to speak in complete sentences if she really tries.

   b. Kathy passed the border of sanity some time ago, even so she is able to speak in complete sentences if she really tries.

   c. Kathy passed the border of sanity some time ago, but she is able to speak in complete sentences if she really tries.

33

   a. She's attracted to sentence fragments, which appeal to something in her character.

   b. She's attracted to sentence fragments, as they appeal to something in her character.

   c. She's attracted to sentence fragments, for they appeal to something in her character.

34

   a. "Finish what you start," her mother often exclaimed, "You don't know when you're going to face a grammar judge."

   b. "Finish what you start," her mother often exclaimed. "You don't know when you're going to face a grammar judge."

   c. "Finish what you start." Her mother often exclaimed, "You don't know when you're going to face a grammar judge."

35

   a. While she is free, Kathy intends to burn grammar textbooks for fuel.

   b. As long as she's free, Kathy intends to burn grammar textbooks for fuel.

   c. During she is free, Kathy intends to burn grammar textbooks for fuel.

36

   a. Grammar books burn exceptionally well, though some people prefer history texts for fuel.

   b. Grammar books burn exceptionally well; nevertheless, some people prefer history texts for fuel.

   c. Grammar books burn exceptionally well, yet some people prefer history texts for fuel.

37

   a. History books create a satisfactory snap and crackle while they are burning, the flames are also a nice shade of orange.

   b. History books create a satisfactory snap and crackle while they are burning, and the flames are also a nice shade of orange.

   c. History books create a satisfactory snap and crackle; while they are burning, the flames are also a nice shade of orange.

38

   a. Because she loves history, Kathy rejected *The Complete History of the Grammatical World,* but she burned *Participles and You* instead.

   b. Because she loves history, Kathy rejected *The Complete History of the Grammatical World,* she burned *Participles and You* instead.

   c. Because she loves history, Kathy rejected *The Complete History of the Grammatical World* and burned *Participles and You* instead.

Setting the Tone with Endmarks

When you're speaking, the listener knows you've arrived at the end of a sentence because the thought is complete and your tone says that you're done. In writing, the tone part is taken care of by a period, question mark, or exclamation point. In formal English you must have one, and only one, of these marks at the end of a sentence. On the internet and in texts where rules shatter all the time, it's common to pile on a bunch of punctuation marks to show strong emotion (or to omit punctuation entirely). But when you want to write in Standard English, you need an endmark at the end of a sentence. Periods are for statements, question marks are for (surprise) questions, and exclamation points scream at the reader. Endmarks become complicated when they tangle with quotation marks. (For tips on endmark/quotation mark interactions, check out Chapter 10.)

Go to work on this section, which is filled with sentences desperately in need of an endmark. Write the appropriate endmark in the blank provided.

EXAMPLE

Q. Did Lola really ride to the anti-noise protest on her motorcycle _____

A. **?** (question mark). You're clearly asking a question, so the question mark fits here.

39 No, she rode her motorcycle to the mathematicians' convention _____

40 You're not serious _____

41 Yes, Lola is a true fan of triangles _____

42 Does she bring her own triangles or expect to find what she needs at the convention _____

43 I'm not sure, but I think I heard her say that her math colleagues always bring triangles that are awesome _____

44 Do you think that she really means they're awful _____

45 I heard her scream that everyone loves triangles because they're the best shape in the universe _____

46 Are you going also _____

47 I'd rather have dental surgery than attend a math convention _____

48 I heard Lola exclaim that equilaterals turn her on _____

49 Are you sure that Lola loves equilaterals _____

50 I always thought that she was fond of triangles _____

51 Who in the world wants an "I love math" T-shirt _____

52 I can't believe that Lola actually bought one _____

53 Will she give me her old "I love grammar" hat _____

Proper Sentence or Not? That Is the Question

If you've plowed your way through this entire chapter, you've practiced each sentence skill separately. But to write well, you have to do everything at once — create subject/verb pairs, finish a thought, combine thoughts properly, and place the appropriate endmark. Take a test drive with the questions in this section.

EXAMPLE

Analyze each sentence and label it as follows:

>> **Fragment.** If the sentence lacks a subject-verb pair or a complete thought, it's a fragment.

>> **Missing endmark.** If the sentence has no endmark, choose this label.

>> **Run-on.** If more than one complete sentence is improperly joined, call it a run-on.

>> **Correct**. If all is well, call it correct and move on.

Q. Though the spaghetti sticks to the ceiling above the pan on rainy days when even one more problem will send me over the edge.

A. **Fragment.** The statement has no complete thought. Possible correction: Omit *Though* and begin the sentence with *The*.

54 Bill's holiday concert, occurring early in October, honors the longstanding tradition of his hometown and the great Elvis Presley.

_____

55. The holiday, which is called Hound Dog Day in honor of a wonderful dog breed.

_____

56. Tradition calls for blue suede shoes.

_____

57. Having brushed the shoes carefully with a suede brush, which can be bought in any shoe store.

_____

58. The citizens lead their dogs to the town square, Heartbreak Hotel is located there.

_____

59. "Look for the ghost of Elvis," the hotel clerk tells every guest, "Elvis has often been seen haunting these halls."

_____

60. Elvis, ghost or not, apparently does not attend the Hound Dog Day festivities because no one has seen an aging singer in a white jumpsuit there.

_____

61. Why should a ghost attend Bill's festival

_____

62. How can you even ask?

_____

63. The blue suede shoes are a nostalgic touch, consequently, the tourists always wear them.

_____

64. Personally, I prefer blue patent leather pumps, but my opinion isn't important.

_____

65. Patent leather is amazing

_____

66. Stay off of my shoes!

_____

67. While we were talking about shoes, Bill was creating a playlist for the Hound Dog Concert.

_____

68. You should plan to arrive early, everyone in town will be there.

_____

Calling All Overachievers: Extra Practice with Complete Sentences

I can't let you go without pitching one more curveball at you. Read the letter in the following figure, introducing a new employee to customers who apparently have good reason to be upset. Only five sentences are complete and correct; the other five have problems. Can you find the five that don't make the grade?

To Our Valued Customers:

[1]Announcing that Abner Grey is our new Director of Customer Satisfaction, effective immediately. Abner brings a wealth of experience to our company. [2]He served as Assistant VP of marketing for Antarctic Icebergs, Inc., until last year, when the cold finally became too much for him. [3]His first task, to introduce himself to every customer, finding out what has been done in the past and how our relationship may be improved. [4]Expect a phone call or a personal visit from him soon! [5]Recognizing that our previous director was not always attentive to your needs (occupied as she was with the lawsuit, prison, and so forth), we have told Abner to work at least 90 hours per week. [6]No more embezzlement either! Abner is completely honest, he considers "Integrity" his middle name. [7]Call him whenever you have a problem. [8]You will not be disappointed, furthermore, Abner will actually anticipate your needs. [9]Rest assured that this Director of Customer [10]Satisfaction will never see the inside of a jail cell.

Sincerely,

Vicki Copple

Answers to Complete Sentence Problems

Following are the answers to the practice questions in this chapter.

(1) **Incomplete.** Did you zero in on *sighing*? That's part of a verb (a present participle, if you absolutely have to know), but all by itself it isn't enough to fill the verb category. Likewise, if you try to pair *sighing* with a subject, the only candidate is *Duke*. *Duke is sighing* would be a match, but *Duke sighing* isn't. No subject/verb pair, no sentence.

(2) **Charlie (S)/fed (V).** Start with a verb search. Any action or being verbs? Yes, *fed.* Now ask who or what *fed. Charlie fed.* You have a good subject/verb match.

(3) **Duke (S)/gobbled (V), woofed (V).** Your verb search (always the best first step) yields two, *gobbled* and *woofed.* Who *gobbled* and *woofed? Duke.* There you go — an acceptable subject/verb pair.

(4) **Duke (S)/is (V).** Were you tricked by *entered? Entered* may be a verb in some sentences, but in this one it isn't, because it has no subject. But *is* does have a subject, *Duke.*

(5) **Incomplete.** Something's missing here: a *subject* and a *verb!* What you have, in grammar-speak, is a series of participles. A participle is a part of a verb, but not enough to satisfy the subject/verb rule.

(6) **Duke (S)/sleeps (V).** Start with a verb search, and you immediately come up with *sleeps,* which, by the way, is an action verb, even though sleeping seems like the opposite of action. Who *sleeps? Duke,* bless her snoring little self.

(7) **Incomplete.** You have two participles that express action — *having eaten and increased* — but no subject. Penalty box!

(8) **Incomplete.** The sentence has action *(biting),* but when you ask who's *biting,* you get no answer, because *one biting* is a mismatch.

(9) **Who (S)/would be (V).** Are you surprised to see *who* as a subject? In a question, *who* often fills that role.

(10) **Incomplete.** A quick glance tells you that you have a verb form *(surprised),* but no subject.

(11) **Incomplete.** In this one you have a subject *(cow)* and a description of the subject *(who used to work for NASA until she got fed up with the bureaucracy).* You're waiting to hear what the cow did – quit? write a memoir? sue? Because the sentence leaves you wondering, it's an incomplete thought.

(12) **Complete.** The sentence tells you everything you need to know, so it's complete.

(13) **Complete.** The question makes sense as is, so the sentence is complete.

(14) **Incomplete.** The statement gives you an idea — *milking* — and some descriptions, but it never delivers a complete thought about milking.

(15) **Complete.** Short, but you have everything you need to know about what the *cow* did. She *protested.*

(16) **Complete.** This sentence is even shorter than the one in the preceding question, but it still delivers its complete message.

(17) **Incomplete.** The word *because* implies a cause-and-effect relationship, but the sentence doesn't supply all the needed information.

18 **Incomplete.** This one goes on and on, piling on descriptions of the author. However, it never delivers the punch line. What's *the author* doing? Or, what state of being is *the author* in? The sentence doesn't tell you, so it's incomplete.

TEST ALERT

I've seen many sentences resembling the one in Question 18 on standardized tests, and I've seen many test takers come up with the wrong answer. Length does not imply completeness.

19 **Complete.** You know what NASA is doing, so this sentence is complete.

20 **Incomplete.** What did the mama cow do when she was only a calf? The sentence doesn't actually say, so it's incomplete.

21 **Complete.** This sentence makes a complete and forceful statement about quitting.

22 **Complete.** All you need to know about moon jumping (that it's enough for any cow) is in the sentence.

23 **Complete.** This sentence contains enough information to reform NASA.

24 **Complete.** This question makes sense as is. You may wonder what NASA will do, but you won't wonder what's being asked here because the question — and the sentence — is complete.

25 **Incomplete.** The statement contains several descriptions but no complete thought.

26 **b.** In choices a and c, you have two complete thoughts. Everything before the comma equals one complete thought; everything after the comma is another complete thought. A comma isn't strong enough to hold them together, and *nevertheless* or *consequently* can't do the job. In choice b, the conjunction *and* connects the two thoughts correctly.

27 **a, b.** No problems in choices a and b. In choice a, the extra information about the nickname *(which had been given to him by the court clerks)* is a description, not a complete thought, so it can be tucked into the sentence next to the word it describes *(nickname)*. The *which* ties the idea to *nickname*. In choice b, the conjunction *and* links the two complete sentences. In choice c, a comma tries to do that job, but it's not strong enough.

28 **a.** The *nevertheless* in choice a is not used as a joiner, so it's legal. In choice b, you see an unnecessary semicolon. In choice c, the *and* isn't needed.

29 **a, c.** Did I get you with choice a? The word *for* has another, more common grammatical use in such expressions as *for the love of Pete, for you, for the last time,* and so on. However, *for* is a perfectly fine joiner of two complete thoughts when it means *because*. Speaking of *because*, it legally joins two thoughts in choice c. Choice b bombs because the comma isn't an appropriate punctuation mark to join two complete thoughts.

30 **a, b.** Sentence a has a semicolon to join two complete thoughts correctly. Choice b uses *and* for the same job. In choice c, *consequently* tries to link these ideas, but it's not a conjunction and therefore not correct.

31 **a, b.** To connect these two ideas, choice a uses a semicolon and choice b the conjunction *and*. Choice c fails because a comma can't link complete sentences.

32 **a, c.** The conjunction *although* joins one thought to another, more important, main idea about Kathy's sanity, so choice a is correct. So is choice c because *but* does the job there. Choice b doesn't work because *even so* isn't a conjunction.

33 **a, b, c.** Surprised? Choice a is correct because *which* connects the description *(which appeal to something in her character)* to the word it describes *(fragments)*. Choices b and c use the conjunctions *as* and *for* to do the same task.

34 **b, c.** Just because you're quoting, don't think you can ignore run-on rules. The quotation itself contains two complete thoughts and thus needs to be expressed in two complete sentences. Choice a runs them together illegally. Choices b and c separate the quotations with a period, placed in different spots. Both are correct.

35 **a, b.** No grammatical felonies in choices a and b: Two ideas *(she is free* and *Kathy intends to burn grammar textbooks for fuel)* are linked by two conjunctions: *while* in choice a and *as long as* in choice b. Choice c incorrectly inserts a preposition *(during)* where you need a conjunction.

36 **a, b, c.** Two conjunctions, *though* in choice a and *yet* in choice c, join the ideas properly, as does the semicolon in choice b.

37 **b, c.** One complete thought *(History books create a satisfactory snap and crackle while they are burning)* is glued to another *(the flames are also a nice shade of orange)* with nothing more than a comma in choice a. Penalty box! Use a conjunction *(and)* as in choice b or a semicolon as in choice c, and you're fine.

38 **a, c.** In choice b, one complete thought *(Because she loves history, Kathy rejected* The Complete History of the Grammatical World*)* and another *(she burned* Participles and You *instead)* are attached by a comma. I don't think so! Choice a properly uses a conjunction *(but)* to join these ideas. Choice c drops the second subject *(she)*, so now you have nothing more than a compound verb, not two complete thoughts. No other conjunction or punctuation is needed in that situation.

39 **. (period).** Because this sentence makes a statement, a period is the appropriate endmark.

40 **! (exclamation point).** These words may also form a question or a statement, but an exclamation point is certainly appropriate because the speaker may be expressing amazement that a biker likes math.

41 **. (period).** Another statement, another period.

42 **? (question mark).** The *does* in this sentence signals a question, so you need a question mark.

43 **. (period).** The period is the endmark for this statement.

44 **? (question mark).** Here the question mark signals a request for information.

45 **. (period).** This statement calls for a period.

46 **? (question mark).** This sentence requests information, so place the question mark at the end.

47 **! (exclamation point).** Okay, a period would do fine here, but an exclamation point adds extra emphasis. And shame on you for avoiding math. Some of my best friends are math teachers!

48 **. (period).** This statement needs a period as an endmark.

49 **? (question mark).** The sentence requests information, so a question mark is the endmark you want.

50 **. (period).** I've chosen a period, but if you're bursting with emotion, opt for the exclamation point instead.

51 **? (question mark).** I see this one as a true inquiry, but you can also interpret it as a scream of disbelief, in which case an exclamation point works well.

52 **! (exclamation point).** I hear this one as a strong blast of surprise, suitable for an exclamation point.

53 **? (question mark).** If you're asking for information, you need a question mark.

54 **Correct.** This one has everything: subject-verb pair (*concert, honors*), complete thought, and an endmark. One description (*occurring early in October*) is properly tucked into the sentence, near the word it describes (*concert*).

55 **Fragment.** The sentence is incorrect because it gives you a subject (*the holiday*) and a long description (*which is called Hound Dog Day in honor of a wonderful dog breed*) but doesn't pair any verb with *holiday*. Several corrections are possible. Here's one: The holiday, which is called Hound Dog Day in honor of a wonderful dog breed, requires each citizen to attend dog obedience school.

56 **Correct.** You have a subject-verb pair (*tradition, calls*), a complete thought, and an endmark. No problems here!

57 **Fragment.** This sentence has no subject. No one is doing the brushing or the buying. One possible correction: Having brushed the shoes carefully with a suede brush, which can be bought in any shoe store, Bill proudly displayed his feet.

58 **Run-on.** This sentence is a run-on, because a comma can't join two complete thoughts. Change it to a semicolon or reword the sentence. Here's a possible rewording: The citizens lead their dogs to the town square, where Heartbreak Hotel is located.

59 **Run-on.** Another run-on sentence. The two quoted sections are jammed into one sentence, but each is a complete thought. Change the comma after *guest* to a period.

60 **Correct.** Here you've got two complete thoughts (*Elvis, ghost or not, apparently does not attend the Hound Dog Day festivities* and *no one has seen an aging singer in a white jumpsuit there*). A conjunction, *because*, connects them properly.

61 **Missing endmark.** The sentence is incorrect because it has no endmark. Add a question mark.

62 **Correct.** This one is a proper question, with a subject-verb pair (*you can ask*), a complete thought, and a question mark.

63 **Run-on.** This sentence is a run-on. *Consequently* looks like a fine, strong word, but it can't join two complete thoughts, which you have in this sentence. To correct it, add a semicolon after *touch* and dump the comma.

64 **Correct.** Two complete thoughts are joined by the conjunction *but*.

65 **Missing endmark.** The sentence needs an endmark. I'd go with an exclamation point, but a period is also correct.

66 **Correct.** Surprised? This sentence gives a command. The subject is *you*, even though *you* doesn't appear in the sentence. It's implied.

(67) **Correct.** You see two ideas in this sentence, with a comma in between. That punctuation doesn't work if the ideas are equal. In this sentence, though, the first idea begins with a conjunction (*while*). Yes, conjunctions don't have to appear in between two thoughts. If one thought is dependent on the other, the conjunction may show up at the beginning of the dependent statement. (For more on clauses, turn to Chapter 16.)

(68) **Run-on.** The comma can't connect two complete sentences. Use a semicolon.

Here are the answers to the "Overachievers" section:

Sentence 1 is incorrect because it lacks a subject/verb pair. To make the sentence correct, drop *Announcing that* or add *I am* to the beginning of the sentence.

Sentence 4 is incorrect because although it has two long descriptions, it doesn't complete the thought begun by *His first task.*

Sentence 7 is incorrect because it has neither a subject nor a verb. You could correct this by adding *We'll have* to the beginning of the sentence.

Sentence 8 is incorrect because it links two complete thoughts with a comma. Only a semicolon or a conjunction (a joining word such as *and*) can do that job.

Sentence 10 is incorrect because *furthermore* is not a conjunction. Place a semicolon in front of *furthermore*, and you're fine.

2

Clearing Up
Confusing
Grammar Points

Analyze verb tenses: how each is formed and when each is appropriate.

Select the proper verbs for reporting speech, placing events in order, and other special situations.

Become familiar with irregular verb forms.

Match subjects and verbs so that singular pairs with singular and plural with plural.

Pair pronouns with the word(s) they refer to, making sure that they agree in number and gender.

Choose the proper case for every pronoun.

Create prepositional phrases so that they express your intended meaning.

Master the proper role of adjectives and adverbs.

Form comparisons in standard English.

Chapter 4

Finding the Right Verb at the Right Time

A s short as two letters and as long as several words, verbs communicate action or state of being. Plus, even without a watch or a smartphone, they tell time. In this chapter I hit you with basic time questions. No, not "You're late again because . . . ?" but "Which verb do I need to show what's completed, not yet begun, or going on right now?" The first section goes over the basic tenses (past, present, and future) and the second concentrates on the perfect tenses, which are anything but perfect. After that you can work on irregulars, always a joy.

Using Past, Present, and Future Tense at the Right Times

Verbs tell time with a quality known as *tense*. Before you reach for a tranquilizer, here's the lowdown on the basic tenses. The three basic tenses are *past*, *present*, and *future*, and each has two forms — low-carb and gluten-free. Sorry, I mean *plain* (its basic time designation — present, past, or future) and *progressive* (the *-ing* form of a verb). Progressive places a little more emphasis on process or on action that spans a time period, and the present progressive may reach into the future. In many sentences either plain or progressive verbs may be used interchangeably. Here's a taste of each:

>> *Past tense* tells what happened at a specific, previous time or describes a pattern of behavior in the past. In the sentence *Diane tattooed a skull on her bulging arm*, *tattooed* is a past-tense verb. In *During the Motorcycle Festival, Diane was flexing her bicep*, *was flexing* is a verb in past progressive tense.

>> *Present tense* tells you what's going on now at the present moment, or more generally speaking, what action is recurring. In the sentence *Grace rides her bike*, *rides* is a present-tense verb. In *Grace is always polishing her bike* and *Grace is riding to Florida*, the verbs *is polishing* and *is riding* are in present progressive tense.

>> *Future tense* moves into fortune-teller land. The verb in *Grace will give Diane a ride around the block* is *will give*, which is in future tense. In *Grace will be bragging about her new motorcycle for months*, *will be bragging* is in future progressive tense.

EXAMPLE

Q. Following the sentence, you see the *infinitive* (the grandpappy of each verb family, the verb's original form preceded by *to*). Stay in that family when you fill in the blank, choosing the correct tense. When you're finished with this sample question, try the practice problems that follow.

Yesterday, overreacting to a tiny taste of arsenic, Mike _____ his evil twin brother of murder. *(to accuse)*

A. **accused.** The clue here is *yesterday*, which tells you that you're in the past.

1. Fashion is important to David, so he always _____ the latest and most popular style. *(to select)*

2. Last year's tight, slim lines _____ David, who, it must be admitted, does not have a tiny waist. *(to challenge)*

3. While David _____ new clothes, his fashion consultant is busy on the sidelines, recommending stripes and understated plaids to minimize the bulge factor. *(to buy)*

4. David hopes that the next fashion fad _____ a more mature, oval figure like his own. *(to flatter)*

5. Right now Diane _____ an article for the fashion press stating that so-tight-it-may-as-well-be-painted-on leather is best. *(to write)*

6. She once _____ a purple suede pantsuit, which clashed with her orange "I Love Motorcycles" tattoo. *(to purchase)*

7. While she _____ the pantsuit, the salesperson urged her to "go for it." *(to model)*

8. Two days after Diane's shopping spree, Grace _____ about show-offs who "spend more time on their wardrobes than on their spark plugs." *(to mutter)*

9 However, Diane knows that Grace, as soon as she raises enough cash, _____ in a suede outfit of her own. (to invest)

10 David, as always, _____ in with the last word when he gave Grace and Diane the "Fashion Train Wreck of the Year" award. (to chime)

11 Two minutes after receiving the award, Diane _____ it on a shelf next to her "Best Dressed, Considering" medal. (to place)

12 Every day when I see the medal, I _____ what "considering" means. (to wonder)

13 Grace _____ it to me in detail yesterday. (to explain)

14 "We earned the medal for considering many fashion options," she _____. (to state)

15 David, who _____ Diane tomorrow, says that the medal acknowledges the fact that Grace is fashion-challenged but tries hard anyway. (to visit)

Putting Perfect Tenses in the Spotlight

The perfect tenses tack *has, have,* or *had* onto a verb. Each perfect tense — past perfect, present perfect, and future perfect — also has a progressive form, which includes an *-ing* verb. The difference between plain perfect tense and progressive perfect is subtle. The progressive perfect is a bit more immediate than the plain form and refers to something that's ongoing or takes place over a span of time. In many sentences the plain and progressive forms may be interchanged. Here's when to use the perfect tenses:

>> *Past perfect* **places one event in the past before another event in the past.** The verb in *Mike had dumped his dirty laundry in his mother's basement long before she decided to change the front-door lock* is *had dumped,* which is in past perfect tense. In the sentence *Christy, Mike's mother, had been threatening a laundry strike for years, but the beginning of mud-wrestling season pushed her to the breaking point, had been threatening* is a verb in past perfect progressive tense.

>> *Present perfect* **links the past and the present by describing an action or state of being that began in the past and is still going on.** In the sentence *Despite numerous reports of sightings around the world, Kristin has stayed close to home,* the verb *has stayed* is in present perfect tense. In *Kristin has been living within two miles of the Scottish border for the last decade, has been living* is a verb in present perfect progressive tense.

>> *Future perfect* **implies a deadline sometime in the future.** In the sentence *Before sundown, David will have toasted several dozen loaves of bread, will have toasted* is in future perfect tense. The verb in *By the time you turn on the television,* Eye on Cooking *will have been covering the toasting session for two hours, with six more to go,* is *will have been covering,* which is in future perfect progressive tense.

EXAMPLE

Practice, especially with these verbs, makes perfect. (Perfect tense, get it?) Try this example and then plunge ahead. The verb you're working on appears as an *infinitive* (the basic, no-tense form) at the end of the sentence. Change it into the correct tense and fill in the blank.

Q. Kristin _____ an acceptance speech, but the Spy of the Year title went to Hanna instead. (*to prepare*)

A. **had prepared.** With two events in the past, the *had* signals the prior event. The preparing of the speech took place before the awarding of the title, so *had prepared* is the form you want.

16 Mike _____ on thin ice for two hours when he heard the first crack. (*to skate*)

17 Diane _____ Mike for years about his skating habits, but he just won't listen. (*to warn*)

18 After Mike _____ an hour in the emergency room, the doctor examined him and announced that the skater was free to go. (*to wait*)

19 After today's skating trip ends, David _____ a total of 1,232 hours for his friend and _____ countless outdated magazines in the emergency room family area. (*to wait, to read*)

20 Grace _____ to speak to Mike ever since he declared that "a little thin ice" shouldn't scare anyone. (*to refuse*)

21 Mike, in a temper, pointed out that Grace's motorcycle _____ him to the hospital more frequently than his skates ever had. (*to send*)

22 Before the emergency room visit is over, Kristin _____ quietly to both combatants. (*to speak*)

23 Despite years of practice, Tim _____ success only on rare occasions, but he keeps trying to resolve his brother's conflicts anyway. (*to achieve*)

24 Since childhood, Tim's conflict-resolution technique _____ of violent finger pokes in the fighters' ribs, but he is trying to become more diplomatic. (*to consist*)

25 After Mike _____ that his brother's wisest course of action was to "butt out," Tim simply ignored him. (*to declare*)

Speaking of the Past and Things That Never Change

Humans love to gossip, so I bet that right now you have a story to tell. Because you're telling (actually, retelling) something that already happened, your base of operations is past tense. Note the past-tense verbs in italics:

> She *caught* Arthur with Stella, but he *told* her that he *was* only tying Stella's bow tie and not nibbling her neck. Then she *said* that Arthur *brought* her a box of candy with a note saying that no one else *had* eyes like hers.

The verb tenses are all in the past because that's where a *summary of speech* usually resides. So even if she still *has* incomparable eyes, in this paragraph the verb *had* is better. However, if you're talking about something that will never change, that is forever true, present tense is the only one that makes sense, no matter what else is going on in the sentence. Take a look at this example:

> **Wrong:** Marty told me that the earth was a planet.
>
> **Why it is wrong:** What is the earth now, a bagel? The unchanging fact, that the earth is a planet, must be expressed in present tense, despite the fact that all other summarized speech should be in past tense.
>
> **Right:** Marty told me that the earth is a planet.

TIP

Another important exception to the stay-in-past-tense-for-speech-summary rule pops up when you're writing about a work of art or literature. See "Romeo Lives! Writing about Literature and Art in Present Tense" later in this chapter for more information.

WARNING

A common error is to switch from one tense to another with no valid reason. I often hear people say something like "He finally *texted* me. He *says* that the big dance *is* a waste of time!" The writer begins in past tense *(texted)*, but the next two verbs *(says, is)* are in present tense. Penalty box. If you start in past tense, stay there, unless the content requires a change. The correct way to explain what went on is to say, "He finally texted me. He said the big dance was a waste of time."

EXAMPLE

Circle the right verb from the choices in parentheses. Just to be sure you're paying attention, I sneak in a few verbs that don't summarize speech, as well as a few forever-true statements.

Q. At yesterday's tryouts for the reality show *Grammarian Survival*, Roberta (tells/told/will tell) the producer that she (likes/liked/will like) selecting pronouns while dangling 20 feet above the ground.

A. **told, liked.** The first answer is easy. If the tryouts were yesterday, the fact that Roberta lied to the producer (she actually hates pronouns) has to be in past tense. *Told* is past tense. The second part is trickier. Roberta may continue to like selecting pronouns, but past tense is the way to go, because a person's feelings can always change.

26 The director of *Grammarian Survival* explained to the candidates that he (has/had/will have) to select a maximum of 30 contestants.

27 Most of the contestants eagerly replied that they (want/wanted/would want) to make the final 30.

28 Those selected were set to compete against 14 other candidates, because the producers made two separate groups, and 15 (equals/equaled) half of 30.

29 Roberta, who (likes/like/had liked) to play hard to get, screamed at the director that he (doesn't/didn't) have the faintest idea how to select the best applicants.

30 One contestant who didn't make the cut, Michael Hooper, told me that Roberta (is/was/had been) the clear winner of the first two challenges — the noun toss and the pronoun shuffle.

31 For the first challenge, a noun, which (is/was) a word naming a person, place, thing, or idea, (is/was) thrown into a container resembling a basketball hoop.

32 During the second contest, the pronoun *I*, which (is/was) always capitalized, (is/was) moved around the racetrack by contestants who (wear/wore) blindfolds.

33 Michael whispered something surprising: Roberta (fails/failed/had failed) the psychological test.

34 The test comes from Austria, which (is/was) in Europe.

35 A month ago, when the psychologist (asks/asked) Roberta her feelings about various parts of speech, Roberta said that the linking verbs (do/did) present a problem.

36 "Why (don't/didn't) you like linking verbs?" (continues/continued) the psychologist.

37 Roberta explained that any form of the verb *to be* (annoys/annoyed) her; she also said she hated any verb she (encounters/encountered) in science class.

38 Her science teacher (is/was) not Roberta's favorite, she explained, although she (admires/admired) his vegetarian diet.

39 Vegetarians (don't/didn't) eat meat.

40 "I (try/tried) to avoid sentences about science," said Roberta in her interview.

41 She went on to say that adjectives (are/were/had been) her favorite part of speech.

42 The psychologist later reported that he (is/was/had been) worried about Roberta's reaction to punctuation.

43 Roberta apparently said that commas (are/were/had been) "out to get her."

44 She remarked that exclamation points (threaten/threatened/had threatened) her also.

45. An exclamation point (is/was) formed by placing a dot under a vertical line; vertical lines (run/ran) up and down, not side to side.

46. Roberta related well to the psychologist, who complained that quotation marks (hem/hemmed) him in and (make/made) him feel trapped.

47. Roberta and the psychologist disagreed, however, when Roberta said that the semicolon (is/was) the best punctuation mark.

48. The director said that he (doesn't/didn't) know what to make of Roberta's punctuation obsession.

49. He declared that she (is/was) too unstable for a show that relies heavily on question marks.

50. The assistant director, on the other hand, whispered that Roberta (is/was) faking a punctuation phobia just to attract attention.

51. "She answered only half of the questions correctly," he continued; because half of 100 (is/was) 50, Roberta (fails/failed).

52. Marty, rejected by *Grammarian Survival*, probably won't be hired as a science teacher because he told the interviewer that each molecule of water (has/had) three oxygen atoms.

53. Science has never been Marty's best subject, as I realized when he explained that water (covers/covered) nine tenths of the planet.

54. In fact, land (makes/made) up about a quarter of the earth's surface.

55. Marty sniffed and said that he (has/had) a cold and couldn't think about the earth anyway.

Romeo Lives! Writing about Literature and Art in Present Tense

At the end of Shakespeare's *Romeo and Juliet* (spoiler alert!) the title characters die. Yet every time you open the book or go to the theater, they live again. Because the events in the book or play are always happening, present tense is generally the best choice when you're writing about literature. Not always, of course. At times you want to explain that one event in the story occurred before another. In such a situation, past tense may be the only way to talk about the earlier event. Other types of art also rely on present tense. In Picasso's famous portrait of Gertrude Stein, for example, her massive form *looks* — not *looked* — like a monument carved from a block of stone.

TIP

If you write about the act of creating art, past tense is best, as in "Picasso *painted* Gertrude Stein's portrait." (*Painted* is a past-tense verb.)

EXAMPLE

In the blank, write the correct form of the verbs (actually, the infinitives, the leaders of each verb family) that appear in parentheses at the end of the sentence. To keep you off balance, I mix sentences about artworks (present tense usually preferred) with sentences about the artistic process or the artist (often in past tense). After the sample question, I base the exercise on nonexistent artworks. Have fun.

Q. In Jane Austen's *Sense and Sensibility*, Marianne _____ her ankle. *(to sprain)*

A. **sprains.** To write about this event in Austen's novel, present tense is best.

56. The horizontal bands in Lola's paintings _____ random, but she _____ the width of each band using a complex formula involving horses at her local racetrack. *(to appear, to calculate)*

57. Lola, who also _____ a mystery novel, _____ a character who _____ his lunch money every day and often _____. *(to write, to create, to bet, to win)*

58. The character's name _____ William, and in every scene he _____ a hat. *(to be, to wear)*

59. William _____ the murder of a veterinarian; in one scene a parrot _____ a vital clue, but William _____ the bird perhaps because earlier the parrot _____ William. *(to investigate, to provide, to ignore, to bite)*

60. When asked about her writing, Lola _____ that William _____ loyalty, honor, and the need for a reliable birdseed provider. *(to maintain, to represent)*

61. Followers of Lola's blog _____ for years on William's fear of parrots, which they _____ "parrot-noia"; in fact, today someone _____ about that topic. *(to comment, to call, to write)*

62. The parrot _____ a poet; he _____ sonnets and sometimes _____ them loudly. *(to be, to favor, to recite)*

63. As of today Lola _____ 17 copies of her novel, which _____ place in New York City. *(to sell, to take)*

Hitting Curveballs: Irregular Forms

Designed purposely to torture you, irregular verbs stray from the usual *-ed* form in the past tense. The irregularity continues in a form called the *past participle*. You don't need to know the terms; you just need to know what words replace the usual *-ed* verb configurations (*sang* and *sung* instead of *singed*, for example).

TIP

You can't memorize every possible irregular verb. If you're unsure about a particular verb, look it up in the dictionary. The definition will include the irregular form.

EXAMPLE

Fill in the blanks with the correct irregular form, working from the verb (actually, the infinitive, the basic form of the verb family) indicated in parentheses. Check out the following example:

Q. With one leg 3 inches shorter than the other, Natalie seldom _____ into first base, even when the team was desperate for a base hit. *(to slide)*

A. **slid.** No *-ed* for this past tense! *Slid* is the irregular past form of *to slide*.

64 If you discover a piece of pottery on the floor, look for Natalie, who has _____ many vases because of her tendency to dust far too emotionally. *(to break)*

65 Once Natalie _____ with sadness at her first glimpse of a dusty armchair. *(to shake)*

66 David, a duster himself, _____ a manual of daily furniture maintenance. *(to write)*

67 The manual, entitled *Dust or Die*, _____ to the top of the best-seller list. *(to rise)*

68 Nearly all the copies had been _____ by fanatical cleaners. *(to buy)*

69 David once dusted the fire alarm so forcefully that it went off; the firefighters weren't amused because David had _____ the fire alarm a little too often. *(to ring)*

70 The fire chief promptly _____ to speak with the mayor about David's false alarm. *(to go)*

71 The mayor has _____ an investigation into a new category of offenses, "False Dust Alarms"; almost immediately, David _____ to protest. *(to begin)*

72 "I have _____ to a new low," sighed David. "I hear that Natalie has _____ a new hobby. Maybe I can get one too." *(to sink, to find)*

73 Natalie _____ David to a fly-catching meet, and soon his interest in grime _____ the dust. *(to take, to bite)*

74 Natalie, inspired by fly catching, _____ a tapestry with a delicate fly pattern. *(to weave)*

75 David, worried about Natalie's enthusiasm for winged pests, _____ help. *(to seek)*

76 "Leave the flies," _____ David. *(to say)*

77 "Never!" Natalie declared as she _____ her coffee. *(to drink)*

78. David soon _____ up on Natalie and her new hobby. (*to give*)

79. Every day when Natalie _____, she thought about flies. (*to wake*)

80. Her friends avoided the fly cage, which _____ in her yard. (*to stand*)

81. Last Saturday, Natalie _____ hours watching public television, which _____ fly-catching tips. (*to spend, to give*)

82. Eventually, Natalie _____ to realize that fly catching _____ too much. (*to come, to cost*)

83. She and David _____ a new hobby. (*to choose*)

84. They _____ miniature houses out of paper that had been _____ out. (*to build, to throw*)

85. First, David _____ a floor plan for each house. (*to draw*)

86. Next, Natalie _____ "logs" from twisted paper strips. (*to make*)

87. Unfortunately, David _____ some dog food near the houses, and his dog _____ them. (*to leave, to eat*)

88. Natalie _____ betrayed and _____ with David about what Natalie called his "criminal carelessness." (*to feel, to fight*)

Getting a Handle on Common Irregulars: Be and Have

Two irregular verbs, *to be* and *to have*, appear more frequently than a movie star with a new film to promote. And like a movie star, they tend to cause trouble. Both change according to time and according to the person with whom they're paired. (Amazing that the movie-star comparison works on so many levels!) Because they're common, you need to be sure to master all their forms, as Table 4-1 shows.

Table 4-1   Verb Forms for the Irregular Verbs *To Be* and *To Have*

Pronoun(s)	Present-Tense Verb for "To Be"	Past-Tense Verb for "To Be"	Present-Tense Verb for "To Have"	Past-Tense Verb for "To Have"
I	am	was	have	had
you/we/they	are	were	have	had
it/he/she	is	was	has	had

Note: The form of "to be" used with helping verbs is *been*.

EXAMPLE

Fill in the blanks with the correct form of *to be* or *to have*, as in this example and the following exercises:

Q. Joyce the lifeguard _____ out in the sun long enough to fry her brain, but she intends to go inside soon because the Picnic Olympics is on television tonight.

A. **has been.** *Been* is the form used with helping verbs, such as *has.*

89 If pickling _____ necessary, I'll bring my own vinegar.

90 Who ever _____ enough cucumbers on this sort of occasion?

91 Mike replied, "I _____ totally comfortable with the amount of green vegetables in my refrigerator."

92 Kristin, never outdone, _____ a different idea.

93 "Grace and I _____ firmly in the anti-vegetable camp," she commented.

94 Two hours from now, Kristin _____ three trophies for carbo-loading.

95 Diane _____ Champion of the Potato Salad Competition for three years in a row, counting this year.

96 Yesterday, Grace _____ second thoughts about her entry choice; she now thinks that she should have picked sides instead of main dishes.

97 The soon-to-be-announced winners in each category _____ extremely pleased with the prizes this year.

98 Give me a taste because I _____ a judge.

99 "No kidding!" exclaimed Kristin. "I thought you _____ a participant."

100 Kristin says that Grace _____ certain to win, but I _____ not sure.

101 Grace _____ a heavy hand with hot sauce.

102 You _____ to taste her dish anyway.

103 It _____ unlikely that Grace's food will actually catch fire.

Calling All Overachievers: Extra Practice with Verbs

Time to sharpen all the tools in your verb kit. Read the memo in the following figure, a product of my fevered brain, and correct all the verbs that have strayed from the proper path.

EXAMPLE

To: All Employees

From: Christy

Subject: Paper Clips

It had come to my attention that some employees will be bending paper clips nearly every day. A few clerks even bended an entire box. The clips we use these days were made of steel. Steel was a metal, and metal items are expensive. In my ten years of superior performance as your boss, I gave you a fair deal. You all been very disrespectful, but I thinked you were responsible employees. Therefore, I began inspecting desks next Monday. I will check every single one. Because I had warned you about paper clips last week, I expect to find no bent clips. If I find any, you will find yourself out of a job.

Answers to Problems on Verbs and Verb Tenses

Have all these verb questions made you tense? If so, take a deep breath and relax. Now, check your answers to see how you did.

1. **selects.** Notice the time clues? The first part of the sentence contains the present-tense verb *is*, and the second part includes the word *always*. You're in the present with a recurring action.

2. **challenged.** Another time clue: *last year's* places you in the past.

3. **is buying** or **buys.** The second verb in the sentence (*is*) takes you right into the store with David, watching the unfolding action. Present progressive tense gives a sense of immediacy, so *is buying* makes sense. The plain present tense (*buys*) works nicely also.

4. **will flatter.** The key here is *next*, which puts the sentence in the future.

5. **is writing.** The time clue *right now* indicates an ongoing action, so the present progressive form *is writing* works well here.

6. **purchased.** Diane's bad-taste splurge happened *once*, which means it took place in the past.

7. **was modeling** or **modeled.** The second part of the sentence includes the verb *urged*, which places the action in the past. I like the past progressive (*was modeling*) here because the word *while* takes you into the process of modeling, which went on over a period of time. However, the sentence makes sense even when the process isn't emphasized, so *modeled* is also an option.

8. **muttered** or **was muttering.** The clue to the past is *two days after*. The second answer gives more of a "you are there" feel, but either is correct.

9. **will invest.** The time words here, *as soon as*, tell you that the action hasn't happened yet.

10. **chimed.** If he *gave*, you're in past tense.

11. **placed.** The expression *two minutes after* tells you that you're in the past, so you know that the action of placing the award on the shelf is in past tense.

12. **wonder.** The time clue here is *every day*, which tells you that this action is still happening at the present time and should be in present tense.

13. **explained.** The *yesterday* is a dead giveaway; go for past tense.

14. **stated.** The saga of Grace and Diane's award is in past tense, and this sentence is no exception. Even without the story context, you see the first verb (*earned*) is in past tense, which works nicely with the past-tense verb *stated*.

15. **will visit.** The time clue is *tomorrow*, which places the verb in the future.

16. **had been skating** or **had skated.** You have two actions in the past — the skating and the hearing. The two hours of skating came before the hearing, so you need past perfect tense. Either the plain or the progressive form works here also.

(17) **has been warning** or **has warned.** The second half of the sentence indicates the present (*won't listen*), but you also have a hint of the past (*for years*). Present perfect is the best choice because it links past and present. I like the immediacy of progressive here (I can hear Diane's ranting), but plain present perfect is okay as well.

(18) **had waited** or **had been waiting.** The waiting preceded the doctor's announcement, so you should use past perfect. Progressive adds a "you are there" feel but isn't necessary.

(19) **will have waited, will have read.** The deadline in the sentence (*the end of today's trip*) is your clue for future perfect tense.

(20) **has refused.** Notice the present-past link? Mike declared and Grace is acting now. Hence you need present perfect tense.

(21) **had sent.** The pointing and the hospital-sending are at two different times in the past, with the hospital occurring first. Go for past perfect for the earlier action.

(22) **will have spoken.** The future perfect needs an end point (in this sentence, the end of the hospital visit) before which the action occurs.

(23) **has achieved.** Because the sentence states that he keeps trying, you have a present-tense idea that's connected to the past (*despite years of practice and on rare occasions*). Present perfect connects the present and past.

(24) **has consisted.** This sentence has a past-tense clue (*since childhood*). The sentence tells you about the past (*at times*) and the present (*is trying*), so present perfect is the one you want.

(25) **had declared.** The *after* at the beginning of the sentence is your clue that one action occurs before another. Because both are in the past, you need past perfect tense for the earlier action.

(26) **had.** The tip-off is the verb *explained*, which tells you that you're summarizing speech. Go for the past tense *had.*

(27) **wanted.** *Replied* is a clue that you're summarizing speech, so *wanted*, the past tense, is best. The last choice, by the way, imposes a condition (he *would* do something under certain circumstances). Because the sentence doesn't impose a condition, that choice isn't appropriate.

(28) **equals.** Math doesn't change, so the verb must be in present tense.

(29) **likes, didn't.** The first choice has nothing to do with summary of speech and is a simple statement about Roberta. The present tense works nicely in this spot. The second choice *is* a speech summary (well, a *scream* summary, but the same rule applies), so the past-tense verb *didn't* fills the bill.

(30) **was.** The sentence tells you that *Michael Hooper told.* The past tense works here for summary of speech.

(31) **is, was.** The definition of a noun won't change, so you need present tense for the first parenthesis. In the second, you're simply telling what happened on the show, so past tense rules.

(32) **is, was, wore.** The rules of grammar are constant, and permanent conditions are best expressed by present tense, so *is* should be your choice in the first parenthesis. The next two verb choices require past tense because they express actions that took place in the past.

(33) **failed.** You can arrive at the answer in two separate ways. If Michael *whispered*, the sentence is summarizing what he said. Another way to look at this sentence is to reason that Michael is telling you something that already happened, not something happening in the present moment. Either way, the past tense *failed* is best.

34 **is.** Austria isn't going anywhere, so this sentence expresses an unchangeable condition. Go for present tense.

35 **asked, did.** The first answer comes from the fact that the psychological test was in the past. The second is summary of speech (Roberta's words) and calls for past tense.

36 **don't, continued.** Give yourself a pat on the back if you got this one. The quotation marks indicate that the words are exactly what the psychologist said. The speech isn't summarized; it's quoted. The present tense makes sense here because the tester is asking Roberta about her state of mind at the moment. The psychologist's action, however, took place in the past, so *continued*, a past-tense verb, is what you want for the speaker tag.

37 **annoyed, encountered.** Straight summary of speech here, indicated by the verb *explained*. Therefore, past tense is best for both parentheses.

38 **was, admired.** Once again, this sentence summarizes speech and thus needs past-tense verbs.

39 **don't.** The definition of *vegetarian* is unchangeable; opt for present tense.

40 **try.** This statement isn't a summary, but rather a direct quotation from Roberta. She's speaking about her current actions, so present tense fits.

41 **were.** Roberta's comments are summarized, not quoted, so past tense is appropriate.

42 **was.** The psychologist may still be worried (I would be, if I were treating Roberta!), but the summary of what he said should be in simple past tense.

43 **were.** The parentheses contain two past-tense verbs, *were* and *had been*. The *had* form is used to place one event further in the past than another, a situation that isn't needed here, when you're simply summarizing what someone is saying and not placing events in order. Go for simple past tense.

44 **threatened.** Roberta's remark about exclamation points is summarized speech calling for past tense.

45 **is, run.** Present tense is your choice here because the description of punctuation marks doesn't change.

46 **hemmed, made.** The psychologist's comments should, like all summarized speech, be reported in simple past tense.

47 **was.** I like semicolons too, though I hesitate to say that they're the best. Whatever I say about them, however, must be summarized in simple past tense.

48 **didn't.** *The director said* is your cue to chime in with simple past tense, because you're reporting his speech.

49 **was.** *He declared* tells you that you're reporting what he said. Thus, past tense is the way to go.

50 **was.** The word *whispered* is the key here because it indicates summarized speech, which calls for simple past tense.

51 **is, failed.** Because 50 is half of 100, an unchangeable fact, you need present tense. The second part of the sentence relates what Roberta did, so past tense is best here.

52 **had.** The composition of a water molecule is a constant, but this sentence talks about what Marty said, not about an unchangeable fact. Therefore, past tense is correct here.

53. **covered.** The verb *explained* tells you that you're in summary-of-speech land, where past tense rules.

54. **makes.** The amount of land doesn't change; go with present tense.

55. **had.** Colds come and go; they aren't unchangeable conditions. The summary of speech rule doesn't change. Past tense is what you want.

56. **appear, calculated.** The first part of the sentence describes a work of art, so the present-tense verb *appear* is what you want. The second part of the sentence explains how the art-work was created, an event that took place in the past. Therefore, opt for the past-tense verb *calculated*.

57. **wrote, created, bets, wins.** The first two verbs describe the process of making art, and because the process is over, past tense works well here. The second two verbs apply to the artwork (the novel), so you need present tense.

58. **is, wears.** For these simple statements about a literary work, use present tense.

59. **investigates, provides, ignores, bit.** The first three statements are in present tense, as comments about literature and art generally are. The last verb is a little tricky; the sentence explains why William ignores the bird by citing an earlier event. Because the order of events is important, the past-tense verb *bit* is best.

60. **maintained, represents.** The verb *asked* tells you that Lola's comments also took place in the past, so the past-tense verb *maintained* is correct. The symbolic meaning, however, doesn't change and should be expressed in present tense.

61. **have commented, call, wrote.** The first choice that confronts you in this sentence is the actions of Lola's readers. Because their actions span past and present, present perfect tense is best for the first parenthesis. Moving on: The second parenthesis addresses the comments that exist on the blog. While blogs don't generally rise to the level of literature, they are writ-ten works, so present tense applies in this situation. The last part of the sentence describes what someone did in the past, so you need a past-tense verb.

62. **is, favors, recites.** These three verbs talk about events in Lola's novel, so present tense is what you need.

63. **has sold, takes.** The first part of the sentence spans past and present, and present perfect tense is (pardon the pun) perfect for that sort of situation. The novel's setting is described in present tense, because that's the tense for writing about literature.

64. **broken.** The verb *to break* has two irregular forms, *broke* and *broken*.

65. **shook.** *To shake* has two irregular forms, *shook* and *shaken*.

66. **wrote** or **has written.** For correct writing, use *wrote* or *has written*.

67. **rose** or **has risen.** Be sure to rise to the occasion and choose *rose* or *has risen*, not *rised*.

68. **bought.** Let this verb remind you of other irregulars, including *caught*, *taught*, and *thought*. Here's a sentence to help you remember: I *thought* I was in trouble because I *caught* a cold when I *taught* that class of sneezing kids, but fortunately I had *brought* tissues.

69. **rung.** The bell *rings*, *rang*, or *has/had rung*.

70. **went.** Take a memo: I *go*, he *goes*, I *went*, and I *have* or *had gone*.

71. **begun, began.** The plain past tense form is *began*, and the form that combines with *has, have,* or *had* is *begun*.

72. **sunk, found.** *To sink* becomes *sank* in the past tense and *has* or *have sunk* in the perfect tenses. *To find* becomes *found* in both past and present/past perfect.

73. **took, bit.** These two forms are in simple past; the perfect forms use *taken* and *bitten*.

74. **wove.** The past tense of *to weave* is *wove*.

75. **sought.** This irregular form wandered far from the original. The past tense of *to seek* is *sought*.

76. **said.** This irregular verb is the past tense of *to say*.

77. **drank.** Three forms of this verb sound like a song to accompany a beer blast: *drink, drank,* and *drunk*. The middle form, which is past tense, is the one you want here. The form that combines with *has* and *have* (in case you ever need it) is *drunk*.

78. **gave.** The verb *to give* becomes *gave* in the plain past tense (and *given* in the perfect tenses).

79. **woke.** The verb *to wake* changes to *woke* (plain past tense) or *woken* (with *has, have,* or *had*).

80. **stood.** This irregular form works for the plain past and the perfect forms of *to stand*.

81. **spent, gave.** *To spend* turns into *spent* in the plain past and perfect tenses. *To give* becomes *gave* in past tense.

82. **came** or **has come, cost.** Write it down: Natalie *came* or *has come*. Just to confuse you, the past tense of *to cost* is *cost* (in both the plain past tense and perfect tenses).

83. **chose.** They *chose* and we *have chosen*. No one *choosed*, ever!

84. **built, thrown.** Don't even consider *builded*. The correct past tense form is *built*. *To throw* becomes *threw* (plain past) or *thrown* (perfect tenses).

85. **drew.** You can't *drawed*. You either *drew* or *have/had drawn*.

86. **made.** *To make* changes into *made* for all past and perfect forms.

87. **left, ate.** Don't leave this section before you memorize this irregular form of *to leave!* The plain past form of *to eat* is *ate*. Opt for *eaten* when you have a helping verb.

88. **felt, fought.** You'll feel better when you know that *felt* works for plain past tense and the perfect tenses. *To fight* also has one form, *fought*, for both jobs.

89. **is.** Here you're in the present tense.

90. **has.** You need a singular, present-tense verb to match *who* in this sentence.

91. **am.** The verb *to be* changes to *am* when it's paired with *I*.

92. **has** or **had.** This answer depends on the tense. If you're speaking about a past event, choose *had*, but if you're speaking about something in the here and now, *has* is your best bet.

93. **are.** You need a plural to match *Grace and I*.

94. **will have.** The sentence speaks about the future.

(95) **has been.** The sentence requires a link between past and present, so simple past won't do. You need present perfect, the bridge between those two time periods. *Has been* does the job.

(96) **had.** The sentence calls for a contrast with *now*, so opt for past tense.

(97) **will be.** Once more into the future!

(98) **am** or **will be.** You may choose either present or future, depending upon the context.

(99) **were.** The past tense of *to be* is required for this sentence.

(100) **is, am.** The *says* tells you that present tense is needed in this sentence.

(101) **has.** Here you need the singular, present tense form of *to have*.

(102) **have.** The verb, *have*, doesn't express ownership in this context. Instead it implies obligation.

(103) **is.** The singular subject *it* pairs with the singular verb *is*.

Refer to the following figure for the answers to the "Overachiever" question.

To: All Employees

From: Christy

Subject: Paper Clips

It ~~had~~ **has come** to my attention that some employees ~~will be~~ **have been** [1] [2]

bending paper clips nearly every day. A few clerks even ~~bended~~ **bent** an [3]

entire box. The clips we use these days ~~were~~ **are** made of steel. Steel [4]

~~was~~ **is** a metal, and metal items are expensive. In my ten years of [5]

superior performance as your boss, I always ~~gave~~ **have given** you a fair [6]

deal. You **have** all been very disrespectful, but I ~~thinked~~ **thought** you [7] [8]

were responsible employees. Therefore, I ~~began~~ **will begin** inspecting [9]

desks next Monday. I will check every single one. Because I ~~had~~

~~warned~~ **warned** you about paper clips last week, I expect to find no bent [10]

clips. If I find any, you will find yourself out of a job.

1. *Had come* is wrong because the *had* places an action prior to another action in the past. The paper-clip issue is ongoing, so present perfect is better.

2. *Will be* places the action in the future, but the memo places the problem in the past and present. To connect these two time periods, use present perfect tense.

3. *Bended* is not proper English. The correct, irregular form is *bent*.

4. *These days* is a phrase implying present, so you need a present tense verb.

5. Steel is always a metal, so you need present tense here.

6. Past and present are joined in this sentence, so opt for present perfect tense.

7. Once more, past and present are referenced, so go for present perfect tense.

8. The irregular past tense of *think* is *thought*.

9. *Next Monday* places you in the future, so you need a future tense verb.

10. The *had* form (past perfect) is what you need when you place one event before another in the past — not the case here. Simple past is best.

Chapter 5

Agreement: Choosing Singular or Plural Verbs and Pronouns

I n Grammarland, the difference between singular (just one) and plural (anywhere from two to a crowd) is a big deal. In this respect grammar follows real life. When an obstetrician reports on an ultrasound, the difference between one and more than one is a matter of considerable interest. In this chapter I show you how to tell the difference between the singular and plural forms of subjects, verbs, and pronouns and explain how to pair them up correctly.

Meeting Their Match: Pairing Subjects and Verbs

To make a good match, as every online-dating service knows, you have to pair like with like. So too in grammar: With two important exceptions (explained in this section), singular subjects pair with singular verbs and plural subjects with plural verbs — a principle that grammarians call *agreement*. First, I take you though the basics of subject-verb agreement. Then I hit you with some tricky subject-verb situations and some deceptive subjects.

Sentences with mismatched subjects and verbs often appear on standardized tests. You have to point out the error or choose a better version of the sentence the error appears in. Number-two pencil pushers, pay special attention to this section!

Boning up on the basics

The good news is that most of the time English verbs have only one form for both singular and plural. "I *burp*" and "the dinosaurs *burp*" are both correct, even though *I* is singular and *dinosaurs* is plural. You have to worry only in these few special circumstances. Here are the rules, with italicized subjects and verbs in the examples so you can locate them quickly:

>> **Talking about someone in the present tense requires different verb forms for singular and plural.** The singular verb ends in *s*, as in "he spits" (singular) and "they spit" (plural).

>> **Verbs that include *does/do* or *has/have* change forms for singular and plural.** Singular verbs use *does* or *has*. ("*John does paint* his toenails blue. He *has stated* that fact.") Plurals use *do* and *have*. ("*Do* the toenails *need* more polish? No, *they have* plenty already.")

>> ***I* pairs with plural action verbs.** The pronoun *I* is always singular, but "I go" is correct, not "I goes."

>> ***You* may be either singular or plural, but it always pairs with plural verbs.** So *you catch* a robber, whether *you* refers to one person or ten.

>> **The verb *to be* changes form according to the noun or pronoun paired with it.** I cover this topic in Chapter 4.

>> **Two subjects joined by *and* make a plural and take a plural verb.** As you discovered in kindergarten, one plus one equals two, which is a plural. ("*John and Dana plan* a bank job every two years.")

>> **Two singular subjects joined by *or* take a singular verb.** The logic here is that you're saying one *or* the other, but not both, so two singles joined by *or* don't add up to a double. ("*Dana or John is cooking* tonight.")

>> **Ignore interrupters when matching subjects to verbs.** *Interrupters* include phrases such as "of the books" and "except for . . ." and longer expressions such as "who golfs badly" and "which takes the cake." ("*Kristin*, as well as all her penguins, *is marching* to the iceberg today.")

WARNING

Some interrupters *(as well as, in addition to)* appear to create a plural, but grammatically they aren't part of the subject and, like all interrupters, have no effect on the singular/plural issue.

>> ***Here* and *there* can't be subjects.** In a *here* or *there* sentence, look for the subject after the verb. ("Here *are* five *beans*. There *is* a *bean* in your nose.")

>> **The subject usually precedes the verb but may appear elsewhere.** ("Around the corner *speed* the *robbers*, heading for the getaway car.")

EXAMPLE

Test yourself with these examples. In the blank, write the correct form of the verb in parentheses.

Q. John's teacher _____ uninterested in his excuses for missing homework. *(remain/remains)*

A. **remains.** The subject, *teacher*, is singular, so the verb must also be singular. The letter *s* creates a singular verb.

1 Hinting delicately that the teacher's attitude _____ unfair, John _____ his eyebrows. *(is/are, raises/raise)*

2 John, whose homework _____ been late every day this year, says that he _____ from a toe condition. *(has/have, suffer/suffers)*

3 We _____ not buying his story. *(am/is/are)*

4 You probably _____ John because you _____ everyone the benefit of the doubt. *(believe/believes, give/gives)*

5 _____ you think that John's friends always _____ the truth? *(Does/Do, tell/tells)*

6 _____ his story fallen on disbelieving ears? *(Has/Have)*

7 I never _____ when John _____ avoiding reality. *(know/knows, am/is/are)*

8 Sometimes he _____ very odd tales. *(tells/tell)*

9 Why _____ everyone believe him? *(does/do)*

10 Nadine, who used to be one of John's closest friends, _____ completely dismayed by John's dishonest tendencies. *(was/were)*

11 He, along with some other students, _____ on tests all the time. *(cheats/cheat)*

12 The principal, in addition to everyone else on the faculty, _____ wanted to expel John for years. *(has/have)*

13 Recently, John _____ spent a lot of time in detention. *(has/have)*

14 There _____ six teachers taking turns as detention-supervisor. *(is/are)*

15 During today's detention, John and Dana _____ texting each other instead of studying math. *(was/were)*

16 When he works on a math problem, John often _____ his cellphone from his pocket and _____ for the correct answer. *(removes/remove, searches/search)*

17. "In every single one of my pockets _____ a math formula," John once remarked. (*is/are*)

18. John, as well as his friend Dana, _____ recently caught cheating on a midterm exam. (*was/were*)

19. His suspension on a variety of charges _____ being processed as we speak. (*is/are*)

20. There _____ a movie director and a literary agent in the principal's office trying to gain access to John. (*was/were*)

21. John's offers, in addition to a "how to cheat" podcast, _____ a chance to be on a reality television show. (*includes/include*)

22. Imagine the show: Formally dressed as always, across the screen _____ John and Dana, while the label "World's Best Cheaters" _____. (*strolls/stroll, scrolls, scroll*) underneath.

Taming the tough guys: Difficult subjects

A few pronouns may trip you up when you form subject–verb pairs. With a little extra attention, though, you can tame these difficult subjects. Check out these rules:

» **Pronouns ending in *-one*, *-thing*, and *-body* (*everyone*, *something*, and *anybody*, for example) are singular.** So are *each* and *every*. Even though they sometimes sound plural, *everyone is* here and *nobody needs* more grammar rules. And no matter what follows *each* or *every*, you're in singular territory and need a singular verb ("*each* of the computers *is*, *every* tablet and laptop *has*).

» ***All, some, most, none,* and *any* can be either singular or plural.** Subjects that can be counted are plural. ("*All* of the ears *are sticking* out. *Some* of the ears *are going* to be super-glued to scalps.") A subject that is measured but not counted is singular. ("*Most* of the sugar in his diet *comes* from his doughnut habit. *None* of his food *contains* anything nutritious.")

» ***Either* and *neither* alone, without *or* and *nor*, are singular.** These pronouns are often followed by a prepositional phrase that makes you think you're in plural territory, but you're not. (*Either* of my cousins *is* happy to escort you to the ball.)

» **In *either/or* and *neither/nor* sentences, match the verb to the closest subject.** You can do these sentences by measuring the distance between the subject and the verb with a ruler! ("*Neither* of my uncles *has agreed* to take me to the movies this afternoon." "Either *Josh* or his *partners are going* to jail. Either his *partners* or *Josh is going* to jail.")

Q. Neither the fire marshal nor the police officers (*was/were*) aware of the bowling tournament.

EXAMPLE

A. **were.** The subject *police officers* is closer to the verb than *marshal*. Because *police officers* is plural, the verb must also be plural.

23 All the dancers in Lola's musical (is/are) required to get butterfly tattoos.

24 Either of the principal singers (has/have) enough talent to carry the musical.

25 Every orchestra seat and balcony box (is/are) sold already.

26 Why (does/do) no one understand that Lola's musical is extremely boring?

27 Most of the songs (has/have) been written already, but the out-of-town tryouts suggest that more work is needed.

28 Everyone (has/have) invested a substantial amount in *Whatever Lola Wants,* but no one (is/are) expecting a profit, despite the strong ticket sales.

29 Neither her partners nor Lola (is/are) willing to speculate on the critical reception.

30 Any of the reviews (has/have) the ability to make or break the production.

31 (Has/Have) either the director or the musicians agreed on a contract?

32 Everyone (agrees/agree) that Lola should cut the fifth song, "Why I Tattoo."

33 Lola is much more interested in tattoos than most of the members of the audience (is/are).

34 I don't understand the tattoo fixation because neither of Lola's parents (has/have) any tattoos.

35 Perhaps every one of Lola's 20 tattoos (is/are) a form of rebellion.

36 Some of the tattoos (is/are) to be covered by makeup, because Lola's character is an innocent schoolgirl.

37 However, each of the tattoos (has/have) special meaning to Lola, who is reluctant to conceal anything.

38 She says, "All the fame in the world (is/are) not as valuable as honesty."

39 Lola talks a good line, but all of her accountants (believes/believe) that she will go along with the necessary cover-up.

40 (Has/Have) someone mentioned the Tony Awards to Lola?

41 Either Lola or her producers (is/are) sure to win at least one award — if nobody else (enters/enter) the contest.

42 Every Tony and Oscar on Lola's shelf (is/are) a testament to her talent.

43 Neither of her Tony awards, however, (has/have) been polished for a long time.

44 Perhaps someone (has/have) neglected to hire a cleaning professional to spruce up Lola's house.

45 Both of Lola's brothers (is/are) in the field of furniture maintenance.

46 (Was/Were) either of her brothers called in to consult about trophy cleaning?

47 If so, perhaps either Lola's brothers or Lola herself (is/are) on the verge of a cleaner future.

48 Most of us, I should point out, (believe/believes) that Lola will never forget to shine her Oscar statuettes.

Dealing with tricksters

The old saying that "appearances are deceiving" certainly applies to the subjects in this section. Take a look:

> » **A few words that appear plural are actually singular.** *Politics, news, economics,* and *thesis* are all singular.
>
> » **Company names are singular, even if they sound plural.** "*Sears is* (not *are*) *having* a great sale on irregular verbs today."
>
> » **Team names usually take a plural verb.** So "the *Yankees have won* again," and "the *Rangers are losing* the game." Team names that sound singular (the *New York Liberty* or the *Utah Jazz,* for example) generally pair with a singular verb.

TIP

The dictionary is the final authority. I can't cover all nouns here, not unless you want a workbook that you can't lift without heavy machinery. Strange words such as *data* (plural), *memorandum* (singular), *scissors* (plural), and others can fool you, unless you check the dictionary.

EXAMPLE

Q. Choose the correct verb from the choices in parentheses.

The news (was/were) announced at noon yesterday.

A. **was.** *News* is singular and takes the singular verb *is.*

49 No matter how little studying Angie does, economics (is/are) an easy A+ for her.

50 The data (shows/show) that Angie never blows an economics test.

51 I wrote a paper on Angie's study habits; the thesis (was/were) that Angie's attention to current events helps her understand economic theory.

52 When I visit Angie, the news (is/are) always on.

53 It's difficult to drag her away from the television, though it's possible if the Giants (is/are) playing.

54 The Miami Heat, on the other hand, (does/do) not draw her attention.

55 Politics (was/were) one of Angie's hobbies when she was young.

56　Now, Angie thinks that the media (has/have) too much power.

57　Angie's fellow alumni (believes/believe) that taxes are evil, and that position is popular with some voters.

58　Angie once screamed at a political rally, "My scissors (cuts/cut) your taxes."

59　The pair of scissors she waved (is/are) in a museum now.

60　The media (loves/love) to cover Angie's career.

61　My memorandum on the subject (makes/make) my ideas perfectly clear.

62　Universal Business and Trade, a giant corporation, (agrees/agree) with me.

63　The corporation's analysis (is/are) that I should pay taxes, not the corporation.

Matching Pronouns and Antecedents

Pronouns take the place of nouns and frequently come in handy. Who can write a paragraph without *I, me, ours, them, us, that,* and similar words? Unfortunately, pronouns can trip you up in a hundred ways, especially when you're matching them to their *antecedents,* the words they replace or refer to. You must follow two basic rules:

>> Replace a singular noun with a singular pronoun.

>> Replace a plural noun with a plural pronoun.

TIP

Pronouns have another characteristic — gender. The rules governing pronoun gender have become more complicated in recent years, as has the topic of gender itself. Traditionally, masculine pronouns (*he, him, himself*) take the place of masculine nouns, and feminine *pronouns* (*she, her, herself*) fill in for feminine nouns. Some pronouns (*it, itself, who, they, which,* and *that,* for example) function in a neutral way — mostly. Because traditional, formal English has no gender-neutral singular form for people, many people employ *they/them/their/theirs* as singular words. Your own beliefs about gender and those of your reader or listener must guide you to a decision about whether to write *his or her,* for example, or *their* when you traditionally need a singular pronoun.

Here are the most common singular and plural pronouns. Following tradition, I've placed *they, them, their,* and *theirs* in the plural slot:

>> **Singular:** *I, me, you, he, she, it, my, your, his, her, its, myself, yourself, himself, herself, itself, either, neither, everyone, anyone, someone, no one, everything, anything, something, nothing, everybody, anybody, somebody, nobody,* and *each*

>> **Plural:** *we, us, you, they, them, our, ours, your, yours, their, theirs, ourselves, yourselves, themselves, both,* and *few*

TIP

When a pronoun shows possession, it never contains an apostrophe. Some possessive pronouns attach to nouns (*my, your, her, its, our, their*), and others take the place of nouns (*mine, yours, hers, ours, theirs*). One pronoun, *his*, can function either way.

WARNING

The *-self* pronouns — *myself, himself,* and so on — have very limited usage. They can add emphasis ("I myself will blow up the mud balloon") or circle back to the person doing the action in the sentence ("She will clean herself later"). Resist the temptation to use a *-self* pronoun without the circling-back action ("Rachel and myself hate mud balloons," for example).

EXAMPLE

Okay, get to work. Without peeking at the answers (and I am watching), decide which pronoun may replace the underlined noun. Consider the singular/plural and gender issues. Write your choice in the blank provided.

Q. I hope that Charlie Burke and Dr. Eileen Burke will attend tonight's symphony, even though Charlie is tone-deaf and <u>Eileen</u> tends to sing along.

_____

A. **she.** Dr. Eileen has been known to hit the doughnut tray a little too often, but Eileen is still just one person. *She* is a singular, feminine pronoun.

64 Eileen wore a plaid hat last year, and <u>the hat</u> made quite an impression on the fashion press. _____

65 "Who is your designer, Eileen?" <u>the photographers</u> screamed.

_____

66 <u>Charlie's</u> hairpiece, on the other hand, attracted almost no attention.

_____

67 At one point during the evening Eileen muttered, "Charlie, you should have ordered a limousine for <u>Charlie and Eileen</u>." _____

68 Unlike his mother, Charlie likes to travel in luxury; <u>Mama</u> usually takes public transportation. _____

69 Charlie and Eileen told <u>Charlie and Eileen</u> that they would never set one foot in a subway. _____

70 Mama says that if you're in trouble, you can always ask the subway conductor and <u>the subway conductor</u> will help. _____

71 Eileen once tried the subway but fainted when the conductor said to her, "Miss, <u>Eileen</u> will need a ticket." _____

72 Until Eileen hit the floor, <u>the subway cars</u> had never before been touched by mink.

_____

73 "Give Eileen a ticket, please," gasped Eileen when she awoke.
_____

74 After Eileen's subway experience, Eileen opted for the bus.
_____

75 The bus driver, Henry Todd, was very gracious to his new passenger, as Henry Todd was to all passengers. _____

76 Because Eileen is a little slow, the driver of the bus parked the bus at the stop for a few extra minutes. _____

77 As Eileen mounted the bus steps, Eileen said, "Thank you, Driver, for waiting for Eileen." _____

78 "I am happy to wait for Eileen," replied the driver. "I have 12 more years until retirement." _____

Tired? Time to switch gears and focus on possessive pronouns (*my, mine, your, yours, his, her, its, our, ours, their, theirs*. All you have to do in this section is pick a word from the choices in parentheses. Consider singular/plural and gender issues and whether the pronoun is attached to a noun or stands alone. Write your choice in the blank provided.

Q. Give me _____ (my, mine) money now! You owe me!

A. my. The possessive pronoun my appears in front of a noun. Mine stands alone.

79 Jessica spent the morning polishing _____ new motorcycle, for which she had paid a rock-bottom price. *(her/hers/she's/her's)*

80 She found two scratches, so she took the cycle back to the store to get _____ fender repaired. *(it/its/their)*

81 When the store employees didn't satisfy her demand for a new fender, Jessica threatened to scratch something of _____. *(their/theirs/their's)*

82 Jessica talks a lot, but she has never taken revenge by damaging a single possession of _____. *(my/mine/mines/mine's)*

83 However, Neil and Rachel claim that Jessica once threw paint on something of _____. *(his/hers/her's/their/their's/theirs)*

84 Also, I heard a rumor that Neil had to bury _____ favorite wig, the one he styled himself, after Jessica got hold of it. *(his/her/he's)*

85 When Rachel's poodle dug up the wig, she had to use paint remover to clean _____ paw. (*it/their/its*)

86 Just to be safe, Neil will never let Jessica borrow another wig of _____ unless she takes out an insurance policy. (*his/his'/he's*)

87 Tomorrow, Neil is going to Matthews Department Store to buy a spare wig. The store is selling wigs at a 50 percent discount, and _____ wigs are Neil's favorites. (*its/their*)

88 Whenever Neil yells at Jessica, she screams, "Don't criticize _____ actions!" (*my/mine*)

89 Neil usually replies, in a voice that is just as loud, "I wouldn't dream of criticizing any action of _____." (*your/your's/yours/yours'*)

90 When Neil speaks to _____ hairdresser, he will request a rush job. (*his/his'/he's*)

91 "Neil will never get his hands on any hairpiece of _____," declared Rachel and Jessica. (*our/ours/our'/ours'/our's*)

92 I think that Rachel took _____ hairpiece, and I told Neil so. (*his/his'/he's*)

93 Neil explained that he itches to get his hands on a wig of _____ someday. (*my/mine*)

94 "Over _____ dead body," I replied. (*my/mine*)

95 "I can't work on _____ dead body," answered Neil in a puzzled voice. (*your/yours/you're*)

96 As she dipped _____ fingers in paint remover, Jessica added, "You can't work on a live one either." (*her/hers/her's*)

97 Jessica and Neil seriously need to work on _____ people skills. (*his/her/their*)

98 I will buy a wig for Jessica, Neil, and myself and then style _____ new hairpieces. (*our/ours/our's*)

Calling All Overachievers: Extra Practice with Hitching Subjects and Verbs

Read this email from a store owner to a very annoying customer. Find and correct errors in subject-verb agreement. Also look for errors in which pronouns do not match the words they refer to or replace. You should find ten errors in all.

To: George Baker

From: E. Neil Johnson

Subject: Watch

Johnson Jewelry Store is proud of their relationship with customers. Your frequent visits to Johnson Jewelry Store is welcome, but each of my sales clerks have found a problem after you leave. Yesterday, for example, Anne Leon noticed that one of the watches were broken after you examined it. Two customers has looked at the watch recently. You was one. The other gave them back undamaged. When you left the store, there was two dents in the watch. Some of the gold were scraped off. Frankly, I do not care about the watch. I care about Anne Leon, who was talking to themselves all afternoon, muttering that "Baker made my blood pressure go sky high." Sadly, I must ban you from Johnson Jewelry unless you agree not to touch the merchandise.

Answers to Subject, Verb, and Pronoun Pairing Problems

I hope you're one singular sensation at pairing subjects and verbs, as well as pronouns and antecedents, now. Check your work in this chapter with the following answers.

1. **is, raises.** You need two singular forms here: *blue is* and *John raises.*

2. **has, suffers.** The verbs *has* and *suffers* are singular, as they should be, because the subject–verb pairs are *hair has* and *he suffers.*

3. **are.** The plural verb *are* matches the plural subject we.

4. **believe, give.** The pronoun *you* always takes a plural verb such as *believe* and *give.*

5. **Do, tell.** Both verbs are plural, matching the plural subjects *you* and *friends.* In the first pair, the subject is tucked between the two parts of the verb because the sentence is a question.

6. **Has.** You need a singular verb here to pair with the singular subject, *story.*

7. **know, is.** The pronoun *I*, though singular, pairs with the plural form *know. John* is singular and matches the singular verb *is.*

8. **tells.** Because *he* is singular, the verb *tells* must also be singular.

9. **does.** The pronoun *everyone* is singular, so it matches the singular form *does.*

10. **was.** The singular verb *was* matches the singular subject *Nadine.*

11. **cheats.** The singular subject is *He*, so you need *cheats*, a singular verb. The interrupter, *along with some other students*, is irrelevant.

12. **has.** Pay no attention to the interrupter, *in addition to everyone else on the faculty.* The real subject, *principal*, is singular and takes the singular verb *has.*

13. **has.** This one's easy. *John* is a singular subject, which pairs nicely with the singular verb *has.*

14. **are.** The subject is *teachers; there* is never a subject. *Teachers* is plural and takes the plural verb *are.*

15. **were.** *John and Dana* — two people, linked together by *and* (not to mention failing math grades) — equal a plural subject, so you need the plural verb *were.*

16. **removes, searches.** Because *John* is singular, the verbs *removes* and *searches* must also be singular.

17. **is.** *Every* has magical powers. Place *every* in front of anything, even *pockets*, and you have a singular subject and a singular verb, *is.*

18. **was.** Ignore the interrupters *(as well as . . . Dana)* and zero in on the real subject, *John.* Match the singular verb *was* to the singular subject.

19. **is.** The subject is *suspension*, not *charges* or *variety. Arrest* is singular, so you need the singular verb *is.*

(20) **were.** Add one *movie director* to one *agent* and what do you get? A big fat check, that's what . . . and a plural subject that takes the plural verb *were*.

(21) **include.** The subject is *offers*, which matches the plural verb *include*. Everything else is camouflage.

(22) **stroll, scrolls.** Two subjects, *John* and *Dana*, appear at the end of the sentence. *John and Dana* = plural, so pair them with the plural verb *stroll. Label* is singular, so it pairs with the singular verb *scrolls*.

(23) **are.** You can count *dancers*, so *are* is best.

(24) **has.** Without a partner, *either* is always singular and rates a singular verb, such as *has*.

(25) **is.** The word *every* has the power to change *seat and balcony box* to a singular concept requiring the singular verb *is*.

(26) **does.** The subject is *no one*, which is singular, so it must be paired with *does*, a singular verb.

(27) **have.** The pronoun *most* may be singular (if it's used with a measurable quantity) or plural (if it's used with a countable quantity). You can count *songs*, so the plural *have* is best.

(28) **has, is.** The pronouns ending in *-one* are always singular, even though they seem to convey a plural idea at times. They need to be matched with singular verbs.

(29) **is.** The closest subject is *Lola*, so the singular verb *is* wins the prize, the only prize likely to be associated with Lola's musical.

(30) **have.** The pronoun *any* may be either singular or plural depending upon the quantity to which it refers. Reviews may be counted (and you can be sure that Lola's investors will count them extremely carefully), so *any* takes the plural verb *have* in this sentence.

(31) **Has.** The sentence has two subjects, *director* and *musicians*. The verb in this sentence has two parts, *has* and *agreed*. The subject *director* is closer to the part of the verb that changes (the *has* or the *have*); *agreed* is the same for both singular and plural subjects. The changeable part of the verb is the one that governs the singular/plural issue. Because that part of the verb is near the singular subject *director*, the singular *has* is correct.

(32) **agrees.** The singular verb *agrees* matches the singular subject *everyone*.

(33) **are.** The pronoun *most* can be either singular or plural. In this sentence, *members* can be counted (and it won't take too long, either, once the reviews are in), so the plural verb *are* is what you want.

(34) **has.** When it's all alone, the pronoun *neither* is always singular and needs to be paired with the singular verb *has*.

(35) **is.** Did I catch you here? The expression *20 tattoos* suggests plural, but the subject is actually *one*, a singular.

(36) **are.** You can count tattoos, so the pronoun *some* is a plural subject and needs to match the plural verb *are*.

(37) **has.** The word *each* has the power to turn any subject to singular; *has* is a singular verb.

(38) **is.** You can measure, but not count, *fame*, so a singular verb matches the singular pronoun *all*.

(39) **believe.** *Accountants* are countable, so *all* is plural in this sentence and needs the plural verb *believe*.

(40) **Has.** The pronoun *someone*, like all the pronouns ending in *-one*, is singular, and so is the verb *has*.

(41) **are, enters.** In an *either/or* sentence, go with the closer subject, in this case, *producers*. Because *producers* is plural, it is paired with *are*, a plural verb. The singular verb *enters* matches the singular pronoun *nobody*. All pronouns ending with *-body* are singular.

(42) **is.** The word *every* has the ability to make the subject singular, matching the singular verb *is*.

(43) **has.** The pronoun *neither* is singular, so the singular verb *has* is needed here.

(44) **has.** Pronouns ending in *-one* are always singular and thus always pair with singular verbs. Here the subject is *someone*, so *has* wins.

(45) **are.** The pronoun *both* is plural, as is the verb *are*.

(46) **Was.** This sentence illustrates a common error. The pronoun *either* is singular and calls for the singular verb *was*.

(47) **is.** A sentence with an *either/or* combo is easy; just match the verb to the closest subject. In this sentence, the singular *Lola* is closer to the verb than *brothers*, so you need a singular verb.

(48) **believe.** The pronoun *most* shifts from singular to plural and back, depending upon context. If it's associated with something that you can count (such as *us*), it's plural. Opt for the plural verb *believe*.

(49) **is.** *Economics* ends in *s*, but it's a singular noun, which matches the singular verb *is*.

(50) **show.** *Data* looks singular because it has no *s*, but it's actually the plural of *datum* (a word no one ever uses!). Match *data* with *show*, a plural verb.

(51) **was.** The subject, *thesis*, is singular, so *was* pairs well with it. In case you're wondering, the plural of *thesis* is *theses*. Strange, huh?

(52) **is.** The *news* is singular and takes the singular verb *is*. This noun has no plural form!

(53) **are.** The team name sounds plural, and it is. Go for *are*, the plural verb.

(54) **does.** The team name sounds singular, so the singular verb *does* works here.

(55) **was.** This subject, *politics*, appears plural because of the *s*, but it's actually singular, as is the verb *was*.

(56) **have.** *Media* is plural and pairs with the plural verb *have*.

(57) **believe.** The subject, *alumni*, is plural and pairs with the plural verb *believe*.

(58) **cut.** For reasons I can't explain, *scissors* is plural and needs a plural verb *(cut)*.

(59) **is.** Now the subject is *pair*, a singular word, so go for the singular verb *is*.

(60) **love.** The subject is *media*, a plural, which pairs with the plural verb *love*.

(61) **makes.** *Memorandum* is singular (and, if you're curious, *memoranda* is plural). Pair *memorandum* with the singular verb, *makes*.

(62) **agrees.** Company names are singular, even if they appear plural. *Agrees* is a singular verb.

(63) **is.** The subject, *analysis*, is singular. (The plural is *analyses*, by the way.) *Is* is a singular verb.

(64) **it.** The hat is singular, and so is *it*.

(65) **they.** More than one photographer means that you need the plural pronoun *they*.

(66) **His.** Charlie is one man, so it's appropriate to refer to him with a singular pronoun. Because *Charlie's* is possessive, *his* is the best choice.

(67) **us.** Two nouns are underlined, so you're in plural territory. Because Eileen is talking about herself and Charlie, *us* fits here.

(68) **she.** Mama is a singular feminine noun, so *she* is your best bet.

(69) **themselves.** Two people make a plural, and the sentence circles back to *Charles and Eileen*, so *themselves*, a plural pronoun, is best.

(70) **he or she, they.** You don't know whether the subway conductor is male or female, though you do know that you're talking about one and only one person. The answer is *he or she*, covering all the bases. Note: Some grammarians now urge the gender-neutral *they*, traditionally plural, as a good substitute for a noun referring to a person whose gender isn't known.

(71) **you.** Because the conductor is talking to Eileen, *you* is the best choice. *You*, by the way, functions as both a singular and a plural.

(72) **they.** *Cars* is a plural noun, so *they* works best.

(73) **me.** Because Eileen is talking about herself, *me* is your answer.

(74) **she.** The singular, feminine *Eileen* calls for a singular, feminine pronoun, in this case, *she*.

(75) **he.** The singular, masculine *Henry Todd* calls for a singular, masculine pronoun, *he*.

(76) **it.** The singular *bus* is a thing, nor a person, *it* fills the bill.

(77) **me.** *Eileen* is talking about herself here, so *me* is appropriate.

(78) **you.** The driver is talking to Eileen, using the pronoun *you*.

(79) **her.** You need a feminine, singular, possessive pronoun. Bingo: *her*.

(80) **its.** The fender is a singular object, and you need a possessive form because the fender belongs to the cycle. Therefore, *its* works well here.

(81) **theirs.** One of the choices — *their's* — doesn't exist in proper English. The first choice, *their*, should precede the thing that is possessed (*their* books, for example). The middle choice is just right.

(82) **mine.** The last two choices don't exist in Standard English. *My* does its job by preceding the possession (*my* blanket, for example). The second choice, *mine*, can stand alone.

(83) **theirs.** You need a word to express plural possession, because you're talking about *Neil and Rachel*. Of the three plural choices (the last three), the first should precede the possession (*their* motorcycle, for example), and the second has an apostrophe, a giant no-no in possessive-pronoun world. Only the last choice works.

(84) **his.** The hairpiece belongs to Neil, so *her*, a feminine pronoun, is out. The last choice is a contraction of *he is*.

(85) **its.** The first choice isn't possessive, so you can rule *it* out easily. The second choice is plural, but the pronoun refers to *poodle,* a singular noun. Bingo: The last choice, a singular possessive, is correct.

Many animal lovers don't consider *it* or *its* appropriate pronouns for family pets. If you know whether an animal is male or female, feel free to use *his/her* or *he/she.*

TIP

(86) **his.** No possessive pronoun ever contains an apostrophe, so the first choice is the only possibility. *He's,* by the way, means *he is.*

(87) **its.** Did I catch you here? In everyday speech, people often refer to stores and businesses as "they," with the possessive form "their." However, a store or a business is properly referred to with a singular pronoun. The logic is easy to figure out. One store = singular. So *Matthews Department Store* is singular, and the possessive pronoun that refers to it is *its.*

(88) **my.** The pronoun *mine* stands alone and doesn't precede what is owned. *My,* on the other hand, is a pronoun that can't stand being alone. A true party animal, it must precede what is being owned (in this sentence, *actions*).

(89) **yours.** This sentence needs a pronoun that stands alone. *Your* must be placed in front of whatever is being possessed — not a possibility in this sentence. All the choices with apostrophes are out because possessive pronouns don't have apostrophes. The only thing left is *yours,* which is the correct choice.

(90) **his.** The contraction *he's* means *he is.* That choice doesn't make sense. The second choice is wrong because possessive pronouns don't have apostrophes.

(91) **ours.** Okay, first dump all the apostrophe choices, because apostrophes and possessive pronouns don't mix. You're left with two choices — *our* and *ours.* The second is best because *our* needs to precede the thing that is possessed, and *ours* can stand alone.

(92) **his.** The possessive pronoun *his,* like all possessive pronouns, has no apostrophe. The last choice, *he's,* means *he is* and isn't possessive at all.

(93) **mine**. The pronoun *mine* works alone (like a private detective in an old movie). In this sentence it has a slot for itself after the preposition *of.* Perfect!

(94) **my.** The form that attaches to the front of a noun is *my.* In this sentence, *my* precedes and is linked to *dead body.*

(95) **your.** The possessive pronoun *your* has no apostrophe. The second choice, *yours,* doesn't attach to a noun, so you have to rule it out in this sentence. The last choice, *you're,* is short for *you are.*

(96) **her.** Right away you can dump the last choice, *her's,* because possessive pronouns are allergic to apostrophes. The pronoun *hers* works alone, but here the blank precedes the item possessed, *fingers. Her* is the possessive you want.

(97) **their.** Because you're talking about both *Jessica* and *Neil,* go for *their,* the plural.

(98) **our.** In this sentence the possessive pronoun has to include *me,* so *our* is the winner. *Ours* isn't appropriate because you need a pronoun to precede what is being possessed (*hairpieces*). As always, apostrophes and possessive pronouns don't mix.

Refer to the following figure for the answers to the "Overachiever" question.

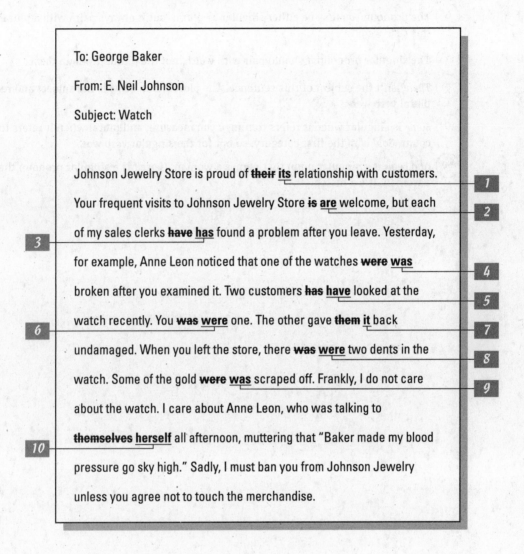

To: George Baker

From: E. Neil Johnson

Subject: Watch

Johnson Jewelry Store is proud of ~~their~~ <u>its</u> relationship with customers.   1

Your frequent visits to Johnson Jewelry Store ~~is~~ <u>are</u> welcome, but each   2

of my sales clerks ~~have~~ <u>has</u> found a problem after you leave. Yesterday,   3

for example, Anne Leon noticed that one of the watches ~~were~~ <u>was</u>   4

broken after you examined it. Two customers ~~has~~ <u>have</u> looked at the   5

watch recently. You ~~was~~ <u>were</u> one. The other gave ~~them~~ <u>it</u> back   6   7

undamaged. When you left the store, there ~~was~~ <u>were</u> two dents in the   8

watch. Some of the gold ~~were~~ <u>was</u> scraped off. Frankly, I do not care   9

about the watch. I care about Anne Leon, who was talking to

~~themselves~~ <u>herself</u> all afternoon, muttering that "Baker made my blood   10

pressure go sky high." Sadly, I must ban you from Johnson Jewelry

unless you agree not to touch the merchandise.

(1) *Their* is wrong because this pronoun refers to *Johnson Jewelry Store*, a single business. The singular pronoun *its* works better here.

(2) *Visits* is the subject of this sentence, so you need the plural verb *are*.

(3) *Each* is singular, even though it comes before a plural *(sales clerks)*. Pair *each* with the singular verb *has*.

(4) *One* is the subject, not *watches*, so you need the singular verb *was broken* to match it.

(5) *Two customers* is a plural and should pair with the plural verb *have looked.*

(6) The pronoun *you* may be either singular or plural, but it always pairs with a plural verb, in this case *were.*

(7) The singular pronoun *it* should pair with *watch,* not the plural pronoun *them.*

(8) *There* isn't the subject of this sentence. The plural noun *dents* is the subject and requires the plural verb *were.*

(9) *Some* is singular when it refers to things you measure, and plural when it refers to things you count. *Gold* is in the first category, so opt for the singular verb *was.*

(10) *Ann Leon* is a singular noun that names a woman. *Herself* is a singular pronoun that refers to a woman. It's a match.

Chapter **6**

Solving Pronoun Case

Have you figured out that pronouns are the most annoying part of speech in the entire universe? Pronouns are the words that most often take the place of nouns — words that name people, places, things, and ideas. Even more annoying is that sometimes pronouns replace other pronouns. In other words, when it comes to error-potential, pronouns are a minefield just waiting to blow up your speech or writing.

I cover the basics of pronoun number (singular or plural) and gender (referring to male, female, or neutral nouns) in Chapter 5. This chapter deals with *case* (the difference, for example, between *they, their,* and *them* or *I, me, my*).

TEST ALERT

Pronouns are very popular with standardized-test writers, so if you plan to bubble little ovals sometime soon, work through these exercises with extra care.

Meeting the Subject at Hand and the Object of My Affection

Subjects and objects have opposite jobs in a sentence. Briefly, the *subject* is the doer of the action or whatever is in the state of being talked about in the sentence. When you say, "He and I are going to the mall," you use the subject pronouns *he* and *I. Objects* receive; instead of acting, they are acted upon. If you scold *him* and *me*, those two pronouns resentfully receive the scolding and thus act as objects. Verbs have objects, and so do some other grammatical elements, such as prepositions. (I deal with prepositions in Chapter 7.) One more complication: If a pronoun follows a linking verb — a verb expressing state of being — and completes the meaning of the subject-linking verb pair, you need a subject pronoun when you're writing in formal English. The logic is that a linking verb acts as a sort of giant equal sign, and the subject and its complement must match. (For more information on complements, turn to Chapter 2.) Here are the contents of the subject- and object-pronoun baskets:

> **Subject pronouns** include *I, you, he, she, it, we, they, who,* and *whoever.*

> **Object pronouns** are *me, you, him, her, it, us, them, whom,* and *whomever.*

Some pronouns, such as *you* and *it,* appear on both lists. They do double duty as both subject and object pronouns. Don't worry about them; they're right for all occasions. Other one-case-fits-almost-all pronouns are *either, most, other, which,* and *that.* Another type of pronoun is a reflexive, or *-self* pronoun (*myself, himself, ourselves,* and so forth). Use these pronouns only when the action in the sentence doubles back on the subject. ("They washed themselves 50 times during the deodorant shortage.") You may also insert the *-self* pronouns for emphasis. ("She herself baked the cake.") You can't use the *-self* pronouns for any other reason. A sentence such as "The cake she gave *myself* was good" is wrong. Opt for "The cake she gave *me.*"

WARNING

Don't unnecessarily buddy up a pronoun and the noun it replaces. "My brother he goes swimming" is fine in many languages, but in English it's wrong because the pronoun *(he)* is meant to replace the noun *(brother).* "My brother goes swimming" or "He goes swimming" are both correct.

EXAMPLE

In the following sentences choose the correct pronoun from the parentheses, if — and only if — a pronoun is needed in the sentence. (If no pronoun is needed, select "no pronoun.") Take care not to send a subject pronoun to do an object pronoun's job, and vice versa.

Q. Peyton took the precious parchment and gave (she/her) a cheap imitation instead.

A. **her.** In this sentence, Peyton is the one taking and giving. The pronoun *her* is on the receiving end because Peyton gave the imitation to *her. Her* is an object pronoun.

1. Maria, Peyton, and (I/me/myself/no pronoun) found a valuable item.

2. The parchment, which Peyton (he/him/no pronoun) discovered in the back pocket of a pair of jeans, is covered with strange symbols.

3. George Morse of Codebusters (he/him/no pronoun) is an expert at decoding ancient parchments.

4. Codebusters may contact Matt first, or the company may wait until Matt realizes that (he/him/himself/no pronoun) needs help.

5. Arthur, the president of Codebusters, knows that Maria (she/her/herself/no pronoun) is good at figuring out obscure symbols.

6. Peyton won't tell (I/me/myself/no pronoun) a thing about the parchment, but Maria (she/her/herself/no pronoun) did nod quietly when I mentioned Martians.

7. Peyton's friends — Lucy and (she/her/herself/no pronoun) — are obsessed with Martians and tend to see Little Green Men everywhere.

8. If the Martians and (she/her/herself/no pronoun) have a message for the world, (they/them/themselves/no pronoun) will make sure it gets maximum publicity.

9. Elizabeth and (I/me/myself/no pronoun) will glue (we/us/ourselves/no pronoun) to the all-news channel just in case Peyton (he/him/himself/no pronoun) decides to talk.

10. Sure enough, Peyton just contacted the authorities, Dan Moore and (he/him/himself/no pronoun), to arrange an interview.

11. Elizabeth (she/her/herself/no pronoun) favors sending NASA and (we/us/ourselves/no pronoun) the parchment.

12. I pointed out that NASA's scientists (they/them/themselves/no pronoun) know a lot about space, but nothing about ancient parchments.

13. Matt checked the internet, but it had little to offer (he/him/himself/no pronoun) except the number for Codebusters.

14. (I/me/I myself/no pronoun) think that the parchment is a fake.

15. Matt told Maria and (I/me/myself/no pronoun) that he would call Codebusters.

16. Yesterday, Elizabeth (she/her/herself/no pronoun) showed Matt and (I/me/myself/no pronoun) some parchment scraps from Peyton's room.

17. When asked who took the parchment scraps, Elizabeth replied, "It was (I/me/myself/no pronoun)."

To "Who" or To "Whom"? That Is the Question

Lately, some grammarians have given up on *whom*. In their view, few people use *whom* and even fewer use it properly. In some circles, the difference between *who* and *whom* still matters. If you're writing or speaking to someone in those circles, you should understand proper usage of these pronouns. *Who* and *whom* tend to occur in complicated sentences. If you untangle the sentence and figure out (pardon the expression) *who* is doing what to *whom*, you'll be fine. Here's the deal: If you need a subject (someone doing the action or someone in the state of being described in the sentence), *who* is your pronoun. If you need an object (a receiver of the action), go with *whom*.

A good trick is to see if you can substitute the words *he* or *she* or *they*. If so, go with *who*. If *him*, *her*, or *them* is a better fit, opt for *whom*.

TIP

Take a ride on the *who/whom* train and select the proper pronoun from the parentheses in the following sentences.

EXAMPLE

Q. (Who/Whom) can decode the message? Codebusters!

A. **Who.** The verb *can decode* needs a subject, someone to do that action. *Who* is for subjects, and *whom* is for objects.

18 Does Peyton know (who/whom) should get the information after Maria has decoded it?

19 Matt will discuss the parchment with (whoever/whomever) the buyer sends.

20 (Who/Whom) is his buyer?

21 His buyer is (whoever/whomever) believes Matt's sales pitch.

22 Also, Matt will sell the parchment to (whoever/whomever) is willing to pay.

23 I don't think NASA is interested, despite Matt's claim that an expert from NASA, (who/whom) isn't saying much, was seen checking "Mars" and "Alien Life Forms" on the internet.

24 Do you know (who/whom) the expert consulted?

25 No one seems to know (who/whom) Matt saw.

26 Peyton remains capable of conspiring with NASA, Codebusters, and (whoever/whomever) else is able to sell a fraudulent document.

27 Matt, (who/whom) I do not trust, has the most sincere face you can imagine.

28 Peyton, (who/whom) Matt once scolded for cutting class, has a reputation for sincerity.

29 I once heard Peyton explain that those (who/whom) have honest faces can get away with anything.

30 "If you are one of those people (who/whom) can fake sincerity," he said, "you can accomplish anything."

You Talkin' to Me, or I? Pronouns as Objects of Prepositions

Prepositions, not to be confused with *propositions* (such as "Are you busy tonight?") are words that express relationships. (Come to think of it, *propositions* concern relationships too.) Common prepositions include *by, for, from, in, on, of, about, after,* and *before.* (For a complete discussion of prepositions, turn to Chapter 7.) Prepositions always have objects, and sometimes those objects are pronouns. Check out the italicized objects of prepositions in these examples:

> Give that umbrella to *me,* or I'll break it over your *head.*

> The embroidery on the *umbrella* was done by *me* alone.

Luckily, you don't have to worry when the object of a preposition is a noun. Nouns don't change no matter where they appear in the sentence. But pronouns do change, depending upon their job in the sentence. And if a pronoun's job is to be an object of a preposition, it must be an object pronoun.

TIP

The *-self* pronouns (*myself, himself, ourselves, themselves,* and the like) can serve as objects of prepositions, but only if the action in the sentence doubles back, as in "I talk to myself all the time." In this example sentence, *myself* is the object of the preposition *to.*

EXAMPLE

Take a stab at the following sentences, selecting the correct pronoun from the pair in parentheses. I cleverly (she said modestly) scatter a few subjects in the exercise.

Q. I won't accept any packages from (he/him) because last week he sent a quart of pickled cabbage to (I/me), and my mailbox was sticky for days.

A. **him, me.** The preposition *from* needs an object, so your first answer has to be *him. To* is also a preposition and should be followed by the object pronoun *me.*

31 Jessica sang songs to Mom and (he/him/himself) whenever the moon was full.

32 Her latest CD is titled *Of Mom, (I/Me/Myself), and the Moon.*

33 I'm going to download some songs, although a lot of issues remain between Jessica and (I/me/myself).

34 Once, she stole my dog Spike and asked for a reward when she returned Spike to (I/me/myself).

35 Spike ran after (she/her) and took a large bite out of her nose, and (I/me) applauded.

36 Aggressive though Spike may be, you can't put much past (he/him), and for that reason (he/him) is a great watchdog.

37 Spike likes to walk behind (we/us) when we approach the house; he growls at (whoever/whomever) comes too close.

38 "At (who/whom) is this dog snarling?" asked Jessica, as she snarled back at (he/him/himself).

39 "(He/Him/Himself) thinks the letter carrier wants to rob us, so Spike tries to keep an eye on (he/him)," I replied as (I/me/myself) pieced together a ripped catalogue.

40 "You have to run around (they/them)," I said to (she/her/herself), speaking of Spike and my mother.

Matching Possessive Pronouns to "-ing" Nouns

A gerund is a noun made from the *-ing* form of a verb (*swimming*, *smiling*, and similar words). Not every noun that ends in *-ing* is a gerund; *king* and *pudding*, for example, aren't, because they don't arise from verbs. When you do run across a gerund, any noun or pronoun in front should be a possessive form if the focus of what you're writing is the action the gerund expresses. Take a look at this sentence:

> Carrie hates (me/my) auditioning for the new reality show, *Nut Search*.

Carrie doesn't hate *me*. Instead, Carrie hates the whole reality-show project. The possessive pronoun *my* is the best choice because it shifts the reader's attention to *auditioning*. The possessive form of a *noun* should also be your choice for the spot in front of an *-ing* noun. In the preceding sample sentence, the correct form is "Carrie hates my auditioning."

TIP

Pronouns in this spot, like all pronouns, should match the word they refer to in number (singular or plural) and gender (masculine, feminine, neuter). For a complete discussion of pronoun gender, turn to Chapter 5.

TEST ALERT

If you're facing a standardized test, don't nod off during this exercise. The SAT and other exams include this topic!

Try your hand at the following example and practice exercises. Circle the pronouns you love and ignore the ones you hate. To keep you alert, I've inserted a few sentences that don't call for possessive pronouns. Keep your eyes open!

EXAMPLE

Q. Although I'm not a literary critic, I think that (he/him/his) writing a novel on his phone is a bad idea.

A. **his.** The bad idea here is the *writing*, not *he* or *him*. The possessive pronoun shifts the attention to the task, which is the point of the sentence.

41. Peter Lincoln of the *Times* needs help with (her/him/his) editing and must hire assistants; Lincoln looks forward to (they/them/their) correcting his grammar.

42. Lincoln said that he loved everything the employment agency did last week except (they/them/their) sending him too many pronoun-obsessed writers.

43. When Lori went for an interview, she saw (her/him/his) reading a review of *The Pronoun Diet*; (she/him/her) saying that the book was "trash" bothered Lincoln.

44. "I object to (she/him/her) insisting on one pronoun per paragraph," he muttered, as he eyed (she/her/his) ring, which made Lori's finger sparkle.

45. When I applied, Lincoln looked favorably upon (I/me/my) editing, but he hated (I/me/my) pronouncing his first name incorrectly.

Missing in Action: Choosing Pronouns for Implied Comparisons

Sometimes, what you don't say is more important than what you do say, especially when it comes to pronouns. In a sentence with an implied, not stated, comparison, you sometimes have to add the missing words before you can select the proper pronoun. In the sentence *George has more cauliflower than I*, the missing word is *have*, and *I* is the subject of the implied verb.

Circle the appropriate pronoun. Think of the missing words before answering.

EXAMPLE

Q. Grandpa always gives Oscar more vegetables than (I/me).

A. **I** or **me**. The answer here depends upon the meaning you're trying to express. If you want to say that *Grandpa gives Oscar more vegetables than I give Oscar*, go for *I*. If your meaning is that *Grandpa gives Oscar more vegetables than Grandpa gives to me*, the answer you want is *me*.

46. Oscar is as careful as (she/her) when he's weeding, but somehow he pulls out more plants than (she/her).

47. The chipmunks consider Oscar their friend because he breaks as much garden fence as (they/them).

48. With the fence down, the chipmunks munch more vegetables than (we/us).

49. Oscar has planted fewer tomato plants than (I/me).

50. Oscar gives more zucchini to the chipmunks than (I/me), because I hate the taste of zucchini.

Calling All Overachievers: Extra Practice with Pronoun Case

Read the following trip report in the following figure from a battle-weary teacher after a particularly bad day. Can you find 18 pronoun errors and correct them?

Three chaperones and myself left school at 10:03 a.m. with 45 fifth graders, all of who were excited about our visit to Adventure Land. The day it passed without incident. My friend Jim and me sat in the Adventure Land Bar and Grill for five hours while the youngsters visited Space Control Center, Pirate Mountain, and other overpriced but popular rides. The students sitting at my table, Arthur and him, objected to me eating such good food and said they wanted some too. The bus driver she explained, looking at Arthur's giant lunch, that all the students could get enough calories by eating her lunch and that Arthur shouldn't assign blame to whomever ate some. Later the students they got in the bus and were scared by it making a lot of noise. "Whom is in charge of maintenance? asked Arthur. "Ourselves are going to die!" he added. We drove to Parker Motors because their mechanics are great. "Myself and the bus driver will pay," I told the owner. "Do you take credit cards?" the driver asked. "Sure. Give the card to my wife or I," answered the owner. "The bookkeepers, Sue and her, will charge you double for the card, but the bus it will be fine soon."

Answers to Advanced Pronoun Problems

I hope all these pronoun problems didn't trip you up too badly. See how you did by taking a look at the answers and explanations.

1. **I.** The pronoun *I* is one of the subjects of the verb *found. Me* is for objects. *Myself* is only for emphasis (*I myself*) or for actions that bounce back on the subject. ("I told myself not to stand under a tree during a thunderstorm!")

2. **No pronoun.** Because the noun *Peyton* is present in the sentence, no pronoun is needed to replace it.

3. **No pronoun.** Because *George Morse* acts as the subject, you don't need a pronoun to act as the subject.

4. **he.** The verb *needs* must have a subject, and the subject pronoun *he* fills the bill.

5. **No pronoun.** *Maria* is the subject of the verb *is,* so you don't have to double up with a pronoun after *Maria.*

6. **me, no pronoun.** In the first part of the sentence, the pronoun receives the action (*Peyton won't tell whom? Me.*) In the second, *Maria* is already nodding, so you don't need an additional pronoun.

7. **she.** The tough part about this sentence is that the pronoun choice is camouflaged by other words (*Peyton's friends* and *Lucy*). If you isolate the pronoun, however, you see that it is *she* who is *obsessed* with Martians. You need the subject pronoun. To add a technical grammatical explanation — stop reading now before you die of boredom! — the subject is *Peyton's friends,* and the expression *Lucy and she* forms an appositive to the subject. An appositive is always in the same case as the word it matches.

8. **she, they.** Two parentheses, two subjects. The verbs *have* and *will make* need subjects; *she* and *they* fill the bill.

9. **I, ourselves, no pronoun.** In the first part of the sentence, you need a subject for *will glue.* You can rule out *me* because *me* is an object pronoun. The pronoun *myself* works only for emphasis, in which case the sentence would read *Elizabeth and I myself.* (*Elizabeth and myself* is never correct, because the *–self* pronouns don't substitute for subject pronouns.) In the second parentheses, you're looking for an object for the verb *will glue.* The pronoun *we* drops out right away because it's for subjects only. The next choice, *us,* is tempting, but because the actor and the receiver are the same, *ourselves* is better. Finally, the noun *Peyton* is the subject of the verb *decides,* so you can immediately eliminate *he* (subject pronoun) and *him* (object pronoun). I don't see a need for emphasis, so *himself* also drops out.

10. **him.** Like Sentence 7, this one has lots of camouflage. Cover everything between *contacted* and the pronoun choice. What's left? *Peyton just contacted he/him/himself.* Can you hear the correct answer? *Peyton contacted he?* I don't think so! You need the object pronoun *him.* You can't use *himself* because the action isn't doubling back on the subject (as in "He told *himself* not to worry"). If you really want a grammatical explanation, and surely you have better things to do with your time, *authorities* is the object of the verb *contacted,* and *Dan Moore and him* forms an appositive. An appositive is always in the same case as its equivalent.

(11) **No pronoun, us.** *Elizabeth* is doing the action, so you have no reason to add a pronoun after her name. Moving to the second parenthesis, you see that the pronoun is on the receiving end of the verb *will glue*. You can't plug in *we* because *we* is for subjects, and receivers are objects. *Ourselves* doesn't fit because the *-self* pronouns are only for emphasis (*we ourselves will go . . .*) or for situations in which the actor and receiver are the same (*I told myself . . .*).

(12) **No pronoun.** A subject for the verb *know* (NASA's scientists) is already present in this sentence. Don't throw in an extra pronoun!

(13) **him.** The verb *offer*, even in the infinitive form (*to offer*), takes the object pronoun *him*.

(14) **I or I myself.** The first choice is an ordinary subject pronoun; the second is emphatic. Do you want to scream this phrase or just say it? Your call.

(15) **me.** *Matt told* is a subject-verb pair, so you need an object pronoun (*me*) to receive the action.

(16) **No pronoun, me.** *Elizabeth* is the subject of the verb *showed*, and doubling up makes no sense. In the second parenthesis, the object pronoun *me* receives the action from the verb *told*. You can probably "hear" the correct answer if you use your thumb to cover the words *Matt and*. By isolating the pronoun, you quickly determine that *Elizabeth showed I* is a nonstarter. *Elizabeth showed me* sounds — and is — correct.

(17) **I.** After the linking verb *was,* you need the subject pronoun *I*.

(18) **who.** Focus on the part of the sentence containing the *who/whom* issue: *who/whom should get the information*. The verb *should get* needs a subject, so *who* is the proper choice.

(19) **whomever.** The buyer is sending someone, so the pronoun you plug in receives the action of *sending*. Receivers are always object pronouns, so *whomever* wins the prize.

(20) **Who.** The verb *is* needs a subject, and *who* is a subject pronoun — a match made in heaven.

(21) **whoever.** The verb *believes* needs a subject. *Whoever* is a subject pronoun.

(22) **whoever.** This one is tricky. When you hear the word *to* (a preposition), you may want to jump for the object pronoun, because *prepositions* are completed by object pronouns such as *whomever*. But in this sentence, the verb *is* needs a subject, and *whoever* fills that role. For those who dig grammar (if you quake at the word, don't read this part), the object of the preposition *to* is the whole clause, *whoever is willing to pay*.

(23) **who.** Somebody *isn't saying*, so you need a subject pronoun. *Who* fills the bill.

(24) **whom.** This sentence is easier to figure out if you isolate the part of the sentence containing the who/whom choice: *who/whom the expert consulted*. Now rearrange those words into the normal subject-verb order: *the expert consulted whom. Whom* is the object of the verb *consulted*.

(25) **whom.** As in the previous sentence, isolating and rearranging are helpful: *who/whom Matt saw, Matt saw whom*. The pronoun *whom* serves as the object of the verb *saw*.

(26) **whoever.** The verb *is* needs a subject, so *whoever* has to do the job.

(27) **whom.** Concentrate on the part of the sentence between the commas. Rearrange the words into the normal subject-verb order: *I do not trust who/whom*. Now do you see that it has to be *whom*? The pronoun *I* is the subject, and *whom* is acted upon, not an actor.

(28) **whom.** The action from the verb *scolded* goes to an object, and the object pronoun *whom* fills that role.

(29) **who.** The verb *have* just has to have a subject (verbs are picky that way), so here you need *who*.

(30) **who.** The verb *can fake* pairs with the subject pronoun *who* in this sentence.

(31) **him.** The preposition *to* needs an object. In this sentence it has two — *Mom and him*. The pronoun *him* works as an object.

(32) **Me.** The preposition *of* has three objects, including *me*.

(33) **me.** The preposition *between* calls for two objects. In this sentence, *Jessica* is one and *me* is the other. Don't fall into the *between-and-I* trap; *between* calls for objects, not subjects. Also, stay away from *myself*. The *-self* pronouns are appropriate only when you're doubling back ("I told *myself*") or emphasizing ("I *myself* will cook the meal").

(34) **me.** The preposition *to* requires the object pronoun *me*.

(35) **her, I.** The preposition *after* needs an object, and *her* takes that role. In the second parenthesis, you're looking for a subject for the verb *applauded*, and *I* does the job.

(36) **him, he.** Did you know that *past* may sometimes be a preposition? The object pronoun *him* works well here. In the second part of the sentence, go for *he* because the verb *is* requires a subject, and *he* is a subject pronoun.

(37) **us, whoever.** This is a hard one; if you got it right, you deserve an ice cream sundae. The pronoun *us* is best as an object of the preposition *behind*. But the preposition *at* is *not* completed by the pronoun *whomever*. Instead, *whoever* functions as the subject of the verb *comes*. The whole thing — *whoever comes too close* — is the object of the preposition *at*.

(38) **whom, him.** Change the first part of this question to a statement and you'll get this one right away: *This dog is snarling at whom.* The preposition *at* is completed by the object *whom*. The second preposition, also *at*, needs an object, which is the object pronoun *him*.

(39) **He, him, I.** The verb *thinks* takes the subject pronoun *he*. The preposition *on* needs an object, and *him* gets the job. Finally, *I* is the subject pronoun paired with the verb *pieced*.

(40) **them, her.** *Around* is a preposition in this sentence, so it takes the object *them*. The object pronoun *her* is the object of the preposition *to*.

(41) **his, their.** *Lincoln* doesn't need help with a person; he needs help with a task (*editing*). Whose editing is it? *His*. Moving on, Lincoln doesn't look forward to a person but to an action (*correcting*). Whose *correcting*? *Their correcting*.

(42) **their.** Lincoln didn't hate the people at the agency, but he didn't love *their sending* pronoun-lovers. The possessive pronoun shifts the focus to the action, where it should be.

(43) **him, her.** I snuck this one in to see if you were awake. *Lori saw him.* What was he doing? *Reading*, but the *reading* is a description tacked onto the main idea, which is that she saw *him*. A possessive isn't called for in the first part of this sentence. In the second part, what bothered Lincoln? Not the person (*she*) but the action (*her* saying that the book was "trash"). Select *her* to keep the emphasis on the action.

(44) **her, her.** The objection isn't to a person (*she*) but to an action (*insisting*). I tucked one regular possessive pronoun problem into the end of the sentence, to see whether you were paying attention. Here, the ring belongs to *her*.

(45) **my, my.** The point in this sentence is Lincoln's reaction to the *editing* and to the *pronouncing*. The possessive pronoun *my* keeps the reader's attention on *editing* and *pronouncing*, not on *me*.

(46) **she, she.** For these implied comparisons, add the missing words. *Oscar is as careful as she is* and *he pulls out more plants than she does.*

(47) **they.** Add in the implied verb (do) and you hear the answer immediately: *as they do.* The pronoun *they* is the subject of the verb *do.*

(48) **we.** The *chipmunks munch more than us munch?* I don't think so! They *munch more than we munch.*

(49) **I.** Tack the missing words to the end of the sentence, and you hear *than I have planted.* You need a subject (I) for the implied verb *have planted.*

(50) **me.** The missing words are in the middle of the sentence. *Oscar gives more zucchini to the chipmunks than he gives to me.* The object pronoun *me* is required here. If you chose, *I,* the meaning of the sentence is quite different: *Oscar gives more zucchini to the chipmunks than I do.*

Refer to the following figure for the answers to the "Overachiever" questions.

[1] Three chaperones and ~~myself~~ I left school at 10:03 a.m. with 45 fifth

[2] graders, all of ~~who~~ whom were excited about our visit to Adventure Land.

[3] The day ~~it~~ (no pronoun) passed without incident. My friend Jim and ~~me~~ I [4]

sat in the Adventure Land Bar and Grill for five hours while the

youngsters visited Space Control Center, Pirate Mountain, and other

overpriced but popular rides. The students sitting at my table, Arthur and

~~him,~~ he objected to ~~me~~ my eating such good food and said they wanted [5] [6]

some too. The bus driver ~~she~~ (no pronoun) explained, looking at Arthur's [7]

giant lunch, that all the students could get enough calories by eating

~~her~~ his lunch and that Arthur shouldn't assign blame to ~~whomever~~ whoever [8] [9]

ate some. Later the students ~~they~~ (no pronoun) got in the bus and were [10]

scared by ~~it~~ its making a lot of noise. "~~Whom~~ Who is in charge of [11] [12]

maintenance? asked Arthur. "~~Ourselves~~ We are going to die!" he added. [13]

We drove to Parker Motors because ~~their~~ its mechanics are great. [14]

"~~Myself~~ I and the bus driver will pay," I told the owner. "Do you take [15]

credit cards?" the driver asked. "Sure. Give the card to my wife or ~~I~~ me," [16]

answered the owner. "The bookkeepers, Sue and ~~her~~ she, will charge [17]

you double for the card, but the bus ~~it~~ (no pronoun) will be fine soon." [18]

(1) Use *myself* only when the action doubles back or when you need strong emphasis. Here neither situation exists, so *I* is better.

(2) The pronoun *whom* is the object of the preposition *of*.

(3) You already have a subject, *day*, so you don't need the pronoun *it*.

(4) *My friend Jim and I* are subjects. *I* is a subject pronoun; *me* isn't.

(5) *Students* is a subject, and *Arthur and he* is the appositive – an equivalent statement that must match the case of the word(s) referred to. In this case, you need *he* because it's a subject pronoun.

(6) The focus here is on *eating*, not on *me*. Go for possessive (*my*) to place the emphasis where it belongs.

(7) Because you already have a subject, you don't need an extra pronoun.

(8) *Arthur* is male, so the pronoun *her* doesn't match. Go for the masculine *his*.

(9) The verb *ate* needs a subject, and *whoever* fills the need.

(10) The subject, *students,* appears in the sentence, so no pronoun is needed here.

(11) The kids weren't scared by the bus but rather by *its making a lot of noise.* The possessive form places the emphasis where it belongs.

(12) The verb *is* needs a subject, so *who* works here.

(13) *Ourselves* shouldn't be a subject; go for *we*.

(14) *Parker Motors* is a business and thus is singular, which should be matched by the singular pronoun *its*, not *their*.

(15) *Myself* shouldn't act as a subject. Go for *I*.

(16) *Me* is suitable for the role as object of the preposition *to*.

(17) The appositive of the subject *bookkeepers* should be a subject pronoun, so *she* is the one you want.

(18) Because the subject *bus* appears, the pronoun *it* is unnecessary.

Chapter 7

Little Words Packing a Lot of Power: Prepositions and Interjections

When I was a kid a few millennia ago, my English teacher made the class memorize a list of prepositions. Not liking detention, I sat down and recited the list until it was seared into my brain. It's still there. Although I hated the assignment, I'm glad I can recognize prepositions and the phrases they appear in. It's a useful skill when you're attempting to write correct sentences.

In this chapter, you practice identifying prepositional phrases and choosing a preposition that expresses the meaning you desire. This chapter also helps you perfect your knowledge of interjections. Fantastic! (*Fantastic*, written that way, is an interjection.)

Pinning Down Prepositions

Prepositions are relationship words, connecting two ideas. If I mention *the grammar book by Geraldine Woods*, I'm connecting the source of my income *(book)* to myself *(Geraldine Woods)* with the preposition *by*. The book can sit *on the shelf*, relating an action *(sit)* to a place *(shelf)*. If I'm lucky, the book can also *sell like hotcakes*, connecting the action *(sell)* to a legendary best-selling item *(hotcakes)* with the preposition *like*. As you've probably noticed, the preposition appears with at least one other word — my name, in the first example, and *shelf* and *hotcakes* in the other examples. Each of those words is the *object of the preposition.* You can have one object or more than one object (in the phrase *near cafes and restaurants*, the preposition *near* has two objects, *cafes* and *restaurants*). A few descriptions may show up between the preposition and its object (*in cheap cafes and expensive restaurants*, for example), but they're not objects.

To locate a prepositional phrase, find the preposition and ask *whom?* or *what?* after it. The most important word in the answer is the object.

You need to know prepositional phrases mostly so you can ignore them. Surprised? Prepositional phrases may camouflage subject–verb pairs, which must match. (For more on pairing off subjects and verbs, turn to Chapter 5.) Also, if the object of a preposition is a pronoun, the pronoun must be an object pronoun, not a subject pronoun. You give money for the book to *me*, not to *I*, because *to* is a preposition and *me* is the object. (Check out Chapter 6 for more on subject and object pronouns.) Finally, recognizing prepositions allows you to fine-tune your understanding of how each is used in everyday language. In the exercises, you practice each of these skills in separate sets.

TEST ALERT

Standardized exams often include questions that test your knowledge of prepositions. If you're taking the SAT, ACT or TOEFL, pay extra attention to this chapter.

EXAMPLE

Underline the prepositional phrases. Write the object of the preposition in the blank.

Q. I water the plant in the basket in the early morning. _____

A. **basket, morning.** I water the plant <u>in the basket</u> <u>in the early morning</u>. In the phrase *in the basket*, *in* is the preposition and *basket* is the object. In the phrase *in the early morning*, *in* is the preposition and *morning* is the object.

1. Take the cat to the veterinary clinic now because Fifi is moaning in pain. _____

2. The dog food bag in the closet is empty, and there's a long rip across the bottom. _____

3. Fifi probably stole food from Spot's supply of doggie treats. _____

4. During the night, I heard noises in the kitchen. _____

5 The flashlight on my nightstand was broken, so I saw nothing of interest. _____

6 Before midnight, I had searched inside every cabinet, without success. _____

7 I had forgotten to look in the closet. _____

8 Spot's food is among the bags behind the door of the closet. _____

9 The vet took Fifi out of the cat carrier. _____

10 According to the vet, Fifi's appetite for dog food is unusual. _____

EXAMPLE

Q. Select the correct pronoun from the pair in parentheses and write it in the blank. To make these questions harder, some of the blanks require subject pronouns and some require object pronouns to act as the object of a preposition.

Metal is chew-proof, so a metal container is safer for _____ (they, them) and every animal who likes to snack.

A. **them.** *Them* is an object pronoun, which fits its role as object of the prepositon *for*. *To snack,* by the way, is an infinitive (a verb form) and not a prepositional phrase.

11 Fifi, give the dog food to _____ (I, me).

12 Don't even think about Spot's food, because it belongs to _____ (he, him).

13 Between you and _____ (I, me), Fifi should eat less food.

14 The vet said that _____ (she, her) should weigh five pounds less.

15 The diet _____ (he, him) recommended is not acceptable to _____ (I, me) because it is very expensive.

EXAMPLE

Now try your hand at selecting the correct preposition. I've provided context clues in each sentence so you know what meaning the sentence should express.

Q. Select the appropriate preposition from the parentheses and write it in the blank.

Billy shouted _____ (at, to, for) me when I broke his computer; it took him ten minutes to calm down.

A. **at.** Billy's anger is key here. He's yelling, so the best choice is *shouted at me.* If he *shouted to me,* he raised his voice so that I could hear his message from some distance away. If he *shouted for me,* he's rooting loudly for my success.

16 Go _____ (in to, into, by) the store and buy more kibble.

17 Teachers and students are frantic _____ (in, at) autumn as the end of vacation nears.

18 I like to buy school supplies _____ (on, by, in) Smith's Stationery _____ (on, at, in) Fifth Avenue.

19 There's no public transportation _____ (to, for) the mall, so everyone goes _____ (in, by) car.

20 At the store, teachers talked _____ (about, concerning) their new students.

Interjections Are Simple!

I lied a little in this heading, but not much. An *interjection*, the part of speech that expresses strong emotion, isn't connected to the structure or content of a sentence. An interjection comments on the content, sometimes within the sentence and sometimes before or after the sentence. Take a look at these examples, in which the interjections are italicized:

Yes! My team won the division championship.

Ouch, my arms hurt. Be more careful with your baseball bat.

You got tickets to the World Series? *Awesome!*

If you try really hard, you can manage to make an error with an interjection. For example, you may mistake it for a subject. In the second example sentence, you'd be wrong to match the verb *hurt* with *ouch*, a word that appears to be singular, instead of the real subject, *arms*, which is plural. Also, on social media or in texts, many people pile on exclamation points after interjections to indicate strong emotion. In formal English, though, one exclamation point is enough.

Q. Mark each sentence as correct or incorrect.

EXAMPLE

Hey!?!?! You mean you don't care?

A. **Incorrect.** After *hey*, one punctuation mark is correct, not five.

21 "No!!!!" Mick screamed as he saw the terms of his new contract. _____

22 "Goodness I've never been paid so little," he explained. _____

23. Boy, was he angry! _____

24. Indeed, he will soon switch to a new agent. _____

25. Rats, I will lose a lot of money because I'm Mick's agent. _____

Calling All Overachievers: Extra Practice with Prepositions and Interjections

Read this letter from a prisoner to his girlfriend. Find and correct errors involving prepositional phrases and interjections. You should find ten errors in all.

Dear Adelie,

Oh!! How I long to be with you in this cold, cold day. The prison bars on my cell have not kept me from dreaming of going at the beach with you. Between you and I, there may be a way to escape. Hank, the guard, loves cake. Please when you come to visit, bring a cake with a file baked in side. Offer a slice to he and the other guards. Careful! Be sure not to cut in to the side of the cake with the file in it. When the guards leave, I will file down the bars and come at you. Soon we will be free and happy together.

Love,
Pete

Answers to Questions About Prepositions and Interjections

Will it be *Hooray! I got them all right* or *Bummer, I got some wrong?* Check to see how you fared.

(1) **clinic, pain.** Take the cat to the veterinary clinic now because Fifi is moaning in pain. The object of the preposition *to* is *clinic*, and the object of *in* is *pain*.

(2) **closet, bottom.** The dog food bag in the closet is empty, and there's a long rip across the bottom. Find the object by asking *whom? what?* after the preposition: *in what? in the closet, across what? across the bottom.*

(3) **supply, treats.** Fifi probably stole food from Spot's supply of doggie treats. Notice that you have two prepositional phrases here, one after the other. Each has its own object.

(4) **night, kitchen.** During the night, I heard noises in the kitchen. Ask *during what?* and *in what?* and the object of the preposition becomes clear.

(5) **nightstand, interest.** The flashlight on my nightstand was broken, so I saw nothing of interest. Ask *on what? on my nightstand.* Ask *of what? of interest.*

(6) **midnight, cabinet, success.** Before midnight, I had searched inside every cabinet, without success. Three prep phrases are tucked into this short sentence, explaining when, where, and how *I had searched.*

(7) **closet.** I had forgotten to look in the closet. Did I trick you with *to look?* It's an infinitive, the head of a verb family, not a prepositional phrase.

(8) **bags, door, closet.** Spot's food is among the bags behind the door of the closet. Three separate prep phrases here, with three different objects.

(9) **carrier.** The vet took Fifi out of the cat carrier. Here the preposition is composed of two words, *out of.*

(10) **vet, dog food.** According to the vet, Fifi's appetite for dog food is unusual. Another two-word preposition: *according to.* The second prep phrase begins with a one-word preposition, *for.*

(11) **me.** The object of the preposition *to* is the object pronoun *me.*

(12) **him.** The object of the preposition *to* is the object pronoun *him.*

(13) **me.** The phrase *between you and I* has become more common lately, but *me,* the object pronoun, is proper. *I* has not yet been accepted by most traditional grammarians.

(14) **she.** Did I fool you? In this sentence, *she* is the subject of the verb *should weigh.*

(15) **he, me.** First up is a subject, *he,* which you need for the verb *recommended.* Next is an object, *me,* for the preposition *to.*

(16) **into.** In Standard English, you go *into a store,* not *in to* or *by.*

(17) **in.** When you state an exact time (say, 12:30 a.m.) you use the preposition *at.* When you refer to a longer period of time, such as a season, *in* is better.

(18) **in, on.** You go into the store and buy *in* the store. When you give a general location, *on* works best. For a specific address (say, 660 Fifth Avenue), use *at.*

(19) **to, by.** The standard phrases are *to the mall* and *by car*. If you insert *a* into that last phrase, you can go *in a car*.

(20) **about.** *About* begins a prepositional phrase attached to the verb *talk*.

(21) **Incorrect.** Four exclamation points are three too many.

(22) **Incorrect.** You need an exclamation point or a comma after *goodness*.

(23) **Correct.** No problems with the interjection, *boy*.

(24) **Correct.** This sentence correctly places and punctuates *indeed*.

(25) **Correct.** The financial situation may be bad, but the sentence is fine.

See the following figure for the answers to the "Overachievers" section.

Dear Adelie,

Oh!~~!~~ **[omit extra exclamation point]** How I long to be with you ① ~~in~~ **on** this cold, cold day. The prison bars ~~on~~ **of** my cell have not kept me ③ from dreaming of going ~~at~~ **to** the beach with you. Between you and ~~I~~ **me**, ⑤ there may be a way to escape. Hank, the guard, loves cake. Please, **[add comma after "please"]** when you come to visit, bring a cake with a ⑥ file baked ~~in side~~ **inside**. Offer a slice to ~~he~~ **him** and the other guards. ⑧ Careful! Be sure not to cut ~~in to~~ **into** the side of the cake with the file in ⑨ it. When the guards leave, I will file down the bars and come ~~at~~ **to** you. ⑩ Soon we will be free and happy together.

Love,

Pete

(1) In Standard English, one exclamation point is enough.

(2) *In* is wrong because you're talking about a specific, relatively short period of time. The better choice for this spot is *on*.

(3) *Of* is the preposition you want, not *on*, because the bars are part of the cell, not an addition to it.

(4) In Standard English, you go *to the beach*, not *at*.

(5) *Between* is a preposition, so it should be followed by object pronouns, such as *me*, not *I*.

6. *Please,* an interjection, should be separated from the sentence by a comma.

7. The expression you want is *inside* (an adverb), not two words (*in side*).

8. The object pronoun *him* is best here as the object of the preposition *to.*

9. *Into* should be written as one word, not two.

10. *Come at* implies an attack. *Come to* is neutral, showing only direction of movement.

» Deciding whether an adjective or an adverb is appropriate

» Selecting articles: *a* or *an* or *the*

» Choosing *good* or *well* and *bad or badly*

» Creating comparisons with adjectives and adverbs

Chapter **8**

Writing Good or Well: Adjectives and Adverbs

D o you write good or well — and what's the difference? Does your snack break feature a apple or an apple or the apple? Is your cold worse or more bad? If you're stewing over these questions, you have problems . . . specifically, the problems in this chapter. Here you can practice choosing between two types of descriptions, adjectives and adverbs. This chapter also helps you figure out whether *a*, *an*, or *the* is appropriate in any given situation. Finally, here you practice making comparisons with adjectives and adverbs.

Identifying Adjectives and Adverbs

Adjectives describe nouns — words that name a person, thing, place, or idea. They also describe pronouns, which are words that stand in for nouns (*other, someone, they*, and similar words). Adjectives usually precede the word they describe, but not always. In the following sentence the adjectives are italicized:

The *rubber* duck with his *lovely orange* bill sailed over the *murky bath* water. *(Rubber* describes *duck; lovely* and *orange* describe *bill; murky* and *bath* describe *water.)*

An *adverb*, on the other hand, describes a verb, usually telling how, where, when, or why an action took place. Adverbs also indicate the intensity of another descriptive word or add information about another description. In the following sentence the adverbs are italicized:

> The alligator snapped *furiously* as the duck *quite violently* flapped his wings. *(Furiously* describes *snapped; violently* describes *flapped, quite* describes *violently.)*

When you're speaking or writing, you should take care to use adjectives and adverbs correctly. But first you have to recognize them. To locate an adjective, check each noun and pronoun. Ask *which one? what kind? how many?* about each noun or pronoun. If you get an answer, you've found an adjective. To locate an adverb, first check every verb. Ask *how? when? where? why?* If you get an answer, you've identified an adverb. Also look at the adjectives. Does any word intensify (*very*, for example) or weaken (*less*, perhaps) that description? That's an adverb at work.

Sometimes when you ask the adjective or adverb questions, the answer is a group of words. Don't panic. You've probably found a prepositional phrase (see Chapter 7) or a clause (see Chapter 16). In this exercise, concentrate on one- or two-word adjectives and adverbs.

WARNING

Q. Underline every adjective or adverb in each sentence. Write *ADJ* above an adjective and *ADV* above an adverb.

EXAMPLE

Debbie slowly crosses the dark street followed by three little dogs.

A. **slowly (ADV), dark (ADJ), three (ADJ), little (ADJ).** How does *Debbie cross? Slowly. Slowly* is an adverb describing the verb *crosses.* What kind of *street? The dark street. Dark* is an adjective describing the noun *street.* In case you're wondering, *the* is also a type of adjective — an *article.* You can find out more about articles later in this chapter. For now, ignore *a, an,* and *the.* What kind of *dogs? Little dogs. Little* is an adjective describing the noun *dogs.* How many dogs? *three dogs. Three* is an adjective describing *dogs.*

1. Slipping onto her comfortable, old sofa, Lola quickly grabbed the black plastic remote.

   _____

2. "I arrived early, because I desperately want to watch that new motorcycle show," she said to George.

   _____

3. George, who was intently watching the latest news, turned away silently.

   _____

4. Everyone present knew that Lola would get her way. She always did!

   _____

5. George struggled fiercely, but he was curious about the show, which featured a different motorcycle weekly.

   _____

6. If he held out a little longer, he knew that Lola would offer something nice to him.

_____

7. Lola's purse always held a few goodies, and George was extremely fond of chocolate brownies.

_____

8. He could almost taste the sweet, hazelnut flavor that Lola sometimes added to the packaged brownie mix.

_____

9. George sighed loudly and waved a long, thin hand.

_____

10. "You can watch anything good," he remarked in a low, defeated voice, "but first give me two brownies."

_____

The Right Place at the Right Time: Placing Adjectives and Adverbs

You don't need to stick labels on adjectives and adverbs, but you do need to send the right word to the right place in order to avoid arrest by the grammar police. A few wonderful words (*fast, short, last,* and *likely,* for example) function as both adjectives and adverbs, but for the most part, adjectives and adverbs are not interchangeable. In this section you choose between adjectives and adverbs and insert them into sentences.

TIP

Most adverbs end in *-ly,* but some adverbs vary, and adjectives can end with any letter in the alphabet, except maybe *q.* If you're not sure which form is an adjective and which is an adverb, check the dictionary. Most definitions include both forms with handy labels telling you what's what.

EXAMPLE

Which word is correct? The parentheses contain both an adjective and an adverb. Circle your selection.

Q. The water level dropped (slow/slowly), but the (intense/intensely) alligator-duck quarrel went on and on.

A. slowly, intense. How did the water *drop?* The word you want from the first parentheses must describe an action (the verb *dropped*), so the adverb *slowly* wins the prize. Next up is a description of a *quarrel,* a thing, so the adjective *intense* does the job.

11 The alligator, a (loyal/loyally) member of the Union of Fictional Creatures, (sure/surely) resented the cartoon duck's presence near the drainpipe.

12 "How dare you invade my (personal/personally) plumbing?" inquired the alligator (angry/ angrily).

13 "You don't have to be (nasty/nastily)!" replied the duck.

14 The two creatures (swift/swiftly) circled each other, both looking for a (clear/clearly) advantage.

15 "You are (extreme/extremely) territorial about these pipes," added the duck.

16 The alligator retreated (fearful/fearfully) as the duck quacked (sharp/sharply).

17 Just then a (poor/poorly) dressed figure appeared in the doorway.

18 The creature whipped out a bullhorn and a sword that was (near/nearly) five feet in length.

19 When he screamed into the bullhorn, the sound bounced (easy, easily) off the tiled walls.

20 "Listen!" he ordered (forceful/forcefully). "The alligator should retreat (quick/quickly) to the sewer and the duck to the shelf."

21 Having given this order, the (Abominable/Abominably) Snowman seemed (happy/ happily).

22 The fight in the bathtub had made him (real/really) angry.

23 "You (sure/surely) can't deny that we imaginary creatures must stick together," explained the Snowman.

24 Recognizing the (accurate/accurately) statement, the duck apologized to the alligator.

25 The alligator retreated to the sewer, where he found a (lovely/lovingly) lizard with an urge to party.

26 "Come (quick/quickly)," the alligator shouted (loud/loudly) to the duck.

27 The duck left the tub (happy/happily) because he thought he had found a (new/newly) friend.

28 The alligator celebrated (noisy/noisily) because he had discovered an enemy (dumb/ dumbly) enough to enter the sewer, the alligator's turf.

29 "Walk (safe/safely)," murmured the gator, as the duck entered a (particular/particularly) narrow tunnel.

30 The duck waddled (careful/carefully), beginning to suspect (serious/seriously) danger.

How's It Going? Choosing Between Good/Well and Bad/Badly

For some reason, adjective and adverb pairs that pass judgment (*good* and *well, bad* and *badly*) cause a lot of trouble. Here's a quick guide: *Good* and *bad* are adjectives, so they have to describe nouns — people, places, things, or ideas. ("I gave a *good* report to the boss." The adjective *good* describes the noun *report*. "The *bad* dog ate my slippers this morning." The adjective *bad* describes the noun *dog*.) *Well* and *badly* are adverbs used to describe action. ("In my opinion, the report was particularly *well* written." The adverb *well* describes the verb *written*. "The dog slept *badly* after his slipper-fest." The adverb *badly* describes the verb *slept*.) *Well* and *badly* also describe other descriptions. In the expression *a well-written essay,* for example, *well* describes *written,* which describes *essay.*

TIP

Well can be an adjective in one particular circumstance: health. When someone asks how you are, the answer (I hope) is "I am well" or "I feel well." You can also — and I hope you do — feel *good,* especially when you're talking about your mental state, though this usage is a bit more informal. Apart from health questions, however, *well* is a permanent member of the adverb team. In fact, if you can insert the word *healthy* in a particular spot, *well* works in the same spot also.

When a description follows a verb, danger lurks. You have to decide whether the description gives information about the verb or about the person/thing who is doing the action or is in the state of being. If the description describes the verb, go for an adverb. If it describes the person/thing (the subject, in grammatical terms), opt for the adjective.

Circle the right word in each set of parentheses.

EXAMPLE

Q. The trainer works (good/well) with all types of dogs, especially those that don't outweigh him.

A. **well.** How does the trainer work? The word you need must be an adverb because you're giving information about an action (work), not a noun.

31 My dog Caramel barks when he's run (good/well) during his daily race with the letter carrier.

32 The letter carrier likes Caramel and feels (bad/badly) about beating him when they race.

33 Caramel tends to bite the poor guy whenever the race doesn't turn out (good/well).

34 Caramel's owner named him after a type of candy she thinks is (good/well).

35 The letter carrier thinks high-calorie snacks are (bad/badly).

36 He eats organic sprouts and wheat germ for lunch, though his meal tastes (bad/badly).

37 Caramel once caught a corner of a dog-food bag and chewed off a (good/well) bit.

38 Resisting the urge to barf, Caramel ate (bad/badly), according to his doggie standards.

39 Caramel, who didn't feel (good/well), barked quite a bit that day.

40 Tired of the din, his owner confiscated the kibble and screamed, "(Bad/Badly) dog!"

Mastering the Art of Articles

Three little words — *a, an,* and *the* — pop up in just about every English sentence. Sometimes (like my relatives) they show up where they shouldn't. Technically, these three words are adjectives, but they belong to the subcategory of articles. As always, forget about the terminology. Just know how to use them:

» *The* refers to something specific. When you say that you want *the book,* you're implying one particular text, even if you haven't named it. *The* attaches nicely to both singular and plural words.

» *A* and *an* are more general in meaning and work only with singular words. If you want *a book,* you're willing to read anything. *A* precedes words beginning with consonants and words that begin with a long *u* sound, similar to what you hear when you say "you." *An* comes before words beginning with vowels *(an ant, an encyclopedia, an uncle)* except for the long *u* sound *(a university). An* also precedes words that sound as if they begin with a vowel *(hour,* for example) because the initial consonant is silent.

TIP

If you want a general term but you're talking about a plural, try *some* or *any* instead of *a* or *an,* because these last two articles can't deal with plurals.

Write the correct article in each blank in the sentences that follow.

EXAMPLE

Q. When Lulu asked to see _____ wedding pictures, she didn't expect Annie to put on _____ twelve-hour slide show.

A. **the, a.** In the first half of the sentence, Lulu is asking for something specific. Also, *wedding pictures* is a plural expression, so *a* and *an* are out of the question. In the second half of the sentence, something more general is appropriate. Because *twelve* begins with the consonant *t, a* is the article of choice.

41 Although Lulu was mostly bored out of her mind, she did like _____ picture of Annie's Uncle Fred snoring in the back of the church.

42 _____ nearby guest, one of several attempting to plug up their ears, can be seen poking Uncle Fred's ribs.

43 At Annie's wedding, Uncle Fred wore _____ antique bow tie that he bought in _____ department store next door to his apartment building.

44 _____ clerk who sold _____ tie to Uncle Fred secretly inserted _____ microphone and _____ miniature radio transmitter.

45 Uncle Fred's snores were broadcast by _____ obscure radio station that specializes in embarrassing moments.

46 Annie, who didn't want to invite Uncle Fred but was forced to do so by her mother, placed _____ buzzer under his seat.

47 Annie's plan was to zap him whenever he snored too loudly; unfortunately, Fred chose _____ different seat.

For Better or Worse: Forming Comparisons

If human beings weren't so tempted to compare their situations with others', life (and grammar) would be a lot easier. In this section, I tell you everything you need to know about creating comparisons, whether they show up as one word (*higher, farthest*) or two words (*more beautiful, least sensible*). For information on longer comparisons, see Chapter 19.

Visiting the -ER (and the -EST): One- or two-word comparisons

Adjectives and *adverbs* serve as the basic construction material for comparisons. Regular unadorned adjectives and adverbs are the base upon which two types of comparisons may be made: the *comparative* and the *superlative*. Comparatives (*dumber, smarter, neater, more interesting, less available,* and the like) deal with only two elements. Superlatives (*dumbest, smartest, neatest, most interesting, least available,* and so forth) identify the extreme in a group of three or more. To create simple comparisons, follow these guidelines:

» **Tack -er onto the end of a one-syllable descriptive word to create a positive comparative form.** When I say *positive,* I mean that the first term of the comparison comes out on top, as in "parakeets are noisier than canaries," a statement that gives more volume to *parakeets.* Occasionally a two-syllable word forms a comparative this way also (*lovelier,* for example).

» **To make the comparative forms of a word with more than one syllable, you generally use *more* or *less,* not -er.** This guideline doesn't hold true for every word in the dictionary, but it's valid for most. Therefore, you'd say that "canaries are more popular than parakeets," not "canaries are popularer." Just to be clear: *populer* isn't a word!

» **Glue -est to one-syllable words to make a positive superlative.** A positive superlative gives the advantage to the element cited in the comparison. For example, *canaries* have the edge in "canaries are the finest singers in the bird world." Also, a few two-syllable words use -est to create a superlative (such as *loneliest*).

>> **Add *most* or *least* to longer words to create a superlative.** Again, the definition of *longer* isn't set in stone, but a word containing two or more syllables, such as *beautiful,* generally qualifies as long. The superlative forms are *most beautiful* or *least beautiful.*

>> **Negative comparative and superlative forms always rely on two words.** If you want to state that something is *less* or *least,* you have to use those words and not a tacked-on syllable. Therefore, "the canary's song is *less pretty* when he has a head cold," and "my parakeets are *least annoying* when they're sleeping."

>> **Check the dictionary if you're not sure of the correct form.** The entry for the plain adjective or adverb normally includes the comparative and superlative forms, if they're single words. If you don't see a listing for another form of the word, take the *less/more, least/most* option.

A few comparatives and superlatives are irregular. I discuss these in the next section, "Going from bad to worse (and good to better): Irregular comparisons."

WARNING

Never add *-er* or *-est* AND *less/more* or *least/most.* These forms together are not correct.

Ready for some comparison shopping? Insert the comparative or superlative form as needed into the blanks for each question. The base word is in parentheses at the end of the sentence.

EXAMPLE

Q. Helen is the _____ of all the women living in Troy, New York. (*beautiful*)

A. **most beautiful.** The sentence compares *Helen* to other women in Troy, New York. Comparing more than two elements requires the superlative form. Because *beautiful* is a long word, *most* creates a positive comparison. (*Least beautiful* is the negative version.)

48 Helen, who manages the billing for an auto parts company, is hoping for a transfer to the Paris office, where the salaries are _____ than in New York but the night life is _____. (*low, lively*)

49 Helen's boss claims that she is the _____ and _____ _____ of all his employees. (*efficient, valuable*)

50 His secretary, however, has measured everyone's output of P-345 forms and concluded that Helen is _____ and _____ than Natalie, Helen's assistant. (*slow, accurate*)

51 Natalie prefers to type her P-345s because she thinks the result is _____ _____ and _____ than handwritten work. (*neat, professional*)

52 Helen notes that everyone else in the office writes _____ than Natalie, whose penmanship has been compared to random scratches from a blind chicken; however, Natalie types _____. (*legibly, fast*)

53 Helen has been angry with Natalie ever since her assistant declared that Helen's coffee was _____ and _____ than the tea that Natalie brought to the office. (*drinkable, tasty*)

54 Helen countered with the claim that Natalie brewed tea _____
    than the office rules allow, a practice that makes her _____
    than Helen. *(frequently, productive)*

55 Other workers are trying to stay out of the feud; they know that both women are
    capable of making the work day _____ and _____
    _____ than it is now. *(long, boring)*

56 The _____ moment in the argument came when Natalie claimed
    that Helen's toy duck "squawked _____ than Helen herself."
    (petty, annoyingly)

57 That duck was the _____ and _____ toy
    in the entire store! *(expensive, cute)*

58 Knowing about Helen's transfer request, I selected a duck that sounded _____
    _____ and _____ than the average American
    rubber duck. *(international, interesting)*

59 The clerk told me my request was the _____ he had ever
    encountered, but because he holds himself to the _____
    standards of customer service, he did not laugh at me. *(silly, high)*

60 I replied that I preferred to deal with store clerks who were _____
    _____ and _____ than he. *(snobby, knowledgeable)*

61 Anyway, Helen's transfer wasn't approved, and she is in the _____
    _____ mood imaginable, even _____ than she was when her
    desk caught fire. *(nasty, annoyed)*

62 We all skirt Natalie's desk _____ than Helen's, because Natalie
    is even _____ than Helen about the refusal. *(widely, upset)*

63 Natalie, who considers herself the _____ person in the com-
    pany, wanted a promotion to Helen's rank or an even _____ job.
    (essential, important)

64 Larry is sure that he would have gotten the promotion because he is the _____
    _____ and _____ of all of us in his donations to the
    Party Fund. *(generous, creative)*

65 "Natalie bakes a couple of cupcakes," he commented _____
    than a boxing champion, "and the boss thinks she's executive material." *(forcefully)*

66 "I, on the other hand, am the _____ of the three clerks in my
    office," he continued, "and I am absent _____ than everyone
    else." *(professional, often)*

67 When I left the office, Natalie and Larry were arm wrestling to see who was _____
    _____, and Helen was surfing Internet job sites _____
    _____ than usual. *(strong, carefully)*

Going from bad to worse (and good to better): Irregular comparisons

A couple of basic descriptions form comparisons irregularly. Irregulars don't add *-er* or *more/less* to create the comparative form, a comparison between two elements. Nor do irregulars tack on *-est* or *most/least* to point out the top or bottom of a group of more than two, also known as the superlative form of comparisons. (See the preceding section, "Visiting the -ER (and the -EST)," for more information on comparatives and superlatives.) Instead, irregular comparisons follow their own strange path, as you can see in Table 8-1.

Table 8-1   **Forms of Irregular Comparisons**

Description	Comparative	Superlative
Good or well	Better	Best
Bad or ill	Worse	Worst
Much or many	More	Most

EXAMPLE

Choose the correct comparative or superlative form of the word in parentheses and write your answer in the blank.

Q. Edgar's scrapbook, which contains souvenirs from his trip to Watch Repair Camp, is the _____ example of a boring book that I have ever seen. (*good*)

A. **best.** Once you mention the top or bottom experience of a lifetime, you're in the superlative column. Because *goodest* isn't a word, *best* is the one you want.

68 Edgar explains his souvenirs in _____ detail than anyone would ever want to hear. (*much*)

69 Bored listeners believe that the _____ item in his scrapbook is a set of gears, each of which Edgar can discuss for hours. (*bad*)

70 On the bright side, everyone knows that Edgar's watch repair skills are _____ _____ than the jewelers' downtown. (*good*)

71 When he has the flu, Edgar actually feels _____ when he hears about a broken watch. (*bad*)

72 Although he is only nine years old, Edgar has the _____ timepieces of anyone in his fourth grade class, including the teacher. (*many*)

73 The classroom clock functions fairly well, but Ms. Appleby relies on Edgar to make it run even _____. (*well*)

74 Edgar's scrapbook also contains three samples of watch oil; Edgar thinks Time-Ola Oil is the _____ choice. (*good*)

75. Unfortunately, last week Edgar let a little oil drip onto his lunch and became sick; a few hours later he felt _____ and had to call the doctor. *(ill)*

76. "Time-Ola Oil is the _____ of all the poisons," cried the doctor. *(bad)*

77. "But it's the _____ for watches," whispered Edgar. *(good)*

Calling All Overachievers: Extra Practice with Descriptors

EXAMPLE

Read this page from a dress catalogue. Twenty-five words or phrases are underlined and numbered. Some are correct, and some aren't. Look for adjectives trying to do an adverb's job and vice versa, articles that should be changed, and comparisons that need some work. When you find an error, correct it. If the underlined expression is fine, leave it alone.

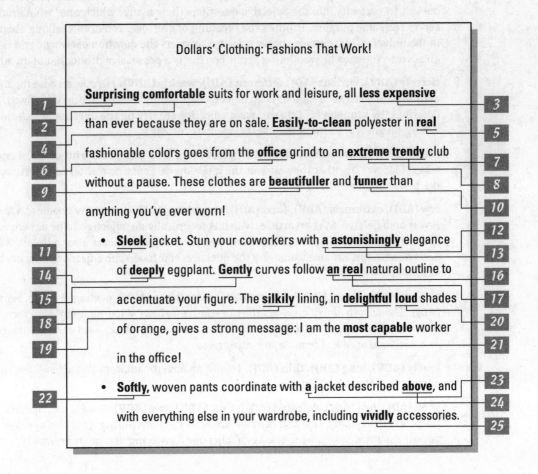

Dollars' Clothing: Fashions That Work!

Surprising comfortable suits for work and leisure, all **less expensive** [1] [3]

than ever because they are on sale. **Easily-to-clean** polyester in **real** [2] [5]

fashionable colors goes from the **office** grind to an **extreme trendy** club [4] [7]

without a pause. These clothes are **beautifuller** and **funner** than [6] [8]

anything you've ever worn! [9] [10]

- **Sleek** jacket. Stun your coworkers with **a astonishingly** elegance [11] [12] [13]

of **deeply** eggplant. **Gently** curves follow **an real** natural outline to [14] [16]

accentuate your figure. The **silkily** lining, in **delightful loud** shades [15] [17]

of orange, gives a strong message: I am the **most capable** worker [18] [20]

in the office! [19] [21]

- **Softly,** woven pants coordinate with **a** jacket described **above**, and [22] [23] [24]

with everything else in your wardrobe, including **vividly** accessories. [25]

Answers to Adjective and Adverb Problems

I hope the challenging exercises in this short chapter on descriptive words didn't give you too much trouble. Find out how you did by comparing your work to the following answers.

1. **comfortable (ADJ), old (ADJ), quickly (ADV), black (ADJ), plastic (ADJ).** The adjectives *comfortable* and *old* tell you what kind of *sofa*. The adverb *quickly* tells you how Lola *grabbed*. The adjectives *black* and *plastic* tell you what kind of *remote*.

2. **early (ADV), desperately (ADV), new (ADJ), motorcycle (ADJ).** The adverb *early* tells you when she *arrived*. The adverb *desperately* tells you how she *wanted*. The adjectives *new* and *motorcycle* answer the question *what kind of show?*

3. **intently (ADV), latest (ADJ), away (ADV) silently (ADV).** The adverb *intently* answers the question *watching how? Latest*, an adjective, tells you *what kind of news. Away* and *silently*, both adverbs, answer *turned how?*

4. **present (ADJ) always (ADV).** *Present* is an adjective describing the pronoun *everyone*. This adjective breaks the pattern because it appears after the word it describes, not before. It also doesn't fit perfectly into the adjective questions (how many? which one? what kind?), but it serves the same purpose. It limits the meaning of *everyone*. You aren't talking about everyone in the universe, just *everyone present. Always* answers the question *did when?* and is therefore an adverb. You may be wondering about *her. Her* is a possessive pronoun, not an adjective.

5. **fiercely (ADV), curious (ADJ) different (ADJ), weekly (ADV).** *Fiercely*, an adverb, answers the question *struggled how? Curious* is an adjective appearing after a linking verb *(was). Curious* describes the pronoun *he. Different* is an adjective answering the question *which motorcycle? Weekly*, an adverb, answers the question *features when?*

6. **little (ADV), longer (ADV), nice (ADJ).** The adverb *little* changes the intensity of another adverb, *longer*. Together they answer the question *held out when? Nice*, an adjective, describes the pronoun *something*.

7. **few (ADJ), extremely (ADV), fond (ADJ), chocolate (ADJ).** How many goodies? *A few* goodies. *Few* is an adjective. (*A* is an article, which is technically an adjective.) The adverb *extremely* intensifies the meaning of the adjective *fond. Fond*, which appears after a linking verb, describes *George. Extremely* answers the question *how fond?* The adjective *chocolate* answers *what kind of brownies?*

8. **almost (ADV) sweet (ADJ), hazelnut (ADJ) sometimes (ADV), packaged (ADJ), brownie (ADJ).** The adverb *almost* answers the question *taste how?* What kind of *flavor? Sweet, hazelnut.* Both are adjectives. *Added* when? *Sometimes* — an adverb. What kind of *mix? Packaged, brownie mix.* Both *packaged* and *brownie* are adjectives.

9. **loudly (ADV), long (ADJ), thin (ADJ).** *Loudly*, an adverb, answers *sighed how? Long* and *thin*, adjectives, tell you what kind of *hand*.

10. **good (ADJ), low (ADJ), defeated (ADJ), first (ADV), two (ADV).** *Good* is an adjective describing the pronoun *anything. Low* and *defeated* are adjectives answering *what kind of voice? First* is an adverb answering *give when? Two* is an adjective answering *how many brownies?*

(11) **loyal, surely.** What kind of *member* is the *alligator*? A *loyal member*. Because you're describing a noun (*member*), you need the adjective *loyal*. In the second part of the sentence, the adverb *surely* explains how the duck's presence was resented. *Resented* is a verb and must be described by an adverb.

(12) **personal, angrily.** In the first part of the sentence, *personal* describes a thing (*plumbing*). How did the alligator *inquire*? *Angrily*. The adverb tells about the verb, *inquire*.

(13) **nasty.** The adjective *nasty* describes *you*. Of course I don't mean you, the reader. You earned my undying affection by buying this book. The *you* in the sentence is *nasty!*

(14) **swiftly, clear.** The adverb *swiftly* describes the action of circling. The adjective *clear* explains what kind of advantage the creatures were seeking.

(15) **extremely.** The adverb *extremely* clarifies the intensity of the descriptive word *territorial*. (If you absolutely have to know, *territorial* is an adjective describing *you*.)

(16) **fearfully, sharply.** Both of these adverbs tell how the actions (*retreated* and *quacked*) were performed.

(17) **poorly.** The adverb *poorly* gives information about the descriptive word *dressed*.

(18) **nearly.** This was a tough question, and if you got it right, treat yourself to a spa day. The expression *five feet* is a description of the sword. The adverb *nearly* gives additional information about the description *five feet in length*.

(19) **easily.** The adverb *easily* describes the verb *bounced*.

(20) **forcefully, quickly.** The adverb *forcefully* tells how he *ordered*, a verb. The adverb *quickly* describes how the alligator should *retreat*.

(21) **Abominable, happy.** You can cheat on the first part of this one just by knowing the name of the monster that supposedly stalks the Himalayas, but you can also figure out the answer using grammar. A snowman is a thing (or a person) and thus a noun. Adjectives describe nouns, so *abominable* does the trick. In the second half you need an adjective to describe the snowman, who was *happy*. You aren't describing the action of seeming, so an adverb isn't correct.

(22) **really.** This sentence presents two commonly confused words. Because *angry* is an adjective, you need an adverb to indicate its intensity, and *really* fills the bill.

(23) **surely.** That horse in the fifth race might be a sure thing, because *thing* is a noun and you need an adjective to describe it. But the verb *deny* must be described by an adverb, so *surely* is the one you want.

(24) **accurate.** *Statement* is a noun that must be described by the adjective *accurate*.

(25) **lovely.** A *lizard* is a noun, which may be described by the adjective *lovely* but not the adverb *lovingly*. Incidentally, *lovely* isn't an adverb, despite the fact that it ends with *-ly*.

(26) **quickly, loudly.** The adverb *quickly* describes the verb *come*, and the adverb *loudly* describes the verb *shouted*.

(27) **happy, new.** This sentence presents a puzzle. Are you talking about the duck's mood or the way in which he left the tub? The two are related, of course, but the mood is the primary meaning, so the adjective *happy* is the better choice to describe *duck*. The adjective *new* describes the noun *friend*.

28 **noisily, dumb.** The adverb *noisily* tells you how the alligator *celebrated*. Because *celebrated* is a verb, you need an adverb. The adjective *dumb* tells you about the noun *enemy*. Most, but not all, adjectives are in front of the words they describe, but in this case the adjective follows the noun.

29 **safely, particularly.** The adverb safely tells you about the verb *walk*. The second answer is also an adverb, because *particularly* explains how *narrow* the tunnel is.

30 **carefully, serious.** The adverb *carefully* explains how the duck *waddled*, and *waddled* is a verb. *Danger*, a noun, is described by the adjective *serious*.

31 **well.** The adverb *well* tells you how Caramel *has run*.

32 **bad.** This sentence illustrates a common mistake. The description doesn't tell you anything about the letter carrier's ability to *feel* (touching sensation). Instead, it tells you about his state of mind. Because the word is a description of a person, not of an action, you need an adjective, *bad. To feel badly* implies that you're wearing mittens and can't *feel* anything through the thick cloth.

33 **well.** The adverb *well* describes the action *to turn out* (to result).

34 **good.** What is her opinion of chocolate caramels? She *thinks* they are *good*. The adjective is needed because you're describing the noun *candy*.

35 **bad.** The description *bad* applies to the *snacks*, not to the verb *are*. Hence, an adjective is what you want.

36 **bad.** The description tells you about his *meal*, a noun. You need the adjective *bad*.

37 **good.** The adjective (*good*) is attached to a noun (*bit*).

38 **badly.** Now you're talking about the action (*ate*), so you need an adverb (*badly*).

39 **well.** The best response here is *well*, an adjective that works for health-status statements. *Good* will do in a pinch, but *good* is better for psychological or mood statements.

40 **Bad.** The adjective *bad* applies to the noun *dog*.

41 **the.** The sentence implies that one particular picture caught Lulu's fancy, so *the* works nicely here. If you chose *a*, no problem. The sentence would be a bit less specific but still acceptable. The only true clinker is *an*, which must precede words beginning with vowels (except for a short *u*, or *uh* sound) — a group that doesn't include *picture*.

42 **A.** Because the sentence tells you that several guests are nearby, *the* doesn't fit here. The more general *a* is best.

43 **an or the, the.** In the first blank you may place either *an* (which must precede a word beginning with a vowel) or *the*. In the second blank, *the* is best because it's unlikely that Fred is surrounded by several department stores. *The* is more definitive, pointing out one particular store.

44 **The, the, a, a.** Lots of blanks in this one! The first two seem more particular (one *clerk*, one *tie*), so *the* fits well. The second two blanks imply that the clerk selected one from a group of many, not a particular microphone or transmitter. The more general article is *a*, which precedes words beginning with consonants.

45 **an.** Because the radio station is described as *obscure*, a word beginning with a vowel, you need *an*, not *a*. If you inserted *the*, don't cry. That article works here also.

46 **a.** The word *buzzer* doesn't begin with a vowel, so you have to go with *a*, not *an*. The more definite *the* could work, implying that the reader knows that you're talking about a particular buzzer, not just any buzzer.

47 **a.** He chose any old seat, not a particular one, so *a* is what you want.

48 **lower, livelier.** The comparative form is the way to go because two cities, Paris and New York, are compared. One-syllable words such as *low* form comparatives with the addition of *-er*. Most two-syllable words rely on *more* or *less*, but *lively* is an exception.

49 **most efficient, most valuable.** In choosing the top or bottom rank from a group of three or more, go for superlative. *Efficient and valuable*, both long words, take *most* or *least.* In the context of this sentence, *most* makes sense.

50 **slower, less accurate.** Comparing two elements, in this case *Helen* and *Natalie*, calls for comparative form. The one-syllable word takes *-er*, and the longer word relies on *less*.

51 **neater, more professional.** Here the sentence compares typing to handwriting, two elements, so the comparative is correct. The one-syllable word becomes comparative with the addition of *-er*, and the two-syllable word turns into a two-word comparison.

52 **more legibly, faster.** After you read the word *everyone*, you may have thought that superlative (the form that deals with comparisons of three or more) was needed. However, this sentence actually compares two elements (Natalie and the group composed of everyone else). *Legibly* has three syllables, so *more* creates the comparative form. Because *fast* is a single syllable, *-er* does the job.

53 **less drinkable, less tasty.** In comparing *coffee* and *tea*, go for the comparative form. Both *more drinkable* and *less drinkable* are correct grammatically, but Helen's anger more logically flows from a comment about her coffee's inferiority. Negative comparisons always require two words; here, *less tasty* does the job.

54 **more frequently, less productive.** The fight's getting serious now, isn't it? Charges and countercharges! Speaking solely of grammar and forgetting about office politics, each description in this sentence is set up in comparison to one other element (how many times Natalie brews tea versus how many times the rules say she can brew tea, Natalie's productivity versus Helen's). Because you're comparing two elements and the descriptions have more than one syllable, go for a two-word comparative.

55 **longer, more boring.** When you compare two things (how long and boring the day is now and how long and boring it will be if Natalie and Helen get angry), go for the comparative, with *-er* for the short word and *more* for the two-syllable word.

56 **pettiest, more annoyingly** or **less annoyingly.** The argument had more than two moments, so superlative is what you want. The adjective *petty* has two syllables, but *-est* is still appropriate, with the letter *y* of *petty* changing to *i* before the *-est*. The second blank compares two (the duck and Helen) and thus takes the comparative. I'll let you decide whether Natalie was insulting Helen or the duck. Grammatically, either form is correct.

57 **most expensive, cutest.** A store has lots of toys, so to choose the one that has the highest price (the meaning that fits the sentence), go for superlative. Because *expensive* has three syllables, tacking on *most* is the way to go. The superlative for a single-syllable word, *cute*, is formed by adding *-est*.

58 **more international, more interesting.** Comparing two items (the sound of the duck you want to buy and the sound of the "average American rubber duck") calls for comparative, which is created with *more* because of the length of the adjectives *international* and *interesting*.

59 **silliest, highest.** Out of all the requests, this one is on the top rung. Go for superlative, which is created by changing the *y* to *i* and adding *-est* (resulting in *silliest*) and adding *-est* to *high*, a one-syllable word.

60 **less snobby, more knowledgeable.** Two elements (*he* and *a group of store clerks*, with the group counting as a single item) are being compared here, so comparative is needed. The add-on *less* does the job for the first answer; *more* is what you want for the second comparison.

61 **nastiest, more annoyed.** I can imagine many moods, so the extreme in the group calls for the superlative. The final *y* changes to *i* before the *-est* to create *nastiest*; in the second blank, *more* creates a two-word comparative form.

62 **more widely, more upset.** Employee habits concerning two individuals (Natalie and Helen) are discussed here; comparative does the job.

63 **most essential, more important.** Natalie is singled out as the extreme in a large group. Hence superlative is the one that fits the first blank. Three-syllable words need *most* to form the superlative *most essential*. In the second blank, two jobs are compared — one of Helen's rank and one that is *more important*, the comparative form of a long word.

64 **most generous, most creative.** *All* includes more than two (*both* is the preferred term for two), so superlative rules. Go for the two-word form because *generous* and *creative* are three-syllable words.

65 **more forcefully.** This sentence compares his force to that of a boxer. Two things in one comparison give you comparative form, which is created by *more*.

66 **most professional, less often.** Choosing one out of three in the first part of the sentence calls for superlative. In the second part of the sentence, the speaker is comparing himself to every other employee, one at a time. Therefore, comparative is appropriate. Because the speaker is bragging, *less often* makes sense.

67 **stronger, more carefully.** Natalie and Larry are locked in a fight to the death (okay, to the strained elbow). In the first part of the sentence, the comparison of two elements requires comparative. Because *strong* is a single syllable, tacking on *-er* does the trick. The second part of the sentence also compares two elements — the way Natalie usually surfs job sites and the way she surfs in this situation. Go for *more carefully*, the comparative form.

68 **more.** Two elements are being compared here: the amount of detail Edgar uses and the amount of detail people want. When comparing two elements, the comparative form rules.

69 **worst.** The superlative form singles out the extreme (in this case the most boring) item in the scrapbook.

70 **better.** The sentence pits Edgar's skills against the skills of one group (*the downtown jewelers*). Even though the group has several members, the comparison is between two elements — Edgar and the group — so comparative form is what you want.

71 **worse.** Two states of being are in comparison in this sentence, Edgar's health before and after he hears about a broken watch. In comparing two things, go for comparative form.

72 **most.** The superlative form singles out the extreme, in this case Edgar's timepiece collection, which included a raw-potato clock until it rotted.

73 **better.** The comparative deals with two states — how the clock runs before Edgar gets his hands on it and how it runs after.

74. **best.** To single out the top or bottom rank from a group of more than two, go for superlative form.

75. **worse.** The sentence compares Edgar's health at two points (immediately after eating the oil spill and a few hours after that culinary adventure). Comparative form works for two elements.

76. **worst.** The very large group of poisons has two extremes, and Time-Ola is one of them, so superlative form is best.

77. **best.** The group of watch oils also has two extremes, and Time-Ola is one of them, so once again you need superlative.

Here are the answers to the "Overachievers" extra practice:

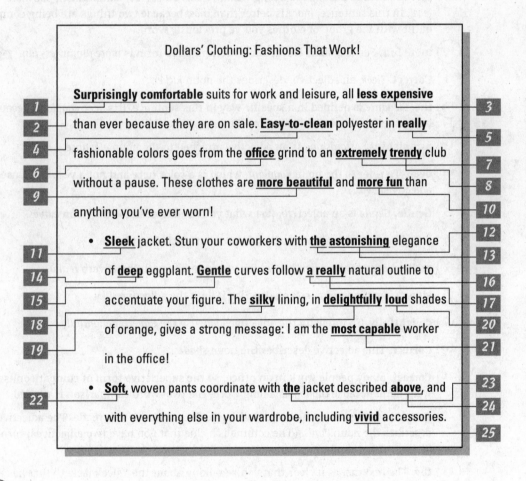

Dollars' Clothing: Fashions That Work!

1 2 4 6 9 — **Surprisingly** **comfortable** suits for work and leisure, all **less expensive** than ever because they are on sale. **Easy-to-clean** polyester in **really** fashionable colors goes from the **office** grind to an **extremely** **trendy** club without a pause. These clothes are **more beautiful** and **more fun** than anything you've ever worn! — 3 5 7 8 10 12 13

- 11 14 15 18 19 — **Sleek** jacket. Stun your coworkers with **the astonishing** elegance of **deep** eggplant. **Gentle** curves follow **a really** natural outline to accentuate your figure. The **silky** lining, in **delightfully** **loud** shades of orange, gives a strong message: I am the **most capable** worker in the office! — 16 17 20 21

- 22 — **Soft,** woven pants coordinate with **the** jacket described **above**, and with everything else in your wardrobe, including **vivid** accessories. — 23 24 25

1. **Surprisingly.** The adverb *surprisingly* is what you need attached to the description *comfortable*, an adjective.

2. **Correct.** The adjective *comfortable* answers *what kind of suits? Suits* is a noun.

3. **Correct.** *Less expensive* is a negative comparison, which is always formed with two words. *Less* is better than *least*, the superlative form, because you're comparing two things — how expensive these suits were before with how expensive they are now.

4. **Easy-to-clean.** *Easily* is an adverb, but the three-word description is attached to a noun, *polyester*. *Easy* is an adjective and is the word you want here. Are you wondering why this phrase is hyphenated? Check Chapter 12 for more information.

5. **really.** The adjective *fashionable* is intensified by the adverb *really*. *Real*, an adjective, is out of place here. By the way, if it were an adjective describing *colors*, *real* would be separated from the next adjective by a comma. For more information on commas, turn to Chapter 11.

6. **Correct.** *Office* can be a noun, but here it functions as an adjective, describing the noun *grind*.

7. **extremely.** How *bright? Extremely bright*. Intensifiers are adverbs.

8. **Correct.** The adjective *trendy* describes the noun *club*.

9. **more beautiful.** *Beautiful* is a long word. To form a correct comparison, use *more, most, less,* or *least.* In this sentence, *more* is better than *most* because two things are being compared: this outfit with the group of clothes you've previously worn.

10. **more fun.** *Fun* is a short word, but its comparative form is *more fun* or *less fun*.

11. **Correct.** *Sleek*, an adjective, describes the noun *jacket*.

12. **the.** *Elegance* is defined in a specific way in this sentence. It's *deep eggplant*. Because you're being specific, *the* is the best article here.

13. **astonishing.** *Astonishing* is an adjective attached to the noun *elegance*.

14. **deep.** To refer to the noun *eggplant*, which is a color here and not a vegetable, use the adjective *deep*.

15. **Gentle.** *Gentle* is an adjective, just what you need to describe the noun *curves*.

16. **a.** Before a word beginning with a consonant, such as *r*, place *a*.

17. **really.** *Natural* is an adjective, which you intensify with the adverb *really*.

18. **silky.** *Lining* is a noun, so you describe it with the adjective *silky*.

19. **delightfully.** To intensify the adjective *loud*, use the adverb *delightfully*.

20. **Correct.** This adjective describes the noun *shades*.

21. **Correct.** Many people work in an office, so the superlative form of comparison is what you want here. Because *capable* is a long word, the two-word comparison is needed.

22. **Soft.** You're describing how the clothing feels, not how it was made. The adjective *soft* describes the noun *pants*. (The comma is a clue that you have two adjectives; turn to Chapter 11 for more information.)

23. **the.** The text makes it clear that you're talking about the "sleek jacket" that has already been identified. To refer to that specific jacket, use *the*.

24. **Correct.** The adverb *above* works perfectly here to explain where the jacket is *described*.

25. **vivid.** You need an adjective, *vivid*, to describe the noun *accessories*.

3

Mastering Mechanics

Insert apostrophes to show possession and shorten words.

Punctuate quotations and titles correctly.

Examine the proper functions of a comma.

Use dashes, hyphens, and colons correctly.

Select capitals or lowercase letters for titles, geography, time periods, titles, events, and abbreviations.

Adapt language and grammar for texts, tweets, social media, blog posts, and presentation slides.

Chapter 9

A Hook That Can Catch You: Apostrophes

An apostrophe is a little raised hook (') that allows writers to show possession and shorten words. Unfortunately, apostrophes have a tendency to snag most writers at some point. With some practice, though, you can confidently insert apostrophes into the proper spots in your writing.

WARNING

The most common apostrophe mistake is to place one where it's not appropriate. Don't use an apostrophe in either of these circumstances:

>> **To create a plural:** You have *one arrow* and *two arrows,* not *two arrow's.* The no-apostrophe-for-plural rule holds true for names. I am one person named *Woods,* and members of my family are the *Woodses,* not the *Woods'.*

>> **With a possessive pronoun:** Don't use an apostrophe in a possessive pronoun (*my, your, his, hers, its, ours, theirs, whose,* and so on).

Hook into the exercises in this chapter so that no apostrophe snags you ever again.

Showing Who Owns What: Possessives

An apostrophe allows you to turn the awkward-sounding phrase "the pen of my aunt" into "my aunt's pen." To show possession with apostrophes, keep these rules in mind:

>> **Singular owner:** Attach an apostrophe and the letter *s* (in that order) to a singular person, place, or thing to express possession ("*Henry's* tooth," "the *platypus's* flipper").

>> **Plural owner:** Attach an apostrophe to a regular plural (one that ends in *s*) to express possession ("the *boys'* ties," "the *octopuses'* arms").

>> **Irregular plural owner:** Add an apostrophe and the letter *s*, in that order, to an irregular plural (one that doesn't end in *s*) to express possession ("the *men's* shoe department").

>> **Joint ownership:** If two or more people own something jointly, add an apostrophe and an *s* (in that order) to the last name ("*Abe and Mary's* sofa").

>> **Separate ownership:** If two or more people own things separately, everyone gets an apostrophe and an *s* ("*James's and Ashley's* pajamas").

>> **Hyphenated owner:** If the word you're working with is hyphenated, just attach the apostrophe and *s* to the end ("*mother-in-law's* office"). For plurals ending in *s*, attach the apostrophe only ("*three secretary-treasurers'* accounts").

>> **Time and money:** Okay, Father Time and Mr. Dollar Bill don't own anything. Nevertheless, time and money may be possessive in expressions such as *next week's test, two hours' homework, a day's pay,* and so forth. Follow the rules for singular and plural owners, as explained at the beginning of this bulleted list.

Easy stuff, right? See whether you can apply your knowledge. Turn the underlined word (or words) into the possessive form. Write your answers in the blanks provided.

EXAMPLE

Q. The style of this <u>year</u> muscle car is <u>Jill</u> favorite.

A. **year's, Jill's.** Two singular owners. *Jill* is the traditional owner — a person — but the time expression also takes an apostrophe.

1 <u>Carol</u> classic car is entered in <u>tonight</u> show. _____

   _____

2 She invested <u>three months</u> work in restoring the finish. _____

3 Carol will get by with a little help from her friends; <u>Jess and Marty</u> tires, which they purchased a few years ago by combining their allowances, will be installed on her car.

   _____

4   The <u>boys</u> allowance, by the way, is far too generous, despite their <u>sister-in-law</u> objections. _____   _____

5   <u>Jill</u> weekly paycheck is actually smaller than the <u>brothers</u> daily income.
    _____   _____

6   Annoying as they are, the brothers donate <u>a day</u> pay from time to time to underfunded causes such as the <u>Children</u> Committee to Protect the Environment.
    _____   _____

7   Carol couldn't care less about the environment; the <u>car</u> gas mileage is ridiculously low.
    _____

8   She cares about the car, however. She borrowed <u>Jess and Marty</u> toothbrushes to clean the dashboard. _____

9   Now she needs her <u>helpers</u> maximum support as the final judging nears.
    _____

10 She knows that the <u>judge</u> decision will be final, but just in case she has volunteered <u>two thousand dollars</u> worth of free gasoline to his favorite charity.
    _____   _____

11 <u>Carol</u> success is unlikely because the <u>court</u> judgments can't be influenced by anything but the law. _____   _____

12 Last week, for example, the judge ruled in favor of a developer, despite his <u>mother-in-law</u> plea for a different verdict. _____

13 <u>Ten hours</u> begging did no good at all. _____

14 Tomorrow the judge will rule on the <u>car show</u> effect on the native <u>animals</u> habitat.
    _____   _____

15 The <u>geese</u> ecosystem is particularly sensitive to automotive exhaust.
    _____

Tightening Up Text: Contractions

Apostrophes shorten words by replacing one or more letters. The shortened word, or *contraction* (not to be confused with the thing pregnant women scream through), adds an informal, conversational tone to your writing.

The most frequently used contractions, paired with their long forms, include those in Table 9-1.

Table 9-1   Frequently Used Contractions

Long Form	Contraction	Long Form	Contraction	Long Form	Contraction
Are not	Aren't	I will	I'll	We are	We're
Cannot	Can't	I would	I'd	We have	We've
Could have	Could've	It is	It's	We will	We'll
Could not	Couldn't	She has	She's	Were not	Weren't
Do not	Don't	She is	She's	Will not	Won't
He has	He's	She will	She'll	Would have	Would've
He is	He's	Should have	Should've	Would not	Wouldn't
He will	He'll	Should not	Shouldn't	You are	You're
He would	He'd	They are	They're	You have	You've
I am	I'm	They have	They've	You will	You'll
I had	I'd	They will	They'll	You would	You'd

TEST ALERT

College entrance tests won't ask you to insert an apostrophe into a word, but they may want to know whether you can spot a misplaced mark or an improperly expanded contraction. An apostrophe shortens a word, and a common mistake is to re-expand a contraction into something it was never meant to be. The contraction *should've*, for example, is short for *should have*, not *should of.* The expressions *should of, could of,* and *would of* don't exist in Standard English. If you see one of these turkeys on the SAT or the ACT, you know you've found a mistake.

You also can slice numbers out of your writing with apostrophes, especially in informal circumstances. This punctuation mark enables you to graduate in 2019, marry in '25, and check the maternity coverage in your health insurance policy by early '27.

EXAMPLE

Feel like flexing your apostrophe muscles? Look at the underlined words in these sentences and change them into contractions. Place your answers in the blanks.

Q. Adam said that <u>he would</u> go to the store to buy nuts. _____

A. **he'd.** This apostrophe is a real bargain. With it, you save four letters.

16 "Peanuts <u>are not</u> the best choice for an appetizer, because of allergies," commented Pam. _____

17 "<u>I am</u> sure that <u>you will</u> choose a better appetizer," she added.

_____   _____

18 The store <u>will not</u> take responsibility for your purchase. _____

19 <u>Do not</u> underestimate the power of a good appetizer. _____

20 <u>You are</u> cheap if you <u>do not</u> provide at least one bowl of nuts.
_____ _____

21 "Adam <u>would have</u> bought caviar, but I <u>would not</u> pass the walnut counter without buying something," commented Pam. _____
_____

22 "You <u>cannot</u> neglect the dessert course either," countered Adam.
_____

23 Adam usually recommends a fancy dessert such as a maple walnut ice cream sundae, but <u>he is</u> watching his weight. _____

24 "If they created a better diet ice cream," he often says, "<u>I would</u> eat a ton of it."
_____

25 "Yes, and then <u>you would</u> weigh a ton yourself," snaps Pam.
_____

26 <u>She is</u> a bit testy when faced with diet food. _____

27 Of course, Adam <u>could have</u> been a little more diplomatic when he mentioned Pam's "newly tight" slacks. _____

28 Adam is planning to serve a special dessert wine, Chateau Adam <u>1999</u>, to his guests.
_____

29 He always serves that beverage at reunions of the class of <u>2006</u>.
_____

30 <u>We are</u> planning to attend, but <u>we will</u> bring our own refreshments!
_____ _____

Calling All Overachievers: Extra Practice with Apostrophes

Marty's to-do list, shown in the following figure, needs some serious editing. Check the apostrophe situation. You need to find nine spots to insert and ten spots to delete an apostrophe.

Thing's to Do This Week

A. Call Johns doctor and arrange for a release of annual medical report.

B. Check on last springs blood pressure number's to see whether they need to be changed.

C. Ask John about his rodent problem's.

D. Find out why network's cant broadcast Tuesdays speech live, as John needs prime-time publicity.

E. Ask whether his' fondness for long speeches' is a problem.

F. Send big present to network president and remind him that you are both Yale 06.

G. Order bouquet's for secretary and National Secretaries Week card.

H. Rewrite speech on cat litter' to reflect sister-in-laws ideas'.

I. Tell opposing managers assistant that "you guys wouldnt stand a chance" in the old day's.

Answers to Apostrophe Problems

Did you get caught on any of the apostrophe questions in this chapter? Check your answers to see how you did.

1. **Carol's, tonight's.** Carol owns the car, so you just need to attach an apostrophe and an *s* to a singular form to create a singular possessive. The second answer illustrates a time/money possessive expression.

2. **three months'.** The value of time and money can be expressed with a possessive form. Because you're talking about *months*, a plural, the apostrophe goes after the *s*.

3. **Jess and Marty's.** The sentence tells you that the boys own the tires together, so only one apostrophe is needed. It's placed after the last owner's name. The possessive pronoun *her*, like all possessive pronouns, has no apostrophe.

4. **boys', sister-in-law's.** The plural possessive just tacks an apostrophe onto the *s* in regular, end-in-*s* plurals. Hyphenated forms are easy too; just attach the apostrophe and an *s* to the end.

5. **Jill's, brothers'.** The first form is singular, so you add an apostrophe and an *s*. The second form is a regular plural, so you just add the apostrophe.

6. **a day's, Children's.** The first form falls into the time/money category, and because *day* is singular, you add an apostrophe and an *s*. The second is an irregular plural (not ending in *s*), so you tack on an apostrophe and an *s*.

7. **car's.** A singular possessive form calls for an apostrophe and an *s*.

8. **Jess's and Marty's.** Okay, the brothers are close, but they draw the line at shared toothbrushes. Each owns a separate brush, so each name needs an apostrophe.

TIP

If a word ends in *s* (*Jess*, for example), adding an apostrophe and another *s* creates a spit factor: People tend to spray saliva all over when saying the word. To avoid this unsanitary problem, some writers add just the apostrophe (*Jess'*), even though technically they've neglected the extra *s*. Grammarians generally allow this practice, perhaps because they too dislike being spit on. In all but the strictest situations, either form is acceptable.

9. **helpers'.** To create a plural possessive of a word ending in *s*, just attach an apostrophe.

10. **judge's, two thousand dollars'.** The first answer is a simple, singular possessive, so an apostrophe and an *s* do the trick. The second is a time/money possessive, and *two thousand dollars* is plural, so just an apostrophe is needed.

11. **Carol's, court's.** These two words are singular, so only an apostrophe and the letter *s* are needed to make each possessive.

12. **mother-in-law's.** The apostrophe and the letter *s* follow the last word of the hyphenated term.

13. **Ten hours'.** The apostrophe creates an expression meaning *ten hours of begging*. Because *hours* is plural, only an apostrophe is added.

14. **car show's, animals'.** The first is a singular possessive, and the second is plural.

(15) **geese's.** The word *geese* is irregular. In an irregular plural, an apostrophe and the letter *s* are added.

(16) **aren't.** The contraction drops the letter *o* and substitutes an apostrophe.

(17) **I'm, you'll.** In the first contraction, the apostrophe replaces the letter *a*. In the second, it replaces two letters, *w* and *i*.

(18) **won't.** This contraction is irregular because you can't make an apostrophe–letter swap. Illogical though it may seem, *won't* is the contraction of *will not*.

(19) **Don't.** Drop the space between the two words, eliminate the *o*, and insert an apostrophe to create *don't*.

(20) **You're, don't.** The first contraction sounds exactly like the possessive pronoun *your*. Don't confuse the two.

(21) **would've, wouldn't.** Take care with the first contraction; many people mistakenly re-expand the contraction *would've* to *would of* (instead of the correct expansion, *would have*). The second contraction, *wouldn't*, substitutes an apostrophe for the letter *o*.

(22) **can't.** Did you know that *cannot* is written as one word? The contraction also is one word, with an apostrophe knocking out an *n* and an *o*.

(23) **he's.** The same contraction works for *he is* (as in this sentence) and *he has*.

(24) **I'd.** You're dropping the letters *woul*.

(25) **you'd.** The same contraction works for *you would* (as in this sentence) and *you had*.

(26) **She's.** The apostrophe replaces the letter *i*.

(27) **could've.** Be careful in re-expanding this contraction. A common mistake is to write *could of*, an expression that's a total no-no.

(28) **'99.** A date may be shortened, especially if you're out with Adam. Just be sure that the context of the sentence doesn't lead the reader to imagine a different century (2099, perhaps). This one is fairly clear, given that we're nowhere near 2099 or 1899.

(29) **'06.** Not much chance of the reader misunderstanding which numbers are missing here (unless he or she is really old)!

(30) **We're, we'll.** The apostrophes replace the letter *a* and *wi*.

Here are the answers to the "Overachievers" section:

1 *Thing/s to Do This Week*

2 A. Call John's doctor and arrange for a release of annual medical report.

3 B. Check on last spring's blood pressure number/s to see whether they **4**

need to be changed.

C. Ask John about his rodent problem/s. **5**

6 D. Find out why network/s can't broadcast Tuesday's speech live, as John **8**

7 needs prime-time publicity.

9 E. Ask whether his/ fondness for long speeches/ is a problem. **10**

F. Send big present to network president and remind him that you are

11 both Yale '06.

12 G. Order bouquet/s for secretary and National Secretaries' Week card. **13**

14 H. Rewrite speech on cat litter/ to reflect sister-in-law's ideas/. **15**

17 I. Tell opposing manager's assistant that "you guys wouldn't stand a **16**

18

19 chance" in the old day/s.

(1) Plural words that aren't possessive need no apostrophes, so remove the apostrophe from Things.

(2) The doctor belongs to John (in a manner of speaking), so the apostrophe is needed to show possession.

(3) This time expression (spring's) needs an apostrophe before the s.

(4) The plural numbers isn't possessive, so it shouldn't have an apostrophe.

(5) A simple plural (not possessive, not a numeral, and so on) takes no apostrophe, so problems shouldn't have an apostrophe.

(6) The networks aren't possessing anything here, so no apostrophe is needed in this plural.

(7) In this contraction (can't), the apostrophe replaces the letters n and o.

(8) Time expressions sometimes use apostrophes, as in Tuesday's.

(9) Possessive pronouns don't have apostrophes, so *his* is the word you want.

(10) A plural (speeches) takes no apostrophe.

(11) Missing numerals (in this case, 20) are replaced by an apostrophe.

(12) A simple plural (bouquets) doesn't take an apostrophe.

(13) This plural possessive form — the *secretaries* own the week, symbolically — adds an apostrophe after the *s*.

(14) In this sentence, *litter* isn't possessive and doesn't need an apostrophe.

(15) A hyphenated singular form takes an apostrophe and an s to become possessive, so *sister-in-law's* is the correct answer.

(16) The plural noun ideas isn't possessive, so it shouldn't carry an apostrophe.

(17) A singular possessive is created by adding an apostrophe and an *s*.

(18) In this contraction, the missing letter *o* is replaced by an apostrophe.

(19) *Days* is just plural, not possessive, so it doesn't take an apostrophe.

Chapter 10

"Can I Quote You on That?" Quotation Marks

Quotation marks can be puzzling because they're subject to many rules, most of which come from custom rather than logic. But if you're willing to put in a little effort, you can crack the code and employ this punctuation mark correctly.

Quotation marks surround words drawn from another person's speech or writing, and, in fiction, they indicate when a character is speaking. However, they don't belong in a sentence that summarizes instead of repeating the actual words someone wrote or said. Quotation marks also enclose the titles of certain types of literary or other artworks. Sometimes quotation marks indicate slang or tell the reader that the writer doesn't agree with the words inside the quotation marks. In this chapter you put quotation marks to work in all these situations. Lucky you!

Quoting and Paraphrasing: What's the Difference?

I have something to tell you: I love Jane Austen's novels and read all six once a year. If you want to convey that fact about me, you have two choices:

"I love Jane Austen's novels and read all six once a year," wrote Woods.

Woods explained that she enjoys Jane Austen's writing and works her way through Austen's six novels annually.

The first example is a *direct quotation*. My exact words are inside the quotation marks. The second example is a *paraphrase*. The sense of what I wrote is there, but the words are slightly different. You don't have to know these terms. You do have to know that quotations, but not paraphrases, belong inside quotation marks.

WARNING

Even when you're paraphrasing, you still have to cite sources for information and ideas that aren't the product of your own brain. Citation format has more rules than the U.S. tax code. For everything you ever wanted to know about citations, check out *Webster's New World Punctuation: Simplified and Applied* (Wiley) or an online source.

EXAMPLE

Now you get to try your hand at distinguishing between quotations and paraphrases. Below is a short paragraph from an imaginary news article. Following the story are sentences about something in the paragraph. Based on the paragraph and what you can infer from it, write "Quotation" if all or part of the sentence is quoted. Or, write "Paraphrase" if no quotation appears. To make your task harder, I haven't inserted quotation marks anywhere in the questions. In real writing, the quotation marks would be present.

> A stunningly positive annual report for Jump-Thru Hoops International is due tomorrow. According to inside sources who wish to remain anonymous, the company will announce that profits have nearly doubled in the last year. The increase is credited to the company's newest product, the Talking Hoop. Buyers moving the hoop around their hips hear a drill sergeant screaming commands as they exercise. Company officials have high hopes for their next product, Ring-Tone Hoops.

Q. The Talking Hoop has been so successful that the company has made twice as much money this year as it did last year. _____

A. **Paraphrase.** The information is from the paragraph, but the wording is different.

1. Jump-Thru Hoops International plans to market a hoop with ring tones.
_____

2. The company is doing well, and profits have nearly doubled in the last year.
_____

3. Go faster, Private! is what you hear when you're playing with this hoop.
_____

4. The annual report should give shareholders cause for celebration.
_____

5. Our best-selling product is the Talking Hoop, said Max Hippo, the president.
_____

6. The Talking Hoop is used for exercise. _____

Giving Voice to Direct Quotations

The basic rule governing quotation marks is simple: Place quotation marks around words drawn directly from someone else's speech or writing, or, if you're writing what is sure to be a best-selling novel, place quotation marks around dialogue. The tricky part is the interaction between quotation marks and other punctuation, such as commas, periods, and the like. You also have to take into account the fact that the rules vary somewhat in different situations. The comma goes one place in a psychology paper, for example, and another place in an English essay. Sigh. Below are the most commonly accepted rules, useful in nearly all situations:

>> **If the quotation has a speaker tag (*he murmured, she screamed,* and so forth), the speaker tag needs to be separated from the quotation by a comma.**

- If the speaker tag is ***before*** the quotation, the comma comes *before* the opening quotation mark: *Sharon sighed, "I hate hay fever season."*

- If the speaker tag is ***after*** the quotation, the comma goes *inside* the closing quotation mark: *"What a large snout you have," whispered Joe lovingly.*

- If the speaker tag appears ***in the middle*** of a quotation, a comma is placed before the first closing quotation mark and immediately after the tag: *"Here's the handkerchief," said Joe, "that I borrowed last week."*

>> **If the quotation ends the sentence, the period goes *inside* the closing quotation mark.** *Joe added, "I would like to kiss your giant ear."*

>> **If the *quotation* is a question or an exclamation, the question mark or the exclamation point goes *inside* the closing quotation mark.** *"Why did you slap me?" asked Joe. "I was complimenting you!"*

Question marks and exclamation points serve as sentence-ending punctuation, so you don't need to add a period after the quotation marks.

>> **If the quotation is *neither* question nor exclamation, but the *sentence* in which the quotation appears is, the question mark or exclamation point goes *outside* the closing quotation mark.** *I can't believe that Joe said he's "a world-class lover"! Do you think Sharon will ever get over his "sweet nothings"?*

TIP

If the quotation is tucked into the sentence without a speaker tag, as in the previous two sample sentences, no comma separates the quotation from the rest of the sentence. Nor does the quotation begin with a capital letter. Quotations with speaker tags, on the other hand, always begin with a capital letter, regardless of where the speaker tag falls. In an interrupted quotation (speaker tag in the middle), the first word of the first half of the quotation is capitalized, but the first word of the second half is not, unless it's a proper name.

EXAMPLE

Enough with the explanations. Your job is to identify the direct quotation and fill in the proper punctuation, in the proper order, in the proper places. To help you, I add extra information in parentheses at the end of some sentences and underline the quoted words. To make your life harder, I omit endmarks (periods, question marks, and exclamation points).

Q. The annual company softball game is tomorrow declared Becky

A. **"The annual company softball game is tomorrow," declared Becky.** Don't count yourself right unless you placed the comma *inside* the closing quotation mark.

7. I plan to pitch added Becky, who once tried out for the Olympics

8. Andy interrupted As usual, I will play third base

9. No one knew how to answer Andy, who in the past has been called overly sensitive

10. Gus said No one wants Andy at third base

11. Who wants to win asked the boss in a commanding, take-no-prisoners tone

12. Did she mean it when she said that we were not hard-boiled enough to play decently

13. Sarah screamed You can't bench Andy (The statement Sarah is making is an exclamation.)

14. The opposing team, everyone knows, is first in the league and last in our company's heart (The whole statement about the opposing team is an exclamation.)

15. The odds favor our opponents sighed Becky but I will not give up

16. The league states that all decisions regarding player placement are subject to the umpire's approval

17. The umpire has been known to label us out-of-shape players who think they belong in the Olympics (The label is a direct quotation.)

18. Do you think there will be a rain delay inquired Harry, the team's trainer

19. He asked Has anyone checked Sue's shoes to make sure that she hasn't sharpened her spikes again

20. Surely the umpire doesn't think that Sue would violate the rule that fair play is essential (Imagine that the writer of this sentence is exclaiming.)

21. Sue has been known to cork her bat commented Harry

22. The corking muttered Sue has never been proved

Punctuating Titles

Punctuating titles is easy, especially if you're a sports fan. Imagine a basketball player, one who tops seven feet. Next to him place a jockey; most jockeys hover around five feet. Got the picture? Good. When you're deciding how to punctuate a title, figure out whether you're dealing with an NBA player or a Derby rider, using these rules:

>> **Titles of full-length works are italicized or underlined.** The basketball player represents full-length works — novels, magazines, television series, plays, epic poems, films, and the like. The titles of those works can be italicized (on a computer) or underlined (for handwritten works).

>> **Titles of shorter works are placed in quotation marks.** The jockey, on the other hand, represents smaller works or parts of a whole — a poem, a short story, a single episode of a television show, a song, an article — you get the idea. The titles of these little guys aren't italicized or underlined; they're placed in quotation marks.

TIP

These rules apply to titles that are tucked into sentences. Centered titles, all alone at the top of a page, don't get any special treatment: no italics, no underlining, and no quotation marks.

When a title in quotation marks is part of a sentence, it sometimes tangles with other punctuation marks. The rules of American English (British English is different) call for any commas or periods *after* the title to be placed *inside* the quotation marks. So if the title is the last thing in the sentence, the period of the sentence comes before the closing quotation mark. Question marks and exclamation points, on the other hand, don't go inside the quotation marks unless they're actually part of the title.

TIP

If a title that ends with a question mark is the last thing in a sentence, the question mark ends the sentence. Don't place both a period and a question mark at the end of the same sentence.

EXAMPLE

All set for a practice lap around the track? Check out the titles in this series of sentences. Place quotation marks around the title if necessary, adding endmarks where needed; otherwise, underline the title. Here and there you find parentheses at the end of a sentence, in which I add some information to help you.

Q. Have you read Sarah's latest poem, Sonnet for the Tax Assessor (The sentence is a question, but the title isn't.)

A. **Have you read Sarah's latest poem, "Sonnet for the Tax Assessor"?** The title of a poem takes quotation marks. Question marks never go inside the quotation marks unless the title itself is a question.

23 Sarah's poem will be published in a collection entitled Tax Day Blues

24 Mary's fifth bestseller, Publish Your Poetry Now, inspired Sarah.

25 Some of us wish that Sarah had read the recent newspaper article, Forget About Writing Poetry

26 Julie, an accomplished violinist, has turned Sarah's poem into a song, although she changed the name to Sonata Taxiana

27 She's including it on her next CD, Songs of April

28 I may listen to it if I can bring myself to stop streaming my favorite series, Big Brother and Sister

29   During a recent episode titled Sister Knows Everything, the main character broke into her brother's blog.

30   In the blog was a draft of a play, Who Will Be My First Love?

Calling All Overachievers: Extra Practice with Quotation Marks

EXAMPLE

Tommy Brainfree's classic composition is reproduced in the following figure. Identify ten spots where a set of quotation marks needs to be inserted. Place the quotation marks correctly in relation to other punctuation in the sentence. Also, underline titles where appropriate.

What I Did during Summer Vacation

by Tommy Brainfree

This summer I went to Camp Waterbug, which was the setting for a famous

poem by William Long titled Winnebago My Winnebago. At Camp Waterbug I

learned to paddle a canoe without tipping it over more than twice a trip. My

counselor even wrote an article about me in the camp newsletter, Waterbug

Bites. The article was called How to Tip a Canoe. The counselor said, Brainfree

is well named. I was not upset because I believed him (eventually) when he

explained that the comment was an editing error.

Are you sure? I asked him when I first read it.

You know, he responded quickly, that I have a lot of respect for you. I

nodded in agreement, but that night I placed a bunch of frogs under his sheets,

just in case he thought about writing How to Fool a Camper. One of the frogs had

a little label on his leg that read JUST KIDDING TOO.

At the last campfire gathering I sang a song from the musical Fiddler on

the Roof. The song was called If I Were a Rich Man. I changed the first line to If I

were a counselor. I won't quote the rest of the song because I'm still serving the

detention my counselor gave me, even though I'm back home now.

Answers to Quotation Problems

It's time to see if you've mastered the use of quotation marks. I'm proud of you for tackling the tough exercises in this chapter. You can quote me on that!

1. **Paraphrase.** Nothing in the sentence reflects the wording in the paragraph.

2. **Quotation.** Part of the sentence is quoted. The phrase "have nearly doubled in the past year" comes directly from the text and should be enclosed in quotation marks.

3. **Quotation.** Although the paragraph doesn't tell you what the drill sergeant says, you can infer that "Go faster, Private!" is a quotation, which should be surrounded by quotation marks.

4. **Paraphrase.** Comb through the paragraph, and you see that these words don't appear.

5. **Quotation.** The first part of the sentence, as far as the word *said*, tells you Max Hippo's exact words.

6. **Paraphrase.** The words in this sentence aren't lifted directly from the paragraph, so they're paraphrased.

7. **"I plan to pitch," added Becky, who once tried out for the Olympics.** The directly quoted words, *I plan to pitch*, are enclosed in quotation marks. The comma that sets off the speaker tag *added Becky* goes inside the closing quotation mark. A period ends the sentence.

8. **Andy interrupted, "As usual, I will play third base."** The speaker tag comes first in this sentence, so the comma is placed before the opening quotation mark. The period that ends the sentence goes inside the closing quotation mark.

9. **No one knew how to answer Andy, who in the past has been called "overly sensitive."** The quotation is short, but it still deserves quotation marks. The period at the end of the sentence is placed inside the closing quotation mark. Notice that this quotation doesn't have a speaker tag, so it isn't preceded by a comma and it doesn't start with a capital letter.

10. **Gus said, "No one wants Andy at third base."** The speaker tag is followed by a comma, and a period ends the sentence.

11. **"Who wants to win?" asked the boss in a commanding, take-no-prisoners tone.** Because the quoted words are a question, the question mark goes inside the closing quotation mark.

12. **Did she mean it when she said that we were "not hard-boiled enough to play decently"?** The quoted words aren't a question, but the entire sentence is. The question mark belongs outside the closing quotation mark.

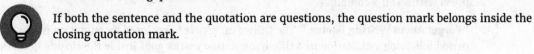

If both the sentence and the quotation are questions, the question mark belongs inside the closing quotation mark.

TIP

13. **Sarah screamed, "You can't bench Andy!"** A comma separates the speaker tag (*Sarah screamed*) from the quotation and precedes the opening quotation mark. Because the quoted words are an exclamation, the exclamation point belongs inside the closing quotation mark.

14. **The opposing team, everyone knows, is "first in the league and last in our company's heart"!** The hint in parentheses gives rationale for the answer. Because the whole statement is an exclamation, the exclamation point belongs outside the closing quotation mark.

15 **"The odds favor our opponents," sighed Becky, "but I will not give up."** Here's an interrupted quotation, with the speaker tag in the middle. This sort of interruption is perfectly proper. The quoted material makes up one sentence, so the second half begins with a lowercase letter.

16 **The league states that "all decisions regarding player placement are subject to the umpire's approval."** This little quotation is tucked into the sentence without a speaker tag, so it takes no comma or capital letter. The period at the end of the sentence goes inside the closing quotation mark.

17 **The umpire has been known to label us "out-of-shape players who think they belong in the Olympics."** Ah yes, the joy of amateur sport! This quotation is plopped into the sentence without a speaker tag, so the first word takes no capital letter and isn't preceded by a comma. It ends with a period, which is slipped inside the closing quotation mark.

18 **"Do you think there will be a rain delay?" inquired Harry, the team's trainer.** Harry's words are a question, so the question mark goes inside the closing quotation mark.

19 **He asked, "Has anyone checked Sue's shoes to make sure that she hasn't sharpened her spikes again?"** This speaker tag *He asked* begins the sentence. It's set off by a comma, which precedes the opening quotation mark. The quoted words form a question, so the question mark belongs inside the quotation marks.

20 **Surely the umpire doesn't think that Sue would violate the rule that fair play is "essential"!** The parentheses tell you that the writer is exclaiming. The whole sentence is an exclamation, and the quoted word is fairly mild, so the exclamation point belongs to the sentence, not to the quotation. Place it outside the closing quotation mark. Because no speaker tag is present, the quotation begins with a lowercase letter and isn't set off by a comma.

21 **"Sue has been known to cork her bat," commented Harry.** A straightforward statement with a speaker tag *commented Harry* calls for a comma inside the closing quotation mark. The quotation is a complete sentence. In quoted material, the period that normally ends the sentence is replaced by a comma, because the sentence continues on — in this case, with *commented Harry*. Periods don't belong in the middle of a sentence unless they're part of an abbreviation.

22 **"The corking," muttered Sue, "has never been proved."** A speaker tag breaks into this quotation and is set off by commas. The one after *corking* goes inside, because when you're ending a quotation or part of a quotation, the comma or period always goes inside. Ditto at the end of the sentence; the period needs to be inserted inside the closing quotation mark.

23 **Tax Day Blues.** If it's a collection, it's a full-length work. Full-length works are not placed in quotation marks but are underlined if you are writing by hand or italicized if you are using a computer.

24 **Publish Your Poetry Now.** The book title is underlined if you're writing by hand or italicized if you writing on a computer.

25 **"Forget About Writing Poetry."** The title of an article is enclosed by quotation marks. The period following a quotation or a title in quotation marks goes inside the closing quotation mark.

26 **"Sonata Taxiana."** The period always goes inside a closing quotation mark, at least in America. In the United Kingdom, the period is generally outside, playing cricket. Just kidding about the cricket. You're using quotation marks here because a "Sonata Taxiana" isn't a full-length work.

27. <u>**Songs of April.**</u> A CD is a full-length work, so the title is underlined or, better yet, italicized.

28. <u>**Big Brother and Sister.**</u> The title of the whole series is underlined. (You can italicize it if you're typing.) The title of an individual episode goes in quotation marks.

29. **"Sister Knows Everything,"** The episode title belongs in quotation marks. The series title gets italicized (or underlined, if you're writing with a pen). The comma around this introductory expression sits inside the quotation marks.

30. <u>**Who Will Be My First Love?**</u> A question mark is part of the title, which is underlined or italicized because a play is a full-length work.

Here are the answers to the "Overachievers" section:

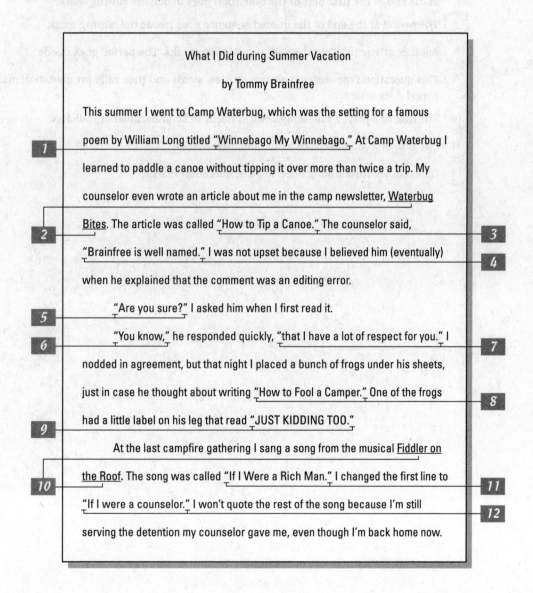

What I Did during Summer Vacation

by Tommy Brainfree

This summer I went to Camp Waterbug, which was the setting for a famous poem by William Long titled "Winnebago My Winnebago." At Camp Waterbug I learned to paddle a canoe without tipping it over more than twice a trip. My counselor even wrote an article about me in the camp newsletter, <u>Waterbug Bites</u>. The article was called "How to Tip a Canoe." The counselor said, "Brainfree is well named." I was not upset because I believed him (eventually) when he explained that the comment was an editing error.

"Are you sure?" I asked him when I first read it.

"You know," he responded quickly, "that I have a lot of respect for you." I nodded in agreement, but that night I placed a bunch of frogs under his sheets, just in case he thought about writing "How to Fool a Camper." One of the frogs had a little label on his leg that read "JUST KIDDING TOO."

At the last campfire gathering I sang a song from the musical <u>Fiddler on the Roof</u>. The song was called "If I Were a Rich Man." I changed the first line to "If I were a counselor." I won't quote the rest of the song because I'm still serving the detention my counselor gave me, even though I'm back home now.

1. Poem titles belong in quotation marks. The title of a collection of poems, on the other hand, needs to be underlined or italicized.

2. The newsletter title should be underlined or italicized.

3. An article title belongs in quotation marks. The period at the end of the sentence belongs inside the closing quotation mark.

4. Directly quoted speech belongs in quotation marks, with the period inside the closing mark.

5. The quoted words are a question, so the question mark goes inside the quotation marks.

6. The interrupted quotation with an inserted speaker tag needs two sets of marks. The comma at the end of the first part of the quotation goes inside the closing mark.

7. The period at the end of the quoted sentence goes inside the closing mark.

8. Another article title, another set of quotation marks. The period goes inside.

9. This quotation reproduces the exact written words and thus calls for quotation marks. The period goes inside.

10. The title of a play, a full-length work, needs to be underlined or italicized.

11. The title of a song needs to be in quotation marks.

12. Quoted lines from a song need to be in quotation marks.

Chapter **11**

Pausing to Consider the Comma

Small though they are, commas nearly always have a significant effect on the meaning of a sentence. They can indicate relationships between items or people, they keep words and numbers from running together, and they point out what's not necessary to the meaning of a sentence. In this chapter you can practice inserting and deleting commas until your writing is clear and correct.

Keeping Lists in Order with Commas and Semicolons

When you're writing a free-standing list, line breaks signal when one item in a list ends and another begins. Commas do the same thing in sentences. Perhaps Professor MacGregor wants you to do the following:

>> Go on the internet.

>> Locate the origin of the handheld meat patty.

>> Write a paper on hamburger history.

Inserted into a sentence, the line breaks in the preceding list turn into commas:

Professor MacGregor wants you to go on the internet, locate the origin of the handheld meat patty, and write a paper on hamburger history.

Notice that the first item isn't preceded by a comma and that the last two items are separated by *and*, which has a comma in front of it. The last comma is a style issue, not a grammatical necessity. In standard American English, most people do insert a comma before the *and* or whatever word joins the last two items of the list. In Britain, most writer don't. My advice is to do what you wish, so long as you always insert a comma to prevent a misreading. For example: "I wish to thank my parents, Abraham Lincoln and Jane Austen." If your readers lack knowledge of history and literature, they may think that your parents are Old Abe and Jane. A comma before *and* indicates that the writer is thanking four people – two parents, a president, and a novelist.

TIP

If the list is very long (and *long* is a judgment call), it may be preceded by a colon (one dot atop another). The words before the colon should be a complete thought. Here's an example:

Ms. Meanie required the following for every homework assignment: 12-point font, green ink, a plastic cover, at least two illustrations, a minimum of three quotations, and a list of sources.

TIP

If any item in a list has a comma *within* it, semicolons are used to separate the list items. Imagine that you're inserting this list into a sentence:

>> Peter McKinney, the mayor

>> Agnes Hutton

>> Jeannie Battle, magic expert

In a sentence using only commas, the reader wouldn't know that Peter McKinney is the mayor and may instead think that Peter and the mayor are two separate people. Here's the properly punctuated sentence:

Because he has only one extra ticket to the magic show, Daniel will invite Peter McKinney, the mayor; Agnes Hutton; or Jeannie Battle, magic expert.

EXAMPLE

Insert the list from each question into a sentence (I supply the beginning) and punctuate it properly. *Note:* I use numbers to separate items on the list. Don't use numbers in your answer sentence.

Q. List of things to buy at the pharmacy: (1) industrial-strength toenail clippers (2) green shoe polish (3) earwax remover

Getting ready for his big date, Rob went to the pharmacy to purchase

A. **Getting ready for his big date, Rob went to the pharmacy to purchase industrial-strength toenail clippers, green shoe polish, and earwax remover.** You have three items and two commas; no comma is needed before the first item on the list.

1 Supermarket shopping list: (1) pitted dates (2) chocolate-covered mushrooms (3) anchovies (4) pickles

Rob planned to serve a tasteful selection of

_____

_____

2 Guests: (1) Helen Ogee, supermodel (2) Natasha Smith, swimsuit model (3) Blair Berry, auto salesperson (4) Hannah Bridge, punctuation expert (5) Jane Fine, veterinarian

Rob's guest list is heavily tilted toward women he would like to date:

_____

_____

3 Activities: (1) juggling cabbages (2) pinning the tail on the landlord (3) playing double solitaire

After everyone arrives, Rob plans an evening of

_____

_____

4 Goals: (1) get three phone numbers (2) arrange at least one future date (3) avoid police interference

Rob will consider his party a success if he can

_____

_____

5 Results: (1) the police arrived at 10:00, 11:00, and 11:30 p.m. (2) no one gave out any phone numbers (3) everyone thought the host's name was Bob

Rob didn't meet his goals because

_____

_____

Directly Addressing the Listener or Reader

If the name or title of the person to whom you're talking or writing is inserted into the sentence, you're in a direct-address situation. Direct-address expressions are set off from everything else by commas. In these examples, *Wilfred* is being addressed:

> Wilfred, you can have the tennis court at 10 a.m.

> When you hit the ball, Wilfred, avoid using too much force.

The most common direct-address mistake is to send one comma to do a two-comma job. In the second example, two commas must set off *Wilfred*.

Can you insert commas to highlight the direct-address name in these sentences?

EXAMPLE

Q. Listen Champ I think you need to get a new pair of boxing gloves.

A. **Listen, Champ, I think you need to get a new pair of boxing gloves.** In this example, you're talking to *Champ*, a title that's substituting for the actual name. Direct-address expressions don't have to be proper names, though they frequently are.

6 Ladies and Gentlemen I present the Fifth Annual Elbox Championships.

7 I know Mort that you are an undefeated Elbox competitor. Would you tell our audience about the sport?

8 Elboxing is about 5,000 years old Chester. It originated in ancient Egypt.

9 Really? Man I can't believe you knew that!

10 Yes Chester the sport grew out of the natural movement of the elbow when someone tried to cut ahead in a line by "elbowing."

11 Excuse me a moment. The reigning champion has decided to pay us a visit. Miss William could you tell us how you feel about the upcoming match?

12 Certainly Sir. I am confident that my new training routine will pay off.

Punctuating Dates and Addresses

When are you reading this book? On 12 September 2022 or on September 12, 2022? Your answer depends on style, and to some extent, the audience you're writing for. In recent years, the rules for placing commas in dates and addresses have changed quite a bit. To make things more complicated, standard American English punctuation sometimes differs from the format used in other parts of the English-speaking world. Here are the basics of the American system, with international variations noted:

>> If the date is alone on a line (say, at the top of a letter), insert a comma after the day of the month: September 12, 2022. Also correct for a date appearing on a separate line, and popular abroad, is a comma-free form: 12 September 2022. A correct but informal version slashes out the comma: 9/12/22 (in the U.S., where the month precedes the day), 12/9/22 (outside the U.S., where the month follows the day).

>> If the date appears inside a sentence, a comma traditionally follows the year if the sentence continues: "Mark started school on September 12, 2022, and graduated four years later." Also correct but not traditional: "Mark started school on 12 September 2022 and graduated four years later."

>> If no year appears, no comma appears: "Mark started his summer vacation on June 12th."

>> In a month-year situation, traditionalists insert a comma between the two (June, 2022). More modern writers omit the comma (June 2022).

Addresses are a bit simpler, and most writers follow these guidelines:

>> For addresses written in "envelope style," with the name, street address, and city-state-postal code on separate lines, place a comma only between the city and state. Use the two-letter state abbreviation approved by the postal service:

   Nell Nixon

   333 Seventh Street

   Barrie, VT 05455

>> For addresses inserted into a sentence, separate the name, street address, city, and state with commas. Don't place a comma before the postal code. If the sentence continues, follow the last element of the address with a comma: "DeDee claimed that she had sent a letter to Ms. Nell Nixon, 333 Seventh Street, Barrie, VT 05455, but no letter arrived at that address."

>> If only the city and state or the city and country appear in a sentence, separate the city and the state or country with a comma. Place a comma after the state or country if the sentence continues: "Nell moved to Augusta, Maine, in 2011.

TIP

With several possible correct formats, what should you do? Check with the Authority Figure who will read your work, or take a look at how other writers producing the same sort of material handle commas.

EXAMPLE

Which of these are correct? Choose one, more than one, or none. To help you decide, I give you the context.

Q. Alone on a line

   I. March 9 1999

   II. March, 9, 1999

   III. March 9, 1999

A. **III.** A comma should separate the day and the year, but not the month and the day.

13 at the end of a sentence

   I.   14 Main Street Chilton CA 09011.

   II. 14 Main Street, Chilton, CA 09011.

   III. 14 Main Street, Chilton CA 09011.

14 in the middle of a sentence

   I.   20 July 1940

   II. July 20, 1940,

   III. July, 20, 1940

15 alone on a line

   I.   Milton Smith

      55 Oak Avenue

      Floral Gardens, WA 98100

   II. Milton Smith

      55 Oak Avenue

      Floral Gardens WA, 98100

   III. Milton Smith

      55 Oak Avenue

      Floral Gardens WA 98100

16 in the middle of a sentence

   I.   Jeannie Wong, 98 East 100th Street, NY NY 10001

   II. Jeannie Wong, 98 East 100th Street, NY, NY, 10001,

   III. Jeannie Wong, 98 East 100th Street, NY, NY 10001,

17 in the middle of a sentence

   I.   June, 1920

   II. June 1920

   III. June, 1920,

Placing Commas in Combined Sentences

Certain words — *and*, *but*, *or*, *nor*, and *for* — are like officials who perform weddings. They link two equals. (Always a good idea in a marriage, don't you think?) These powerful words are *conjunctions.* Forget the grammar term! Just remember to place a comma before the conjunction when you're combining two complete sentences. Here are some examples:

> The wedding cake was pink, and the bride's nose was purple.

> A wedding in the middle of an ice rink is festive, but the air is chilly.

> The bride's nose began to run, for she had forgotten her heated veil.

You get the idea. Each conjunction is preceded by a complete sentence and a comma. The conjunction is followed by another complete sentence. (See Chapter 3 for more information on complete sentences.)

WARNING

When one of these conjunctions links anything other than a complete sentence (say, two verbs), you don't need a comma.

EXAMPLE

Time to scatter commas around these sentences, starting with this example. If no comma is needed, write "no comma" in the margin.

Q. The groom skated to the center of the rink and waited for his shivering bride.

A. **No comma.** The words in front of the conjunction (*The groom skated to the center of the rink*) are a complete sentence, but the words after the conjunction (*waited for his shivering bride*) aren't. Because the conjunction *and* links two verbs (*skated* and *waited*) and words that describe those verbs, no comma is called for. In case you're wondering, *groom* is the subject of *skated* and *waited.*

18 The best man rode in a Zamboni for he was afraid of slipping on the ice.

19 The flowers scattered around the rink and the colorful spotlights impressed the guests.

20 One of the bridesmaids whispered that her own wedding would be on a beach or in a sunny climate with absolutely no ice.

21 The guests sipped hot chocolate but they were still cold.

22 The ice-dancing during the reception made them sweat and then the temperature seemed fine.

23 Do you know who is in charge of the gifts or who is paying the orchestra?

24 I'd like to swipe a present for my blender is broken.

25 I don't need an icemaker but I'll take one anyway.

26 The happy couple drove away in a sled and never came back.

Inserting Extras with Commas: Introductions and Interruptions

Grammatically, *introductory expressions* are a mixed bag of verbals, prepositional phrases, adverbial clauses, and lots of other things. You don't have to know their names; you just have to know that an introductory expression makes a comment on the rest of the sentence or adds a bit of extra information. An introductory statement is usually separated from the rest of the sentence by a comma. Check out the italicized portion of each of these sentences for examples of introductory expressions:

> *Creeping through the tunnel,* Brad thought about potential book deals.

> *No,* Brad didn't blow up the enemy base.

> *While he was crossing the lighted area,* he called his agent instead.

Interrupters (also a grammatical mixed bag) show up inside — not in front of — a sentence. The same principle that applies to introductory expressions applies to interrupters: They comment on or otherwise *interrupt* the main idea of the sentence and thus are set off by commas. Check out these italicized interrupters:

> Cindy, *unmasking the spy,* thought that Hollywood should film her adventures.

> There was no guarantee, *of course,* that Cindy would make it out alive.

You don't need commas for short introductory expressions or interrupters that don't contain verbs and are tied strongly to the main idea of the sentence. For example, "In the morning Brad drank 12 cups of coffee" needs no comma to separate *In the morning* from the rest of the sentence.

EXAMPLE

Up for some practice? Insert commas where needed and resist the temptation to insert them where they're not required in these sentences.

Q. Tired after a long day delivering pizza Elsie was in no mood for fireworks.

A. **Tired after a long day delivering pizza, Elsie was in no mood for fireworks.** The comma sets off the introductory expression, *Tired after a long day delivering pizza.* Notice how that information applies to *Elsie?* She's the subject of the sentence.

TEST ALERT

Introductory verb forms must describe the subject of the sentence. Test writers really want you to know that rule, judging from the questions they create.

27 In desperate need of a pizza fix Brad turned to his cellphone.

28 Cindy on the other hand ached for sushi.

29 Yes pizza was an excellent idea.

30. The toppings unfortunately proved to be a problem.

31. Restlessly Brad pondered pepperoni as the spies searched for him.

32. Cindy wondered how Brad given his low-fat diet could consider pepperoni.

33. Frozen with indecision Brad decided to call the supermarket to request the cheapest brand.

34. Cindy on a tight budget wanted to redeem her coupons.

35. To demand fast delivery was Brad's priority.

36. Lighting a match and holding it near his trembling hand Brad realized that time was almost up.

37. Worrying about toppings had used up too many minutes.

38. Well the survivors would have a good story to tell.

39. With determination Cindy speed-dialed the market and offered "a really big tip" for fast service.

40. As the robbers chomped on pepperoni and argued about payment Brad slipped away.

41. Let's just say that Cindy was left to clean up the mess.

Setting Descriptions Apart

Life would be much simpler for the comma-inserter if nobody ever described anything. However, descriptions are a part of life, so you need to know these punctuation rules:

>> **If the description *follows* the word being described, it is not set off by commas if it's essential, identifying material. If the description falls into the "nice to know but I didn't really need it" (extra) category, surround it with commas.** For example, in the sentence "The dictionary *on the table* is dusty," the description in italics is necessary because it tells *which* dictionary is dusty. In the sentence "Charlie's dictionary, *which is on the table,* is dusty," the description in italics is set off by commas, because you already know *Charlie's dictionary* is the one being discussed. The part about the table is extra information.

TEST ALERT

Standardized tests often require you to decide whether descriptions such as the ones in the preceding bullet point need to be set off by commas.

>> **For descriptions that precede the word described, place commas only when you have a list of two or more descriptions of the same type and importance.** You can tell when two or more descriptions are equally important; they can be written in different order without changing the meaning of the sentence. For example, "the *tan, dusty* dictionary"

and "the *dusty, tan* dictionary" have the same meaning, so you need a comma between the descriptions. However, "*two dusty* dictionaries" is different. One description is a number, and one is a condition. Because the descriptions differ, you don't insert commas.

>> **When descriptions containing verb forms introduce a sentence, they always are set off by commas.** An example: Sighing into his handkerchief, Charlie looked for a dust cloth. The description, *sighing into his handkerchief,* has a verb form (sighing) and thus is set off by a comma from the rest of the sentence.

EXAMPLE

Got the idea? Now try your comma skills on the following sentences. If the italicized words need to be set off, add the commas. If no commas are called for, write "correct" in the margin. *Note:* Some sentences present you with more than one group of italicized words, separated by a nonitalicized word or words. Treat each group of italicized words as a separate task.

Q. The *ruffled striped* shirt is at the closest dry cleaner *Fleur and Sons.*

A. **The *ruffled, striped* blouse is at the closest dry cleaner, Fleur and Sons.** The first two descriptions precede the word being described *(shirt)* and may be interchanged, so a comma is needed between them. The second description (which, the strictest grammarians would tell you is really an equivalent term or *appositive*) follows what's being described *(the closest dry cleaner).* Because you can have only one *closest dry cleaner,* the name is extra, not essential identifying information, and it's set off by commas.

42 *Oscar's favorite* food *which he cooks every Saturday night* is hot dogs.

43 The place *where he feels most comfortable during the cooking process* is next to his *huge brick* barbecue.

44 Oscar stores *his wheat* buns in a *large plastic* tub *that used to belong to his grandpa.*

45 One of the horses *that live in Oscar's barn* often sniffs around *Oscar's lucky* horseshoe *which Oscar found while playing tag.*

46 Oscar rode *his three favorite* horses in a race *honoring the Barbecue King and Queen.*

47 Oscar *who is an animal lover* will never sell one of his horses *because he needs money.*

48 *Being sentimental* Oscar dedicated a song to the filly *that was born on his birthday.*

49 The jockeys *who were trying to prepare for the big race* became annoyed by Oscar's song *which he played constantly;* the jockeys *who had already raced* didn't mind Oscar's music.

50 The *deep horrible* secret is that Oscar can't stay in tune *when he sings.*

51 His guitar *a Gibson* is also missing *two important* strings.

Calling All Overachievers: Extra Practice with Commas

EXAMPLE

The following figure shows an employee self-evaluation with some serious problems, a few of which concern commas. (The rest deal with the truly bad idea of being honest with your boss.) Forget about the content errors and concentrate on commas. See whether you can find five commas that appear where they shouldn't and ten spots that should have commas but don't. Circle the commas you're deleting, and insert commas where they're needed.

Annual Self-Evaluation — October 1, 2019

Well Ms. Ehrlich that time of year has arrived again. I, must think about

my strengths and weaknesses as an employee, of Toe-Ring International.

First and foremost let me say that I love working for Toe-Ring.

When I applied for the job I never dreamed how much fun I would have

taking two, long lunches a day. Sneaking out the back door, is not my idea

of fun. Because no one ever watches what I am doing at Toe-Ring I can

leave by the front door without worrying. Also Ms. Ehrlich I confess that I

do almost no work at all. Upon transferring to the plant in Idaho I

immediately claimed a privilege given only to the most experienced most

skilled, employees and started to take two, extra weeks of vacation. I have

only one more thing to say. May I have a raise?

Answers to Comma Problems

Check your answers to this chapter's problems against the following solutions.

(1) **Rob planned to serve a tasteful selection of pitted dates, chocolate-covered mushrooms, anchovies, and pickles.** Each item on Rob's list is separated from the next by a comma. No comma comes before the first item, *pitted dates.* The comma before the *and* is optional.

(2) **Rob's guest list is heavily tilted toward women he would like to date: Helen Ogee, super-model; Natasha Smith, swimsuit model; Blair Berry, auto salesperson; Hannah Bridge, punctuation expert; and Jane Fine, veterinarian.** Did you remember the semicolons? The commas within each item of Rob's dream-date list make it impossible to distinguish between one dream date and another with a simple comma. Semicolons do the trick. Also, I hope you noticed that this rather long list begins with a colon.

(3) **After everyone arrives, Rob plans an evening of juggling cabbages, pinning the tail on the landlord, and playing double solitaire.** Fun guy, huh? I can't imagine why he has so much trouble getting dates. I hope you didn't have any trouble separating these thrilling activities with commas. The comma before the *and* is optional.

(4) **Rob will consider his party a success if he can get three phone numbers, arrange at least one future date, and avoid police interference.** All you have to do is plop a comma between each item. Add a comma before the *and* if you wish.

(5) **Rob didn't meet his goals because the police arrived at 10:00, 11:00, and 11:30 p.m.; no one gave out any phone numbers; and everyone thought his name was Bob.** I hope you remembered to use a semicolon to distinguish one item from another. Why? The first item on the list has commas in it, so a plain comma isn't enough to separate the list items. The comma before *and* is optional.

(6) **Ladies and Gentlemen, I present the Fifth Annual Elbox Championships.** Even though *Ladies and Gentlemen* doesn't name the members of the audience, they're still being addressed, so a comma sets off the expression from the rest of the sentence.

(7) **I know, Mort, that you are an undefeated Elbox competitor. Would you tell our audience about the sport?** Here you see the benefit of the direct-address comma. Without it, the reader thinks *I know Mort* is the beginning of the sentence and then lapses into confusion. *Mort* is cut away with two commas, and the reader understands that *I know that you are . . .* is the real meaning.

(8) **Elboxing is about 5,000 years old, Chester. It originated in ancient Egypt.** You're talking to *Chester,* so his name needs to be set off with a comma.

(9) **Really? Man, I can't believe you knew that!** Before you start yelling at me, I know that *Man* is sometimes simply an exclamation of feeling, not a true address. But *man* can be a form of address, and in this sentence, it is. Hence the comma slices it away from the rest of the sentence.

(10) **Yes, Chester, the sport grew out of the natural movement of the elbow when someone tried to but ahead in line by "elbowing."** *Chester* is being addressed directly, so you need to surround the name with commas.

11 **Excuse me a moment. The reigning champion has decided to pay us a visit. Miss William, could you tell us how you feel about the upcoming match?** Here the person being addressed is *Miss William.*

12 **Certainly, Sir. I am confident that my new training routine will pay off.** The very polite *Miss William* talks to *Sir* in this sentence, so that term is set off by a comma.

13 **II. 14 Main Street, Chilton, CA 09011.** A comma separates the street address from the city and the city from the state abbreviation.

14 **I and II. 20 July 1940 and July 20, 1940,** In the first correct answer, commas disappear. In the second, commas separate the day from the year and the year from the rest of the sentence.

15 **I.** A comma separates the city and state and nothing else in this envelope-style address.

16 **III. Jeannie Wong, 98 East 100th Street, NY, NY 10001,** Commas separate the name from the street address, the street address from the city, and the city from the state. An additional comma follows the postal code and precedes the rest of the sentence.

17 **II and III. June 1920** or **June, 1920,** In the first correct answer no commas appear. In the second, a comma separates the month and year and the year from the rest of the sentence.

18 **The best man rode in a Zamboni, for he was afraid of slipping on the ice.** The conjunction (*for*) joins two complete sentences, so a comma precedes it.

19 **No comma.** Read the words preceding the conjunction (*and*). They don't make sense by themselves, so you don't have a complete sentence and don't need a comma before the conjunction.

20 **No comma.** Read the words after the conjunction (*or*). You have two descriptions but not a complete sentence. Therefore, you don't need a comma before *or.*

21 **The guests sipped hot chocolate, but they were still cold.** Here you have two complete thoughts, one before and one after the conjunction (*but*). You need a comma in front of the conjunction.

22 **The ice-dancing during the reception made them sweat, and then the temperature seemed fine.** Two complete thoughts sit in front of and behind *and*, so a comma is needed.

23 **No comma.** This one is a little tricky. The conjunction *or* joins *who is in charge of the gifts* and *who is paying the orchestra.* These two questions sound like complete sentences. However, the real question here is *Do you know.* The *who* statements in this sentence are just that: statements. No complete sentence = no comma.

24 **I'd like to swipe a present, for my blender is broken.** Both ideas — before and after the conjunction *for* — are complete, so a comma must precede *for.*

25 **I don't need an icemaker, but I'll take one anyway.** The two statements surrounding *but* are complete sentences, so you have to insert a comma.

26 **No comma.** The words after the conjunction (*and*) don't tell you who *never came back.* Without that information, the statement isn't a complete sentence. No comma needed here!

27 **In desperate need of a pizza fix, Brad turned to his cellphone.** The introductory expression here merits a comma because it's fairly long. Length doesn't always determine whether you need a comma, but in general, the longer the introduction, the more likely you'll need a comma.

28 **Cindy, on the other hand, ached for sushi.** The expression inside the commas makes a comment on the rest of the sentence, contrasting it with the actions of Brad. As an interrupter, it must be separated by two commas from the rest of the sentence.

29 **Yes, pizza was an excellent idea.** *Yes* and *no*, when they show up at the beginning of a sentence, take commas if they comment on the main idea.

30 **The toppings, unfortunately, proved to be a problem.** The *unfortunately* is short and closely tied to the meaning of the sentence. However, setting the word off with two commas emphasizes the emotional, judgmental tone. I've gone with the commas, as you see, but I can accept a case for omitting them.

31 **No comma.** The introductory word *restlessly* is short and clear. No comma is necessary.

32 **Cindy wondered how Brad, given his low-fat diet, could consider pepperoni.** The expression *given his low-fat diet* interrupts the flow of the sentence and calls for two commas.

33 **Frozen with indecision, Brad decided to call the supermarket to request the cheapest brand.** Introductory expressions with verb forms always take commas.

34 **Cindy, on a tight budget, wanted to redeem her coupons.** The phrase *on a tight budget* interrupts the flow of the sentence and comments on the main idea. Hence the two commas.

35 **No comma.** Did I catch you here? This sentence doesn't have an introductory expression. *To demand fast delivery* is the subject of the sentence, not an extra comment.

36 **Lighting a match and holding it near his trembling hand, Brad realized that time was almost up.** Introductory expressions containing verbs always take commas. This introductory expression has two verbs, *lighting* and *holding*.

37 **No comma.** The verb form (*Worrying about toppings*) is the subject of the sentence, not an introduction to another idea, so no comma is needed.

38 **Well, the survivors would have a good story to tell.** Words such as *well, indeed, clearly,* and so forth take commas when they occur at the beginning of the sentence and aren't part of the main idea.

39 **With determination, Cindy speed-dialed the market and offered "a really big tip" for fast service.** I admit that this one's a judgment call. If you didn't place a comma after *determination*, I won't prosecute you for comma fraud. Neither will I scream if you inserted one, as I did.

40 **As the robbers chomped on pepperoni and argued about payment, Brad slipped away.** This introductory statement has a subject and a verb and thus is followed by a comma.

41 **No comma.** The sentence reads seamlessly because of the word *that*, which ties the beginning of the sentence to the end of the sentence so strongly that "Let's just say" doesn't qualify as an introductory statement.

42 *Oscar's favorite* **food, which he cooks every Saturday night, is hot dogs.** Two words tell you more about *food*, but one is a possessive (*Oscar's*) and the other is a description (*favorite*). Because the two descriptions aren't equivalent, they aren't separated by commas. Moving on: After you find out that the food is *Oscar's favorite*, you have enough identification. The information about Oscar's datefree Saturday nights is extra and thus set off by commas. By the way, descriptions beginning with *which* are usually extra.

43 **Correct.** The term *place* is quite general, so the description is an essential identifier. The two descriptions preceding *barbecue* aren't of the same type. One gives size and the other composition. You can't easily reverse them (a *brick huge barbecue* sounds funny), so don't insert a comma.

(44) Correct. The paired descriptions (*his* and *wheat*, *large* and *plastic*) aren't of the same type. *His* is a possessive, and you should never set off a possessive with a comma. *Large* indicates size, and *plastic* refers to composition. The last description nails down which *tub* you're talking about, so it isn't set off by commas. In general, descriptions beginning with *that* don't take commas.

(45) One of the horses *that live in Oscar's barn* **often sniffs around** *Oscar's lucky* **horseshoe,** *which Oscar found while playing tag.* Which horses are you talking about? Without the *barn* information, you don't know. Identifying information doesn't take commas. The two words preceding *horseshoe* aren't equivalent. *Oscar's* is a possessive (never set off by commas), and *lucky* is a quality that we all want in our horseshoes. The last description is extra, because we already know enough to identify which horseshoe is getting sniffed. Because it's extra, a comma must separate the description from the rest of the sentence.

(46) Correct. The three descriptions preceding *horses* aren't of the same type: One (*his*) is possessive, and another (*three*) is a number. Commas never set off possessives and numbers. The second descriptive element, *honoring the Barbeque King and Queen*, explains which race you're talking about. Without that information, the topic could be any race. As an identifier, that phrase isn't set off by a comma.

(47) Oscar, *who is an animal lover,* **will never sell one of his horses** *because he needs money.* Because you know Oscar's name, the information about loving animals is extra and thus set off by commas. The *because* statement is tricky. Without a comma, *because he needs money* is essential to the meaning of the sentence. In this version, Oscar may sell a horse because he hates the animal or wants to please the prospective buyer, but never for financial reasons. With a comma before *because*, the italicized material is extra. The sentence then means that Oscar will never sell a horse, period. The reason — *he needs the money* — may mean that the horses are worth more in Oscar's stable than they would be anywhere else. The first interpretation makes more sense, so don't insert a comma.

(48) *Being sentimental,* **Oscar dedicated a song to the filly** *that was born on his birthday.* The introductory expression (which is also a description) contains a verb, so it must be followed by a comma. The second description is essential because you don't know which filly without the italicized identification. Thus, you need no comma.

(49) The jockeys *who were trying to prepare for the big race* **became annoyed by Oscar's song,** *which he played constantly;* **the jockeys** *who had already raced* **didn't mind Oscar's music.** In this sentence the jockeys are divided into two groups, those who are preparing and those who are done for the day. Because the *who* statements identify each group, no commas are needed. *Oscar's song*, on the other hand, is clear. Even without *which he played constantly*, you know which song the jockeys hate. The italicized material gives you a little more info, but nothing essential, so it must be set off by commas.

(50) The *deep, horrible* **secret is that Oscar can't stay in tune** *when he sings.* The first two descriptions may be reversed without loss of meaning, so a comma is appropriate. The last description also gives you essential information. Without that description, you don't know whether Oscar can stay in tune when he plays the tuba, for example, but not *when he sings*. Essential = no commas.

(51) His guitar, *a Gibson,* **is missing** *two important* **strings.** The *his* tells you which guitar is being discussed, so the fact that it's *a Gibson* is extra and should be set off by commas.

Here are the answers to the "Overachievers" section:

Annual Self-Evaluation — October 1, 2019

Well, Ms. Ehrlich, that time of year has arrived again. I/ must think about | 1 | 3
my strengths and weaknesses as an employee/ of Toe-Ring International. | 2 | 4

First and foremost, let me say that I love working for Toe-Ring. | 5

When I applied for the job, I never dreamed how much fun I would have | 6

taking two/ long lunches a day. Sneaking out the back door/ is not my idea | 7 | 8

of fun. Because no one ever watches what I am doing at Toe-Ring, I can | 9

leave by the front door without worrying. Also, Ms. Ehrlich, I confess that I | 10

do almost no work at all. Upon transferring to the plant in Idaho, I | 11

immediately claimed a privilege given only to the most experienced, most | 12

skilled/ employees and started to take two/ extra weeks of vacation. I have | 13 | 14

only one more thing to say. May I have a raise?

---

(1) Commas surround *Ms. Ehrlich* because she's being directly addressed in this sentence. Also, *well* is an introductory word, so even without *Ms. Ehrlich*, you'd still need a comma after *well*.

(2) See the preceding answer.

(3) The pronoun *I* is part of the main idea of the sentence, not an introductory expression. No comma should separate it from the rest of the sentence.

(4) The phrase *of Toe-Ring International* is an essential identifier of the type of employee being discussed. No comma should separate it from the word it describes *(employee)*.

(5) A comma follows the introductory expression, *First and most important.*

(6) The introductory expression *When I applied for the job* should be separated from the rest of the sentence by a comma.

(7) Two descriptions are attached to *lunches* — *two* and *long*. These descriptions aren't of the same type. *Two* is a number, and *long* is a measure of time. Also, numbers are never separated from other descriptions by a comma. The verdict: Delete the comma after *two.*

(8) In this sentence the expression *Sneaking out the back door* isn't an introductory element. It's the subject of the sentence, and it shouldn't be separated from its verb *(is)* by a comma.

(9) The introductory expression *Because no one ever watches what I am doing at Toe-Ring* should be separated from the rest of the sentence by a comma.

(10) *Also* is an introduction to the sentence. Slice it off with a comma.

(11) A comma follows *Idaho* because it is the last word of an introductory element.

(12) Two descriptions are attached to *employees: most experienced* and *most skilled.* Because these descriptions are more or less interchangeable, a comma separates them from each other.

(13) No comma ever separates the last description from what it describes, so the comma before *employees* has to go.

(14) Two descriptions (in this case *two* and *extra*) aren't separated by commas when one of the descriptions is a number.

Chapter 12

Handling Dashes, Hyphens, and Colons

As your thumbs hover over whatever you're texting, tweeting, or otherwise sending, do you take the time to tap a few punctuation marks on your tiny keyboard? Maybe you don't, and maybe you should. In this chapter, you practice inserting dashes (long or short horizontal lines), hyphens (very short horizontal lines), and colons (one dot atop another). These small marks pack a big punch of meaning.

Dashing Off

Before you dash off somewhere, let me explain what dashes do:

» **Long dashes insert information.** Long dashes — what grammarians call *em dashes* — break into a sentence. Look back at the sentence you just read. I inserted the technical term for a long dash with two long dashes. When you break into one thought with another, you may use a long dash. Often the inserted material is a definition or explanation, but sometimes it reflects a small change in subject. "Terry went to the museum this morning — she loves abstract art — so she can't babysit." The information about Terry's art preferences is only slightly related to the main idea of the sentence, which is that Terry can't babysit.

>> **Long dashes clarify lists containing commas.** If you're dealing with two expressions, each of which contains commas, a long dash can separate them and make your meaning clear. "Jill invited the vice-presidents for marketing, publicity, technology, and manufacturing — Jack, Peggy, Billy, and John." With a comma instead of a long dash, the reader might stumble into the list of names and wonder whether those people received invitations in addition to the vice-presidents. The long dash indicates that the vice-presidents' names are *Jack, Peggy, Billy, and John.*

>> **Long dashes separate general and specific information.** The long dash may take the reader from general to specific: "Ollie has assembled all the ingredients for his favorite meatloaf — mustard, ground turkey, Jell-O, and lollipops." In this example, the general *(ingredients)* becomes specific *(mustard, ground turkey, Jell-O, and lollipops)* after the dash. The same punctuation mark can signal a move in the other direction: "Eggs, ground beef, and bread crumbs — Ollie hated all those ingredients and refused to cook with them." Now the details *(eggs, ground beef, and bread crumbs)* precede the general *(ingredients).*

>> **Long dashes show that speech has broken off.** You see this usage often in mystery novels, when a character starts to give a vital clue and then stops because a dagger has flown through the air: "Marvin shouted, 'The codebook is in the —'"

TIP

Other punctuation marks can do the same jobs as long dashes. Sometimes commas are all you need. Parentheses also insert information and avoid potential comma confusion. Colons separate general and specific information, especially when the general appears first. An ellipsis (three spaced dots) shows an unfinished thought. You never *need* a long dash, but they're perfectly proper and a bit more dramatic than commas, parentheses, colons, and ellipses. Because they're dramatic, be careful. Nobody likes an overdose of drama.

>> **Short, or *en dashes,* show a range.** The range can be distance (the Chicago–New York train) or time (1900–2010). Don't send a long dash to do a short dash's job. Don't send in a hyphen either. (More on hyphens appears in the next section, "Helping Yourself to Hyphens.")

>> **Short dashes pair equal elements.** The short dash often signals a relationship: "Are you worried about the *pitcher–catcher* coordination on that team?"

EXAMPLE

Insert long dashes (em dashes) or short dashes (en dashes) where appropriate in these sentences.

Q. Melanie a passionate defender of animals attends veterinary school.

A. **Melanie — a passionate defender of animals — attends veterinary school.** Strictly speaking, you could surround *a passionate defender of animals* with commas, because that expression gives you extra information about of *Melanie.* (For more information on commas, see Chapter 11.) To add a bit of drama, use a long dash on each side.

1 While she was waiting for a bus, Melanie took out her lunch almonds, steamed broccoli, and a hard-boiled egg.

2 Suddenly she realized that two animals in this case, a squirrel and a pigeon were staring at her.

3 The Bronx Manhattan express bus was late.

4 "Well," thought Melanie, "I'll wait for two four minutes and then leave if it doesn't show up."

5 While thinking about the bus Melanie has always been good at multitasking and eating the egg, she continued to stare at the squirrel and the pigeon.

6 The human animal bond is amazing.

7 Who can imagine what questions go through the mind of a squirrel where's the food supply, how's my tail doing, why's that human looking at me, or something else!

8 Xander Hicksom (1802 1888) theorized that squirrels spend most of the day sleeping, not thinking.

9 Will an actual descendent of Xander Hicksom Melanie prove him right or wrong?

10 Will Melanie can Melanie analyze squirrel psychology?

11 Probably Melanie an animal lover but definitely not a scientist cannot.

12 Nevertheless, she will spend two four years on the project.

13 As the woman squirrel connection deepened, the pigeon flapped its wings.

14 Melanie was concerned about the bus, which was now 10 15 minutes late.

15 "Finally, the bus has " said Melanie, breaking off her thought as the pigeon swooped in and grabbed the last of her almonds.

Helping Yourself to Hyphens

Hyphens are horizontal lines, like dashes, but they're much shorter. Hyphens are versatile. They can connect or separate. Here are a hyphen's main jobs:

>> **Hyphens cut words that don't fit on a line.** Most writers don't have to worry about this function of hyphens because computers, tablets, and phones usually move a word that's too long to the next line or, in some cases, chop the word into pieces and insert the hyphen automatically. If you're hitting a margin and have no way to complete a word, break it off by placing a hyphen at the end of a syllable and continue on the next line. *Picnic,* for example, breaks this way: *pic- nic,* with *pic-* appearing at the end of the line and *nic* on the next line.

>> **Hyphens create compounds.** Where would the world be without *well-meaning mothers-in-law?* The hyphens turn two words into one description *(well-meaning)* and three words into one noun *(mothers-in-law).*

>> **Hyphens clarify numbers.** If you're writing numerals, you don't have to worry about hyphens. And most of the time you should be writing numerals, especially for large amounts. If you have to express an amount in words, hyphenate all numbers from *twenty-one to ninety-nine*. Also hyphenate fractions that function as a description *(two-thirds full)*. Don't hyphenate a fraction used as a noun *(one third of your paycheck)*.

Check the hyphens (or the lack of hyphens) in these questions. Mark each as "correct" or "incorrect."

Q. line 1: ap-

line 2: ology

A. **Incorrect.** *Apology* has four syllables: *a pol o gy.* Break the word only at the end of a syllable. In this case, your best option is write *apol- ogy.* It's not a good idea to leave one letter alone on the first line or only two letters on the second line.

16 third base coach

17 well-planned plot

18 line 1: com-

line 2: plicated

19 attorney-general

20 top-of-the-line

21 top-of-the-line car

22 sixty six

23 star studded cast

24 my great-grandmother, my mother's mother

25 three quarters of a cup

Coming to a Stop: Colons

Have you noticed that most of the section headings in this book contain *colons*? *Colons* are the stacked dots that separate the title from the subtitle. In this section, the title is *Coming to a Stop* and the subtitle is *Colons*. That's one function of a colon. Here are others:

» **Business letters or emails.** This punctuation mark signals formality. Use it after the greeting *(Dear Client:* or *Attention: George Smith)*. A colon also follows the subject line in a memo *(Re: Salary Negotiations)*.

» **In combined sentences.** You don't often see colons in this role. When you link two complete sentences and the second explains the first, a colon is a legal sentence-combiner. *(Arthur was clear about his goal: He wanted to make his first billion before he turned thirty.)*

» **Lists.** You don't need a colon in a short list, but if you've got a lot of items, a colon makes a strong, clean introduction. *(Mercy packed everything she'd need while hiking: boots, food, phone, bug spray, and the phone number of a limo service that would take her to a luxury hotel every night.)* The words preceding the colon should form a complete sentence.

» **Introductory line on a presentation slide.** Most presentation slides are lists. You often need a colon for the top line, unless it is the title of the slide, alone on a line. For all the rules of presentation slides and their punctuation, turn to Chapter 14.

» **Introducing long quotations.** Students, pay attention! If you're tucking a quotation into a sentence, and the quotation is on the short side, don't use a colon. If it's long (yes, you have to use your judgment here), a colon prepares the reader for what's to come. Always use a colon to introduce a quotation that is presented as a block of text, separate from the information surrounding it. *(The new president of the Dog Lovers Club declared: "Ask not what your collie or your terrier or your pug can do for you! Ask what you can do for your beloved canine companions.")*

Correct or incorrect? You decide.

Q. To Whom It May Concern,

A. Incorrect. This extremely formal and somewhat old-fashioned greeting is always followed by a colon.

26 Last week Joe campaigned in ten states, Maine, Vermont, New Hampshire, Massachusetts, Connecticut, Rhode Island, New York, New Jersey, Pennsylvania, and Ohio.

27 Joe stated: "I like states."

28 Quotations from Joe's essay, "A Statement about States: My Position," were widely tweeted.

29 Joe's campaign head remarked: "Joe is very qualified for the position of Regional Transportation Director. He drives. He takes trains and planes. Sometimes he bikes. If he can't avoid it, he walks. He knows a lot about transportation. True, he has never worked in the field, but he does use transportation."

30 Joe's energy level is low: He plans to run for Regional Transportation Secretary if he doesn't win the directorship.

Calling All Overachievers: Extra Practice with Dashes, Hyphens, and Colons

Ten portions of this letter from a florist to a client are underlined. Decide whether the underlined material properly employs dashes, hyphens, or colons. If you find a mistake, correct it. If everything is fine, leave it alone.

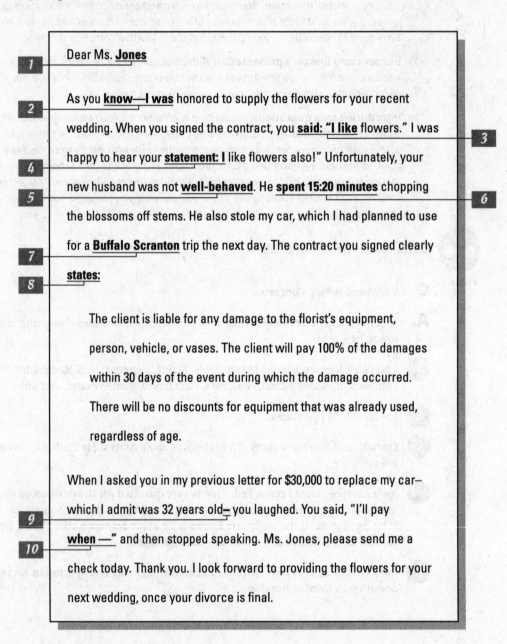

1 Dear Ms. **Jones**

2 As you **know—I was** honored to supply the flowers for your recent wedding. When you signed the contract, you **said: "I like** flowers." I was **3** happy to hear your **statement: I** like flowers also!" Unfortunately, your **4** new husband was not **well-behaved**. He **spent 15:20 minutes** chopping **5** **6** the blossoms off stems. He also stole my car, which I had planned to use for a **Buffalo Scranton** trip the next day. The contract you signed clearly **7** **states: 8**

> The client is liable for any damage to the florist's equipment, person, vehicle, or vases. The client will pay 100% of the damages within 30 days of the event during which the damage occurred. There will be no discounts for equipment that was already used, regardless of age.

When I asked you in my previous letter for $30,000 to replace my car— which I admit was 32 years old— you laughed. You said, "I'll pay **9** **when —"** and then stopped speaking. Ms. Jones, please send me a **10** check today. Thank you. I look forward to providing the flowers for your next wedding, once your divorce is final.

Answers to Problems on Dashes, Hyphens, and Colons

How's your punctuation? Check your answers here before you answer that question!

1. **While she was waiting for a bus, Melanie took out her lunch — almonds, steamed broccoli, and a hard-boiled egg.** The long dash separates a general term, *lunch*, from the components of lunch (*almonds, steamed broccoli, and a hard-boiled egg*). The long dash could be replaced by parentheses, as it is in the preceding explanation sentence. It can't be replaced by a comma, though, because the commas that separate each item in Melanie's lunch would seem to be part of a series starting with *lunch*.

2. **Suddenly she realized that two animals —in this case, a squirrel and a pigeon — were staring at her.** As in question one, you're better off with long dashes than simple commas here, because *in this case, a squirrel and a pigeon* already has a comma. Parentheses, however, would also be fine in this sentence.

3. **The Bronx–Manhattan express bus was late.** The short dash shows a range. The bus travels between the *Bronx* and *Manhattan*.

4. **"Well," thought Melanie, "I'll wait for two–four minutes and then leave if it doesn't show up."** The short dash in this sentence shows a range of time.

5. **While thinking about the bus — Melanie has always been good at multitasking — and eating the egg, she continued to stare at the squirrel and the pigeon.** Here the comment about Melanie's ability to do more than one thing at a time interrupts the statement *While thinking about the bus and eating the egg.* Two long dashes show the interruption.

6. **The human–animal bond is amazing.** A short dash shows a relationship between two categories, *human* and *animal*.

7. **Who can imagine what questions go through the mind of a squirrel — where's the food supply, how's my tail doing, why's that human looking at me, or something else!** The long dash signals the shift from general (*questions*) to specific (the content of those questions). A colon would also serve to introduce the list of possible questions.

8. **Xander Hicksom (1802–1888) theorized that squirrels spend most of the day sleeping, not thinking.** The short dash connects two dates here, the years of birth and death.

9. **Will an actual descendent of Xander Hicksom — Melanie — prove him right or wrong?** Simple commas would also do the job here, much less dramatically.

10. **Will Melanie — can Melanie — analyze squirrel psychology?** The long dashes emphasize the real question, which is whether Melanie *can* figure out what a squirrel thinks. The dash gives the first question, *will she*, less importance.

11. **Probably Melanie — an animal lover but definitely not a scientist — cannot.** The long dashes create a dramatic air in this sentence, as they set apart the statement about Melanie's aptitude for science.

12. **Nevertheless, she will spend two–four years on the project.** The short dash shows a time range.

13. **As the woman–squirrel connection deepened, the pigeon flapped its wings.** The short dash connects *woman* and *squirrel.*

14. **Melanie was concerned about the bus, which was now 10–15 minutes late.** The short dash shows the time range.

15. **"Finally, the bus has — " said Melanie, breaking off her thought as the pigeon swooped in and grabbed the last of her almonds.** The long dash shows that Melanie didn't finish her statement.

16. **Incorrect.** The expression *third base coach* is confusing. Are you talking about the baseball coach who stands near third base (the *third-base coach*) or the third person to hold that position this season *(the third base-coach).* Without a hyphen, your reader may misinterpret your meaning.

17. **Correct.** The two words, *well* and *planned,* function as one description, so a hyphen should link them. If the same two words appear after the word they refer to *(plot),* the grammar changes. If you write, "The plot was well planned," *well* describes *planned,* which is part of the verb *was planned.*

18. **Correct.** *Complicated* breaks into four syllables: *com pli ca ted.* The hyphen properly separates the first syllable from the next three.

19. **Correct.** This title, like many others, is hyphenated. If you're not sure about a particular title, check your dictionary.

20. **Incorrect.** Creating one description such as *top-of-the-line* is correct only when you're describing something. In this expression, you're not.

21. **Correct.** Now *top-of-the-line* does describe something *(car).*

22. **Incorrect.** Numbers from twenty-one to ninety-nine should be hyphenated, so the correct form is *sixty-six.*

23. **Incorrect.** Two words, *star* and *studded,* combine to describe *cast,* so you want a *star-studded cast.*

24. **Correct.** The hyphen tells you that this word refers to a relative, not to a quality (greatness) that a grandmother may possess.

25. **Correct.** Surprised? Used this way, *quarters* is a noun. *Three* is a description, telling you how many *quarters* you have.

26. **Incorrect. Last week Joe campaigned in ten states: Maine, Vermont, New Hampshire, Massachusetts, Connecticut, Rhode Island, New York, New Jersey, Pennsylvania, and Ohio.** A colon introduces this long list.

27. **Incorrect. Joe stated, "I like states."** A comma is fine as an introduction to this short statement.

28. **Correct.** The colon separates the title from the subtitle of Joe's article.

29. **Correct.** This overly long quotation is properly introduced by a colon.

30. **Incorrect.** A colon properly joins two complete sentences, but only if the second portion explains the meaning of the first. Okay, *Joe's energy level is low.* That's nice to know, but his *plans to run for Regional Transportation Secretary if he doesn't win the directorship* don't explain anything about the fact that he naps 20 hours a day. These two sentences need a different connection.

Here are the answers to the "Overachievers" section:

1. Dear Ms. **Jones:**

2. As you **know, I was** honored to supply the flowers for your recent wedding. When you signed the contract, you **said, "I like** flowers." I was

3. happy to hear your **statement: I** like flowers also!" Unfortunately, your

4. new husband was not **well behaved**. He **spent 15–20 minutes** chopping

5. the blossoms off stems. He also stole my car, which I had planned to use

6. for a **Buffalo–Scranton** trip the next day. The contract you signed clearly

7. **states:**

8.

> The client is liable for any damage to the florist's equipment, person, vehicle, or vases. The client will pay 100% of the damages within 30 days of the event during which the damage occurred. There will be no discounts for equipment that was already used, regardless of age.

When I asked you in my previous letter for $30,000 to replace my car, which I admit was 32 years old**,** you laughed. You said, "I'll pay

9. **when —**" and then stopped speaking. Ms. Jones, please send me a

10. check today. Thank you. I look forward to providing the flowers for your next wedding, once your divorce is final.

---

(1) **Incorrect.** A colon follows the greeting in a business letter or email.

(2) **Incorrect.** A comma, not a dash, follows this short introductory phrase.

(3) **Incorrect.** The quotation is short, so a comma is better than a colon.

(4) **Correct.** The second portion of the sentence explains the first, so the colon is correct.

(5) **Incorrect.** The description, *well behaved*, is not hyphenated when it appears after the word it describes, which in this sentence is *husband*.

(6) **Incorrect.** A short dash shows the time range.

(7) **Incorrect.** A short dash shows the path of the trip, from Buffalo to Scranton.

(8) **Correct.** To introduce a blocked quotation, a colon is appropriate.

(9) **Incorrect.** A short dash shows a range, not what you need in this sentence. Here, information is inserted into the main idea of the sentence, so commas work well. The long dash would add a touch of drama and would also be correct here.

(10) **Correct.** The long dash shows an incomplete thought.

Chapter **13**

Hitting the Big Time: Capital Letters

Most people know the basics of capitalization: Capital letters are needed for proper names, the personal pronoun *I*, and the first letter of a sentence. Trouble may arrive with the finer points of capital letters — in quotations (which I cover in Chapter 10), titles (of people and of publications), abbreviations, geography and history, and school or business terms. Never fear. In this chapter you get to practice all those topics. If you want to fine-tune your capitalization skills in texts, tweets, emails, and presentation slides, turn to Chapter 14.

WARNING

The major style-setters in the land of grammar (yes, grammar has style, and no, grammarians aren't immune to trends) sometimes disagree about what should be capitalized and what shouldn't. In this workbook I follow the most common capitalization styles. If you're writing for a specific publication or teacher, you may want to check which 20-pound book of rules (also known as a style manual) you should follow. The most common are those manuals published by the Modern Language Association (*MLA*, for academic writing in the humanities), the American Psychological Association (*APA*, for science and social science writing), and the University of Chicago (*Chicago or CMS*, for general interest and academic publishing).

Paying Respect to People's Names and Titles

Your name, and the personal pronoun *I* that you use to refer to yourself, are always in caps, but titles are a different story. The general rules are as follows:

>> **A title preceding and attached to a name is capitalized** *(Mr. Smith, Professor Wiley)*. Small, unimportant words in titles *(a, the, of,* and the like) are never capitalized *(Head of School Barker)*.

>> **Titles written after or without a name are generally not capitalized** *(George Wiley, professor of psychology)*.

>> **Titles of national or international importance may be capitalized even when used alone** *(President, Vice President, Secretary-General)*. Some style manuals opt for lowercase regardless of rank.

>> **Family relationships are capitalized when they are used in place of a name** ("That building was designed by Mom," but "My mother is an architect").

EXAMPLE

In the following sentences, add capital letters where needed. Cross out incorrect capitals and substitute the lowercase form. Keep your eyes open; not every sentence has an error.

Q. The reverend archie smith, Chief Executive of the local council, has invited senator Bickford to next month's fundraiser.

A. **Reverend, Archie, Smith, chief, executive, Senator.** Personal names are always capitalized, so *Archie Smith* needs capitals. *Reverend* and *Senator* precede the names *(Archie Smith* and *Bickford)* and act as part of the person's name, not just as a description of their jobs. Thus they should be capitalized. The title *chief executive* follows the name and isn't capitalized.

1. Yesterday mayor Victoria Johnson ordered all public servants in her town to conserve sticky tape.

2. Herman harris, chief city engineer, has promised to hold the line on tape spending.

3. However, the Municipal Dogcatcher, Agnes e. Bark, insists on taping reward signs to every tree.

4. My Sister says that the signs placed by dogcatcher Bark seldom fall far from the tree.

5. Did you ask mom whether ms. Bark's paper will freeze in December?

6. Few Dogcatchers care as much as agnes about rounding up lost dogs.

7. The recent dog-show champion, BooBoo, bit uncle Lou last week.

8. My Brother thinks that no one would have been hurt had Agnes found BooBoo first.

9. The Mayor's Cousin, who owns a thumbtack company, has an interest in substituting tacks for tape.

10. Until the issue is resolved, Agnes, herself the chief executive of Sticking, Inc., will continue to tape.

11. Sticking, Inc. has appointed a new Vice President to oversee a merger with Thumbtack, Inc.

12. Vice president Pinkie of Thumbtack, Inc., is tired of jokes about his name.

13. When he was appointed Chief Financial Officer, George Pinkie asked grandma Pinkie for advice.

14. George's aunt, Alicia Bucks, had little sympathy for Pinkie, who is her favorite Nephew.

15. With a name like Bucks, she explained, everyone thinks you should work as a Bank President.

16. Pinkie next asked reverend Holy how he dealt with his unusual name.

17. However, Holy, who has been a Bishop for twelve years, shrugged off the question.

18. "My Brother is The Manager of the New Jersey Devils hockey team, so he faces more jokes than i do," Bishop Holy remarked.

19. Reginald Holy joined the Devils twenty years ago as a Player Development Director.

20. Holy hopes to be appointed President of the National Hockey League someday.

Capitalizing the Right Time and Place

Where are you going on vacation? Are you flying *west* or *West*? During the *winter* or *Winter*? Terms for time periods and places can be confusing. Follow these guidelines:

>> **Geographical areas (Midwest, Soho, East Asia) are capitalized, but not directions.** You fly *south* to the *South* if you live in *New England*.

>> **Geographical features with names are capitalized, but not general terms referring to them.** You should visit the magnificent *Grand Canyon* and perhaps see some smaller *canyons* during your vacation.

>> **Seasons of the year aren't capitalized, but historical eras and events are.** The *Boston Tea Party,* an important event in the *Revolution,* took place in *winter.*

>> **Days of the week and months of the year are always capitalized.** Every *Sunday* in *May,* Eugene and his family have a picnic.

EXAMPLE

Ready to try your capitalization skills? Check every sentence. If you see a capitalization error, correct it.

Q. In march, Ellie drove east to the Rocky mountains and then visited several Cities.

A. **March, Rocky Mountains, cities.** Months of the year always begin with a capital letter. Both words, *Rocky* and *Mountains,* should be capitalized, because they form one name. Because *cities* is a general term, lower case is appropriate.

21 On a Westward voyage, Sindy hoped to reach Europe and visit places associated with world war II.

22 During the Summer, Sindy has about a month off and usually looks for Lakes with cabins nearby.

23 Last monday Sindy spent several hours reading history books about the War.

24 She immediately called a travel agent and tried to book an Eastbound flight to Amsterdam.

25 The fare was too high, so she chose to cross the atlantic on a ship instead.

26 "I love Oceans," remarked Sindy as she searched the horizon, looking for islands.

27 When the ship neared Iceland, Sindy sighed. "A Volcano erupted there last year," she remarked.

28 Sindy planned to continue her trip, moving west across the Continent until she reached the Middle East.

29 The suez canal had been at the top of her "must see" list since December, when she saw a documentary on its construction.

30 Sindy plans to spends some time in old Cairo, a neighborhood rich in history.

Working with Business and School Terms

Whether you bring home a paycheck or a report card, you should take care to capitalize properly. Surprisingly, the worlds of business and education have a lot in common:

>> **The place where it all happens:** Capitalize the name of the company or school (*Superlative Gadgets International* or *University of Rock and Roll*). General words that may refer to a number of businesses or academic institutions (*university, conglomerate,* and so forth) are written in lowercase.

>> **Working units:** Business activities (*management* or *advertising*) and general academic tasks, years, and subjects (*research, sophomore, history*) aren't capitalized. The name of a specific department (*Research and Development Division, Department of Cultural Anthropology*) may be capitalized. Project names (*the Zero Task Force*) and course names (*History of Belly-Button Rings*) are capitalized.

TIP

Course titles and the names of businesses or institutions are capitalized according to the "headline style" rules of titles, which I describe in "Capitalizing Titles of Literary and Media Works" later in this chapter. Briefly, capitalize the first word, all nouns and verbs, and any important words in the title. Short, relational words such as *of, for, by,* and *from* aren't capitalized, nor are articles such as *a, an,* and *the.*

>> **Products:** General terms for items produced or sold (*widgets, guarantees, consultation fee*) aren't capitalized. Neither are academic degrees or awards (*master's* or *fellowship*). If a specific brand is named, however, roll out the big letters (*Columbus Award for Round-Trip Travel* or *Universal Gadget Lever*).

WARNING

Some companies change the usual capitalization customs (*eBay* and *iPad,* for example). As a grammarian, I'm not happy, but people (and companies) have the right to ruin — sorry — *select* their own names.

EXAMPLE

Now that you have the basics, try these questions. If a word needs a capital letter, cross out the offending letter and insert the capital. If a word has an unnecessary capital letter, cross out the offender and insert a lowercase letter. You may also find a correct sentence. If you do, leave it alone!

Q. The eldest daughter of Matt Brady, founder of body piercing international, is a senior at the university of southeast hogwash, where she is majoring in navel repair.

A. **Body Piercing International, University of Southeast Hogwash.** The name of the company is capitalized, as is the name of the school. The year of study (*senior*) isn't capitalized, nor is the major.

31 After extensive research, the united nose ring company has determined that freshmen prefer silver rings, except Psychology majors.

32 The spokesperson for the Company commented that "gold rocks the world" of future Psychologists.

33 "I wore a gold ring to the curriculum committee during the Spring Semester," explained Fred Stileless, who is the student representative to that committee and to the board of trustees.

34 "My gold earring was a turn off for juniors," explained Fred, who hasn't had a date since he was a senior at Smith And Youngtown United high school. "I hope they like my new nose ring."

35 The Spokesperson surveyed competing Products, including a silver–gold combination manufactured by in style or else, inc., a division of Nosy Industrials, where every worker has a College Degree.

36 Nosy's website sells rings to Students in fifty Countries on six Continents.

37 The website manager claims that silver attracts clicks and costs less, though the department of product development can't figure out the difference in the "attractive power" of various metals.

38　Stileless, who originally majored in chemistry, said that "introduction to fashion, a course I took in freshman year, opened my eyes to beauty and made me question my commitment to Science."

39　Stileless expects to receive a bachelor's degree with a concentration in body-piercing jewelry.

40　Import-export Companies plan to switch their focus from gold to silver.

Capitalizing Titles of Literary and Media Works

If you write an ode to homework or a scientific study on the biological effects of too many final exams, how do you capitalize the title? The answer depends on the style you're following:

>> **In the United States, the titles of literary, creative, and general-interest works are capitalized in "headline style."** Headline style specifies capital letters for the first and last word of the title and subtitle, in addition to all nouns, verbs, and descriptive words, and any other words that require emphasis. Articles *(a, an, the)* and prepositions *(among, by, for,* and the like) are usually in lowercase. *For Dummies* chapter titles employ headline style. In Britain, titles of all sorts of works often appear in sentence style, which I describe in the next bullet point.

>> **The titles of scientific works employ "sentence style,"** which calls for capital letters only for the first word of the title and subtitle and for proper nouns. Everything else is lower-cased. (The title of a scientific paper in sentence style: "Cloning fruit flies: Hazards of fly bites.")

EXAMPLE

The following titles are written without any capital letters at all. Cross out the offending letters and insert capitals above them where needed. The style you should follow (headline or sentence) is specified in parentheses at the end of each title. By the way, titles of short works are enclosed in quotation marks. Titles of full-length works are italicized. (See Chapter 10 for more information on the punctuation of titles.)

Q.　"the wonders of homework completed: an ode" *(headline)*

A.　**"The Wonders of Homework Completed: An Ode"** The first word of the title and subtitle *(The, An)* are always capitalized. So are the nouns *(Wonders, Homework)* and descriptive words *(Completed)*. The preposition *(of)* is left in lowercase.

41　moby duck: a tale of obsessive bird-watching *(headline)*

42　"an analysis of the duckensis mobyous: the consequences of habitat shrinkage on population" *(sentence)*

43　"call me izzy smell: my life as a duck hunter" *(headline)*

44　the duck and i: essays on the relationship between human beings and feathered species *(sentence)*

45 duck and cover: a cookbook *(headline)*

46 "the duck stops here: political wisdom from the environmental movement" *(sentence)*

47 duck up: how the duck triumphed over the hunter *(headline)*

48 "moby platypus doesn't live here anymore" *(headline)*

49 "population estimates of the platypus: an inexact science" *(sentence)*

50 for the love of a duck: a sentimental memoir *(headline)*

Managing Capital Letters in Abbreviations

The world of abbreviations is prime real estate for turf wars. Some publications and institutions proudly announce that "*we* don't capitalize a.m." whereas others declare exactly the opposite, choosing "AM" instead. (Both are correct, but don't mix the forms. Notice that the capitalized version doesn't use periods.) You're wise to ask in advance for a list of the publication's or Authority Figure's preferences. These are the general, one-size-fits-most guidelines for abbreviations:

>> **Acronyms** — forms created by the first letter of each word (*NATO, UNICEF,* and so forth) — take capitals but not periods.

>> **Initials and titles** are capitalized and take periods (*George W. Bush* and *Msgr. Sullivan,* for example). The three most common titles — Mr., Mrs., and Ms.— are always capitalized and usually written with periods, though trendy writers skip the period.

>> **Latin abbreviations** such as *e.g.* (for example) and *ibid.* (in the same place) aren't usually capitalized but do end with a period.

>> **State abbreviations** are the two-letter, no-period, capitalized forms created by the post office (*IN* and *AL*).

>> **Abbreviations in texts or tweets to friends** may be informal, written without capitals or periods. If you've *gtg* (got to go), you probably don't have time for capitals. However, avoid these abbreviations when writing to someone you're trying to impress — a boss, client, or teacher.

>> **When an abbreviation comes at the end of a sentence,** the period for the abbreviation does double duty as an endmark.

EXAMPLE Okay, try your hand at abbreviating. Check out the full word, which I place in lowercase letters, even when capital letters are called for. See whether you can insert the proper abbreviation or acronym for the following words, taking care to capitalize where necessary and filling in the blanks with your answers.

Q. figure _____

A. **fig.**

51. illustration _____

52. before common era _____

53. mister Burns _____

54. united states president _____

55. national hockey league _____

56. reverend Smith _____

57. new york _____

58. Adams boulevard _____

59. irregular _____

60. incorporated _____

Calling All Overachievers: Extra Practice with Capital Letters

EXAMPLE

Use the information in this chapter to help you find ten capitalization mistakes in the following figure, which is an excerpt from possibly the worst book report ever written.

Moby, the Life Of a Duck: A Book Report

If you are ever given a book about Ducks, take my advice and burn it. When i had to

read *Moby Duck*, the Teacher promised me that it was good. She said that

"Excitement was on every page." I don't think so! A duckling with special powers is

raised by his Grandpa. Moby actually goes to school and earns a Doctorate in bird

Science! After a really boring account of Moby's Freshman year, the book turns to

his career as a Flight Instructor. I was very happy to see him fly away at the end of

the book.

Answers to Capitalization Problems

Now that you've burned a hole through your thinking cap while answering questions about capitalization, check out the answers to see how you did.

1. **Mayor Victoria Johnson.** Titles that come before a name and proper names take capitals; common nouns, such as *servants* and *tape,* don't.

2. **Harris.** Names take capitals, but titles written after the name usually don't.

3. **municipal dogcatcher, E.** The title in this sentence isn't attached to the name; in fact, it's separated from the name by a comma. It should be in lowercase. Initials take capitals and periods.

4. **sister, Dogcatcher.** Family relationships aren't capitalized unless the relationship is used as a name. The title *Dogcatcher* is attached to the name, and thus it's capitalized.

5. **Mom, Ms.** The word Mom substitutes for the name here, so it's capitalized. The title *Ms.* is always capitalized, but the period is optional.

6. **dogcatchers, Agnes.** The common noun *dogcatchers* doesn't need a capital letter, but the proper name Agnes does.

7. **Uncle.** The title uncle is capitalized if it precedes or substitutes for the name. Did I confuse you with *BooBoo?* People can spell their own names (and the names of their pets) how they want.

8. **brother.** Family titles aren't capitalized unless they substitute for the name.

9. **mayor's, cousin.** These titles aren't attached to or used as names, so they take lowercase.

10. **Correct.** Names are in caps, but the title isn't, except when it precedes the name.

11. **vice president.** A title that isn't attached to a name shouldn't be capitalized.

12. **President.** In this sentence the title precedes the name and thus should be capitalized.

13. **chief financial officer, Grandma.** The first title (chief financial officer) isn't attached to a name. Go for lowercase. The second title (Grandma) is part of a name and must be capitalized.

14. **nephew.** Don't capitalize relationships, like aunt, unless they precede and are part of a name.

15. **bank president.** This title isn't connected to a name; therefore, it should be lowercased.

16. **Reverend.** The title precedes the name and becomes part of the name, in a sense. A capital letter is appropriate.

17. **bishop.** In this sentence bishop doesn't precede a name; lowercase is the way to go.

18. **brother, the, manager, I.** Lowercase is best for *brother, the,* and *manager* because *brother* isn't being used as a name, *the* isn't part of the title, and in any case, the title isn't connected to a name. The personal pronoun *I* is always capitalized.

19. **player development director.** Another title that's all by itself. Opt for lowercase.

20. **president.** To be president is a big deal, but not a big letter.

(21) **westward, World War II.** Directions aren't capitalized. The names of historical events, such as wars, should be capitalized.

(22) **summer, lakes.** Use lower case for seasons and general geographical terms.

(23) **Monday, war.** Days of the week should appear in caps, but the general term war should not. Did I catch you with history? That's a general term, so it appears in lower case.

(24) **eastbound.** Directions aren't capitalized. Amsterdam, the name of a city, is correctly capitalized.

(25) **Atlantic.** The name of the ocean (or any geographical feature) should be capitalized.

(26) **oceans.** General geographical terms, such as oceans and islands, take lower case.

(27) **volcano.** Volcano is a general term, so write it with lower case.

(28) **continent.** Another general term, another lowercase letter. Middle East, the name of a region, is capitalized.

(29) **Suez Canal.** This one is a specific place, so capitals letters do the job. December, like all months, is capitalized.

(30) **Old.** The sentence tells you that Old Cairo is a neighborhood, an area, so capital letters are needed.

(31) **United Nose Ring Company, psychology.** Although college freshmen think they're really important (and, of course, they are), they rate only lowercase. The name of the company is specific and should be in uppercase. Don't capitalize subject areas.

(32) **company, psychologists.** Common nouns such as *company* and *psychologists* aren't capitalized. (And if you've read Chapter 10, you may remember that because the quotation isn't tagged with a name, the quotation doesn't begin with a capital letter.)

(33) **spring semester, Board of Trustees.** The name of the committee is generic and generally would not take capitals, though you have some elbow room here for style. Seasons, both natural and academic, take lowercase letters. The name of an official body, such as the Board of Trustees, is usually capitalized.

(34) **and, High School.** Years in school and school levels aren't capitalized. The name of the school is (and the name includes High School), but an unimportant word such as *and* is written in lowercase.

(35) **spokesperson; products; In Style or Else, Inc.; college degree.** A common noun such as spokesperson or college degree isn't capitalized. The names of companies are capitalized according to the preference of the company itself. Most companies follow headline style, which is explained in the section "Capitalizing Titles of Literary and Media Works" earlier in this chapter.

(36) **students, countries, continents.** Don't capitalize general terms.

(37) **task force, Department of Product Development.** In this sentence, task force isn't a name but rather a common label, which takes lowercase. The name of a department should be capitalized, but the preposition (of) is lowercased.

(38) **Introduction to Fashion, science.** Course titles get caps, but subject names and school years don't.

39 **Correct.** School degrees (bachelor's, master's, doctorate) are lowercased, though their abbreviations aren't (B.A., M.S., and so on). Most school subjects aren't capitalized, except for languages (such as Spanish). Course names, such as Economics I, are capitalized.

40 **companies.** This term isn't the name of a specific company, just a common noun. Lowercase is what you want.

41 **Moby Duck: A Tale of Obsessive Bird-Watching** In headline style, the first word of the title (Moby) and subtitle (A) are in caps. Nouns (Duck, Tale, and Watching) and descriptive words (Obsessive, Bird) are also uppercased. The short preposition of merits only lowercase.

42 **"An analysis of the Duckensis mobyous: The consequences of habitat shrinkage on population"** In sentence-style capitalization, the first words of the title and subtitle are in caps, but everything else is in lowercase, with the exception of proper names. In this title, following preferred scientific style, the names of the genus (a scientific category) and species are in italics with only the genus name in caps.

43 **"Call Me Izzy Smell: My Life As a Duck Hunter"** Per headline style, the article (a) is in lowercase. I caught you on As, didn't I? It's short, but it's not an article or a preposition, so it rates a capital letter.

44 **The duck and I: Essays on the relationship between human beings and feathered species** Sentence style titles take caps for the first word of the title and subtitle. The personal pronoun *I* is always capitalized.

45 **Duck and Cover: A Cookbook** Headline style calls for capitals for the first word of the title and subtitle and all other nouns. The joining word *and* is lowercased in headline style, unless it begins a title or subtitle.

46 **"The duck stops here: Political wisdom from the environmental movement"** Sentence style gives you two capitals in this title — the first word of the title and subtitle.

47 **Duck Up: How the Duck Triumphed over the Hunter** Because this title is in headline style, everything is in caps except articles (the) and prepositions (over).

48 **"Moby Platypus Doesn't Live Here Anymore"** Headline style gives capital letters for all the words here because this title contains no articles or prepositions.

49 **"Population estimates of the platypus: An inexact science"** Sentence style calls for capital letters at the beginning of the title and subtitle. The term platypus isn't the name of a genus, so it's written in lowercase.

50 **For the Love of a Duck: A Sentimental Memoir** Headline style mandates lowercase for articles (the, a) and prepositions (of). The first words of the title and subtitle, even if they're articles or prepositions, merit capital letters.

51 **illus.**

52 **BCE** (The Latin expression *Anno Domini* — abbreviated *AD* — means "in the year of our Lord" and is used with dates that aren't *BC*, or *before Christ*. To make this term more universal, historians often substitute *CE* or *Common Era* for *AD* and *BCE* or *Before the Common Era* for *BC*.)

53 **Mr. Burns**

54 **U.S. Pres.**

55 **NHL** (an acronym)

(56) **Rev. Smith**

(57) **NY** (postal abbreviation) or **N.Y.** (traditional form)

(58) **Adams Blvd.**

(59) **irreg.**

(60) **Inc.**

Here are the answers to the "Overachievers" section:

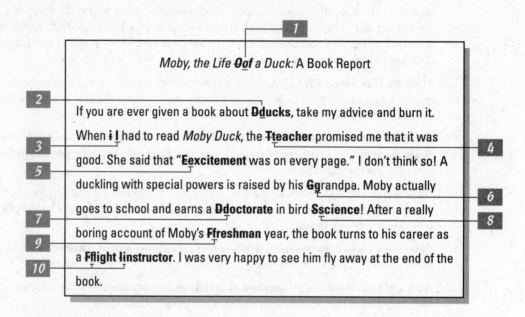

Moby, the Life ~~O~~of a Duck: A Book Report

If you are ever given a book about ~~D~~ducks, take my advice and burn it. When ~~i~~ I had to read *Moby Duck,* the ~~T~~teacher promised me that it was good. She said that "~~E~~excitement was on every page." I don't think so! A duckling with special powers is raised by his ~~G~~grandpa. Moby actually goes to school and earns a ~~D~~doctorate in bird ~~S~~science! After a really boring account of Moby's ~~F~~freshman year, the book turns to his career as a ~~F~~flight ~~I~~instructor. I was very happy to see him fly away at the end of the book.

(1) In a headline-style title, prepositions aren't capitalized.

(2) An ordinary term for animals, in this case *ducks,* is lowercased.

(3) The personal pronoun *I* is always capitalized.

(4) The name of the teacher isn't given, just the term *teacher,* which should be lowercased.

(5) When a quotation is written without a speaker tag, the first word isn't capitalized.

(6) Family relationships are capitalized only when they serve as a name.

(7) Most academic degrees take lowercase.

(8) Most school subjects are written in lowercase. (I must point out that *English* is in caps because it's so important. Okay, I'm lying. It's in caps because it's the name of a language.)

(9) School years are in lowercase too.

(10) Job titles, when they aren't attached to the beginning of a name, are in lowercase.

Chapter **14**

Writing for Electronic Media

When you and your 5,000 closest friends communicate on a social networking site, should you worry about grammar? The answer is a definite maybe. Electronic media — texts, instant messages, tweets, emails, social media posts, and the like — have bent some traditional grammar rules and broken more than a few. I'm not upset about these changes. In fact, I'm happy that the written word is making a comeback. But some rules may be broken without creating confusion, and some may not.

In this chapter I explain what you can get away with — and when — and what sends you to the grammar penitentiary. I also show you the ins and outs of presentation slides, so you can fire off bullet points with confidence.

Knowing Your Audience: The Right Writing for the Right Situation

In some situations you may want to write informally, without sacrificing meaning, of course. If you're dealing with a friend or co-worker, you can generally drop a few words and punctuation marks, especially if you're limited to 200 or so characters (letters and spaces) in your message. Your peers probably don't care about capital letters either (though in my experience every crowd has at least one stickler for the rules, and yes, I'm the stickler in *my* crowd). When you're aiming upward — writing to a boss, teacher, parole board, whatever — proper English is safest. Social media and blog posts fall somewhere in the middle. You may want a relaxed, just-kicked-off-my-shoes tone. In that case, go for informal language. If you want readers to see you as an authority, stick with Standard English.

Most instant messages make do without a "greeting" — the *Dear Sir,* or *Hi, Pamela!* sort of comment — and a closing such as *Sincerely, Best,* and the like. Emails sometimes drop these also. If you *do* include a greeting line and a closing, capitalize the greeting and the name, and the *first* word of the closing. If a closing (*Sincerely yours,* for example) has more than one word, capitalize the first word only.

TIP

Take a look at these excerpts from texts, instant messages, tweets (140-character messages, which may soon increase to 280 characters), blogs or social media posts, and emails. Decide which message, if any, is most appropriate for the intended audience and the medium.

EXAMPLE

Q. Text to co-worker

    I.   meet Luigi's 8 PM ntk

    II.   Dinner at Luigi's 8 p.m.? Let me know asap.

    III. luigi's 8 rsvp

    IV. None

A. **II.** A text to a peer at work can be informal, but not too informal. It must also be understandable. Option II fulfills both of these standards, assuming the co-worker knows where Luigi's is located. The abbreviation *asap* ("as soon as possible") is standard, though it's usually capitalized. The other two texts aren't suitable for a business situation. Not only do they break too many rules (caps for *Luigi's,* for example), but neither includes a question mark. The person receiving the message might see it as an order, not a suggestion. The abbreviation *rsvp* is a standard way to ask for a reply, but option I's *ntk* (need to know) is less common and might be confusing.

1 blog post from cookbook reviewer

    I.   I cooked three chickens tonight, and I'm now on page 5567 of *How to Cook Everything.* It was terrible. Don't ever put a sardine near a chicken.

    II.   i cooked three chickens tonight and im now on p 5567 of How to Cook Everything. It was terible. Don't ever put a sardine near a chicken ever.

    III. 3 chix w/ sards tonight p 5567 *How Cook Everything* terrible

    IV. None

2 text to boss

    I.   Met client. Deal okay if shipping included. Your thoughts?

    II.   shp deal brAkr ok?

    III. The client has accepted the deal on the condition that all shipping costs are included in the price we quoted. I wonder if you would mind getting back to me, at your earliest convenience, so that I have some idea whether this stipulation is all right with you.

    IV. None

3 tweet to voters from lobbyist

I. No on #toothpastebill

II. no toothpaste bill #myteethRmine

III. Tell your representative to vote no on the bill to ban toothpaste. Defy the dental lobby!

IV. None

4 email to teacher

I. no hw cat 8 it better tmrw leo

II. Mr. Smarva, sorry, can't hand in my homework my cat ate it I'll do better tomorrow your friend Leo

III. cat 8 hw do btr 2mrw leo

IV. None

5 comment from archaeologist on a social media post discussing an excavation

I. The horizontal strips of some metallic substance and the marks of a crude pickax show that this was probably a prehistoric mine.

II. Horizontal strips of metal + pickax marks = prehistoric mine.

III. I ascertain from the evidence that the site was a prehistoric mine. The aforementioned evidence (the horizontal strips of some metallic substance and the marks of a crude pickax) is incontrovertible.

IV. None

6 instant-message to a person interviewing for a position at your firm

I. can't come now maybe later

II. not now, maybe L8R

III. cannot come now maybe later

IV. None

7 text to close friend

I. I will have to get back to you. The professor just arrived. I will text again after the class ends.

II. prof l8r

III. prof here ttyl

IV. None

8 email to relative

I. Hi, Grandpa. The speaker was great. Thanks for arranging her visit.

Best, Alice

II. Grandpa the speaker great thanks for arranging

III. great speaker thx

IV. None

9   post on a music blog

    I.   BB's last set = epic fail where do they find those notes?

    II. Bl Bk's last set didn't work. Were do thA find those notes?

    III. Blue Beak's last set was screechy. Seriously, where do they find those notes?

    IV. None

10   tweet to high school students from the class president

    I.   tlion 9s only

    II. #library is 9s only

    III. Library is open now for 9th graders only!

    IV. None

Shortening Your Message

A character in Shakespeare's *Hamlet* proclaims that "brevity is the soul of wit." It's also the soul of most communication these days. Maybe because electronic media zings words back and forth quickly, readers expect you to get to the point fast. Whatever the reason, you need to know how to say more with fewer words when you text, send an instant message, or tweet (send a message that's 140 or 280 characters long).

WARNING

In this section I explain how to cut away elements of Standard English. Before you cut, be sure to consider the identity of the person reading your message. The preceding section, "Knowing Your Audience: The Right Writing for the Right Situation," explains when you can break grammar rules. This section concentrates on how a message may be shortened.

Here are some guidelines for the chopping block:

» **Consider dropping the subject.** If I type "attended meeting," you can probably figure out that *I* attended the meeting. If someone else went, you should include the name ("Bob attended meeting") unless the reader knows whom you're discussing.

» **You can usually drop articles.** *A, an,* and *the* are seldom important.

» **Use abbreviations, but carefully.** Some abbreviations (such as *FYI* for "for your information") are commonly known, but others (*F2F* for "face to face") may mystify readers who don't frequent social-networking sites. Think about your reader as you type an abbreviation. When in doubt, write the whole word.

» **Never drop punctuation that adds meaning.** If you type, "Deal?" you're asking someone to commit. "Deal" either conveys information ("I agree to your terms") or gives a command ("deal with it"). The question mark makes a difference.

I sharpened my knife and whittled down these messages. Which shortenings, if any, are short but understandable? Assume that you're writing to a co-worker or friend and that your goals are accuracy, clarity, and brevity.

Q. I don't know what you mean about Lola.

    I. What about Lola?

    II. Lola?

    III. Lola meaning?

A. **I.** If you're writing to a friend who understands you well and you're talking about a comment you just heard or read, option II or III may be enough. I prefer option I because it's clear even if the person receiving the message hasn't been paying strict attention.

11 You should know that Lola is in jail and needs ten thousand dollars for bail money. She was arrested for driving without a license. She needs your help.

    I. 10K L in jail help

    II. Lola jail 10000! DWL help

    III. FYI: Lola in jail. Driving w/o a license. Needs $10K bail. Help!

12 Her lawyer is hopeful that Lola will be sentenced to probation and community service.

    I. Hope prob and cs

    II. Lawyer hopeful for probation + community service.

    III. sentence probation and community serv fingers Xd lawyer

13 Lulu will visit Lola as soon as possible. Lulu will probably arrive at the jail around noon.

    I. 12 L to L

    II. Lulu > Lola asap 12?

    III. Lulu to visit Lola asap, probably 12 p.m.

14 The bad news for Lola is that the judge, Larry Saunders, was once flattened by a motorcycle. He's bitter and will probably give Lola the maximum penalty because she was riding a motorcycle when she was arrested.

    I. Judge Saunders bad news for Lola b/c bitter about motorcycles after his own accident. Top penalty probable for L's motorcycle arrest.

    II. JS = bad news bitter cycles top penalty

    III. Judge S not good motorcycle accident jail ∧

15 Lola claimed that her license had been shredded when she washed her jeans.

    I. Lola claimed license shredded in wash.

    II. License shredded wash

    III. Claimed license shredded in washing machine.

16 Will you attend the press conference when Lola is released?

    I. Press conference?

    II. Attend press conference on release?

    III. You going to press conference on L's release?

Powering Up Your Presentation Slides

Do you spend your days dodging bullets? I'm not talking about target practice but rather the little round dots, stars, or checkmarks that create lists in PowerPoint-style presentation slides and in other spots (memos, for example). If you are dodging bullets, it may be because you're not sure what to capitalize and where to place punctuation marks. To help you, here are some bullet points on bullet points:

>> **A title or introductory sentence should precede every list.** Notice that *this* list is set up by a sentence *(To help you, here are some bullet points on bullet points).*

>> **Titles should be centered and capitalized.** The rules for capitals are in Chapter 13. Don't place quotation marks around a centered title. Also, avoid full-sentence titles.

>> **Introductory sentences, if complete, may end with a colon.** A colon (one dot on top of another) sets up this bulleted list. Don't place a colon in a partial sentence, such as "Projected earnings for 2018 are." Omit punctuation entirely after that sort of introduction.

>> **If the bullet point is a complete sentence, capitalize the first word and use an endmark (period, question mark, exclamation point).** The bullet points in this list are complete sentences, so they follow this rule.

>> **If the bullet point isn't a complete sentence, don't capitalize the first word or use an endmark.** This sort of list often follows an introductory statement that isn't a complete sentence.

>> **Grammatically, every bullet point should match.** If one bullet point is a complete sentence, all the bullet points should be complete sentences. Or, all the bullet points may be phrases. In grammar terms, the items should be *parallel*. I discuss parallel structure in detail in Chapter 18.

EXAMPLE

Time to target some bullet points. Below are some sample "slides" from a presentation, without capital letters or punctuation. Underneath each slide is a list of corrections. Select all the corrections needed to create a grammatically correct slide.

Q.

parakeet hobbies

- bowling

- they like to toss seeds

- hang-gliding

I. Capitalize *Parakeet*.

II. Capitalize *Hobbies*.

III. Change second bullet to *toss seeds*.

IV. Change second bullet to *seed-tossing*.

A. **I, II, IV.** Capitalize both words of the title. The second bullet doesn't match the other two. Of the two possible changes, IV is better because it matches the *-ing* verb form of the other two bullets.

parakeets need the following items for bowling

- three-toed bowling shoes

- beak-adapted bowling balls

- featherweight pins

I. Capitalize *Parakeets*.

II. Place a comma at the end of the first line of the slide.

III. Place a colon at the end of the first line of the slide.

IV. Place a period at the end of each bullet point.

18

> the best-selling bowling shoes for parakeets have
>
> - they have room for overgrown claws
> - most are in brightly colors
> - many include a complimentary seed stick
> - they have clips rather than laces

I. Capitalize *The.*

II. Place a colon at the end of the first line.

III. Place a period at the end of each bullet point.

IV. Change bullet points to *overgrown claws, bright colors, complimentary seed stic*k, and *clips rather than laces.*

19

> most prominent parakeet bowlers are
>
> - able to think on their feet (claws)
> - sponsored by well-known pet food companies
> - active only for five or six years

I. Capitalize *Most.*

II. Place a colon after *are.*

III. Capitalize the first word of each bullet point.

IV. Place a period at the end of each bullet point.

> **history of parakeet bowling**
>
> - the sport began in the 15th century
>
> - early bowlers used apples to knock down corn stalks
>
> - first professional tour — 1932

I.   Capitalize every word in the title except for *of*.

II. Capitalize the first word in each bullet point.

III. Place a period at the end of each bullet point.

IV. Change the last bullet point to *The first professional tour took place in 1932.*

Calling All Overachievers: Extra Practice with Electronic Media

EXAMPLE

The employee who created the slide presentation in the following figure slept through every single grammar lesson she ever had. Now it's up to you to correct her errors. You should find ten mistakes.

> **Best careers for Parakeets; paper Shredder**
>
> - Every bird earns a good salary
>
> - excellent working conditions
>
> - Each bird has an assistant and
>
> - the veterinary insurance plan has a low deductible
>
> - Seed breaks once an hour.

Answers to Electronic Media Problems

New forms of communication often bring new rules. See if you understand the grammar of electronic media by checking your answers here.

(1) **I.** Option II is filled with problems. No matter who your reader is, you should avoid incorrect spelling (*terible*). Also, why lowercase the personal pronoun *I?* It's not much harder or time-consuming to add an apostrophe to *I'm*. Options III is worse, as it includes abbreviations and shortened words (*chix*) that would be better for a text to a friend than a post on a website. Option I obeys the rules of standard English — not a bad idea for someone who wants to be taken seriously as a reviewer.

(2) **I.** You don't have to write all the information in option III, which is far too wordy for a text. By the time the boss finishes reading those unnecessary words, the client may have moved to another supplier in sheer frustration. All the same ideas come through in option I, which is shorter, and though not formal, stays close enough to Standard English to please a boss. Option II is far too informal for a message to someone with more power than you (*brAkr* isn't standard, for example).

(3) **III.** The meaning as expressed in option III is clear, and because the lobbyist wants to convince voters that the ideas are the product of an intelligent being, proper grammar and spelling are a plus. The other two are vague and more suited for a community that expects informality. The hashtags (the # symbols) are intended to rally like-minded readers to join together, but it's hard to gather support for an ill-defined cause.

(4) **IV.** If Leo seriously wants to be excused for missing a homework assignment, he should unearth every bit of grammar knowledge he has, because the teacher is an Authority Figure and deserves standard English.

(5) **I.** Option III is far too wordy and stuffy, for social media and for anywhere else! Option II is too informal. The plus and equal signs don't belong in a post about archeology from someone who wants the respect due to a professional in that field.

(6) **IV.** Writing in a business setting should be more formal than these three options. Furthermore, if you're postponing an interview, courtesy demands a reason (the building's on fire, you have TB, a comet's about to strike earth — *something*).

(7) **III.** Option I isn't wrong, exactly, but a close friend doesn't need complete and proper sentences, especially when the professor has arrived and you're supposed to be ready for class. Your peers probably understand words you shortened, especially an abbreviation such as *ttyl* ("talk to you later") that frequently appears in texts and informal posts on social media. Option II is a little too vague.

(8) **I.** In option I, the punctuation is correct, and the sentences make sense. Grandpa will be proud. The others may be acceptable (grandparents tend to give their grandchildren a lot of leeway), but it's not particularly polite to leave your best grammar on the shelf when writing to someone older than you, especially when that person has done you a favor.

(9) **III.** The tone of option III is conversational, but that's fine in a blog post. The other options are better suited to a friend-to-friend text.

10) III. The senior class president should come across as friendly, but a bit serious also. Not to mention clear! A tweet to teens can include all sorts of abbreviations. But *tlion*, which appears in option I, is an abbreviation I made up. Inside my head. Just me! It means "the library is open now." Option II doesn't include all the information. Only option III has a clear meaning and sounds friendly but informal.

11) III. Options I and II have cut out too much. Did Lola steal $10,000? Could be, the way these texts read. Option III clarifies the situation. The abbreviation *FYI* ("for your information") is standard, as is *w/o* ("without") and *K* ("thousand"). The last sentence is clearly a plea for bail money.

12) II. Option II gets the job done. I wouldn't mind cutting the *for*, but with that word the message sounds a little more respectable (not like Lola). The plus sign could also be an ampersand (&) or the word *and*. Options I and III aren't clear. What's *cs? Prob?* I made up the abbreviations, so anyone receiving this message isn't likely to understand. The role of the lawyer is also murky in the too-short versions.

13) III. Option III is short, but not too short. The standard abbreviation for "as soon as possible" is *ASAP*, but you don't really need the capital letters here. You could also cut *p.m.* from the message if you wish, as it's unlikely that a jail would allow visitors at midnight. Option I is vague, and II uses the "greater than" math symbol in an attempt to show that Lulu's going to Lola. Too far out for clarity!

14) I. Option I works. The abbreviation *b/c* ("because") is standard, though you wouldn't use it for formal writing. Notice that I deleted the verbs because the meaning comes through without them. I also substituted *top penalty probable* for the longer *will probably give Lola the maximum penalty*. The other options need CIA code-breakers. What are *bitter cycles?* Option I doesn't tell you. Did Lola or the judge have an accident? You can't tell from option III.

15) I. Isn't it fun to put your sentences on a diet? (Much more enjoyable than the other sort of diet.) In option I, you have all the information you need at half the length. Option II has shed too many words. Option III is tempting, and if you know your reader really well, it might be fine. Because three people are involved in the story (the judge, Lola, and the texter), I prefer option I, which names Lola.

16) III. The shorter options don't work because three people (the judge, Lola, and the texter) are possibilities. Only III supplies enough words to clarify the situation.

17) I and III. Because the introductory statement is a complete sentence, it should begin with a capital letter (option I) and end with a colon, which indicates that a list follows (option III). A comma shouldn't introduce a bulleted list. The bullet points aren't complete sentences, so no periods are necessary.

18) I, IV. The first word of the introductory statement needs a capital letter (option I). No punctuation follows *have* because the statement isn't a complete sentence (options II and III). In the original list each item is a complete sentence, so they don't combine well with the introductory statement. *The best bowling shoes for parakeets have they have room . . .* nope, I don't think so. The bullets should be *room for overgrown claws, bright colors, complimentary seed sticks,* and *clips rather than laces* (option IV).

19 **I.** Did I catch you with this one? No punctuation is needed in the first line because *are* doesn't complete the introductory sentence. Nor should you capitalize any of the bullet points, as they complete the sentence begun by the introductory statement. Option IV is tempting, but you've got three half sentences, one in each bullet point, all connected to the introductory line. Placing three periods doesn't make sense. Some grammarians recommend a semicolon after each bullet point, with a period after the last. This is somewhat stuffy. My recommendation is no punctuation at all after the bullet points. The only change is a capital *M* for the first word in the introductory sentence (option I).

20 **I, II, III, IV.** This slide has a title, and titles need capital letters. The first two bullet points are complete sentences, so the third should match.

Here are the answers to the "Overachievers" section:

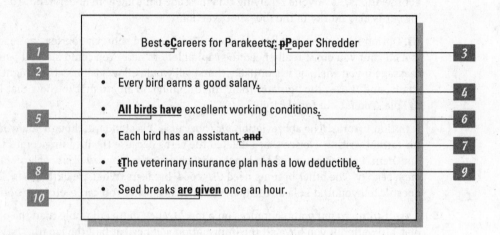

1 Capitalize the important words in a title. (See Chapter 13 for details.)

2 Separate a title from a subtitle with a colon (:).

3 Capitalize the first word of a subtitle.

4 Always place an endmark after a full-sentence bullet point; here a period is best.

5 The first bullet point is a complete sentence, so all the bullet points should also be complete sentences. (Alternate correction: Change all the bullet points to phrases.)

6 A complete sentence that makes a statement ends with a period.

7 One bullet point should not continue on to the next. Delete *and* and place a period at the end of this sentence.

8 This bullet point is a complete sentence, so it should begin with a capital letter.

9 This complete sentence needs an endmark — specifically, a period.

10 The original bullet point was not a complete sentence. To preserve uniformity, change this bullet point to a complete sentence by adding a verb.

4

Going Above and Beyond: The Finer Points of Grammar and Style

Chapter **15**

Going for the Gold: The Finer Points of Verb Usage

I f a grammar Olympics took place every four years, mastering the material in this chapter would give you a shot at a gold medal in verb usage. You can speak and write reasonably well without this knowledge, but you'll be on a much higher level if you have it. Think of the difference between the track times of a high-school champ and those of an Olympic sprinter. Which would you rather have? In this chapter I explain voice (active or passive), mood (yes, verbs have moods), and strength (finding verbs that give much more information than, for example, *be* or *have*).

Voicing an Opinion: Active and Passive Verbs

In the world of grammar, verbs have a *voice* — either *active* or *passive*. With *active voice*, the subject performs the action or is in the state of being expressed by the verb: "Millie *cracked* the priceless vase." (*cracked* = active-voice verb) With *passive voice*, the subject receives the action: "The priceless vase *was cracked*." (*was cracked* = passive-voice verb) Many writers, including me, hold the opinion that active voice is often better than passive. Why? Sometimes active voice gives you more information. If your company insured the *priceless vase* mentioned in the example sentence, you probably want to know who did the cracking, and the active-voice sentence tells you. True, you could tack on *by Millie* after the passive-voice verb, but the resulting sentence sounds a bit awkward.

TIP

Although I'm in favor of active voice, passive does have its uses. Sometimes you don't know who performed the action, and sometimes you don't care: "The winning lottery numbers *were drawn* last night." In that sentence, the focus is on the lottery, not on the person pulling numbered balls out of a container.

EXAMPLE

Q. Label the underlined verb forms as *active voice* (AV) or *passive voice* (PV).

Charles <u>arrived</u> three hours after curfew. He <u>was grounded</u> for three weeks.

A. **arrived (AV), was grounded (PV).** *Charles* is the subject. Because he performs the action in the first sentence *(Charles arrived)*, that verb is in active voice. In the second sentence, someone else grounded him. The subject, *Charles*, receives the action. *Was grounded* is in passive voice.

1. The job opening <u>was posted</u> on a networking site.

2. About a thousand resumes <u>were emailed</u> within an hour.

3. When Pete first <u>heard</u> about the position the day after it <u>was announced</u>, he <u>was</u> already too late.

4. The job <u>had been given</u> to someone else.

5. Pete <u>set</u> an alert on his computer. Now, when resumes <u>are requested</u> for someone with a degree in philosophy, Pete <u>is informed</u> immediately.

6. Philosophers <u>have</u> a high unemployment rate, and Pete <u>must apply</u> for every position he <u>can find</u>.

7. "Only so many burgers <u>can be flipped</u> before boredom <u>sets</u> in," <u>explained</u> Pete.

8. Pete <u>has been given</u> free room and board by friends and relatives for the last year, but they <u>are losing</u> patience with him.

9. Lola <u>offered</u> free tattoo-training, but Pete <u>refused.</u>

10. "I <u>think</u> for a living," he <u>declared</u>.

Now try your hand at changing these passive-voice sentences to active voice. To keep you on your toes, I tucked in a couple where no change is possible.

EXAMPLE

Q. The score was kept by Roger throughout the season.

A. **Roger kept score throughout the season.** In the original, *score* receives the action of the verb, *was kept*. In the new version, *Roger* performs the action of scoring.

11 The ball was hit out of the park by the home team 562 times.

_____

12 Most balls were retrieved by fans and kept as cherished souvenirs.

_____

13 One baseball, though, wasn't found until more than a year after it was hit.

_____

14 It was placed by the team groundskeeper in a glass case in the locker room and labeled "the one that almost got away."

_____

15 According to Joe Smokey, the owner, fans are allowed to see the display only during the off-season.

_____

16 When outsiders were first invited to the locker room, objections were filed with the players' union.

_____

17 After the union's complaint was read by the owner, visits were strictly limited.

_____

18 The coach told the attendant to lock the locker room when players were inside.

_____

19 Some players were not pleased by the new policy.

_____

20 Their friends and family were barred also!

_____

In the Mood: Selecting the Right Verb for All Sorts of Sentences

Verbs have mood swings. One minute they're indicative, the just-the-facts sort of verb. ("The dishes are dirty. No one has washed them. Little colonies of mold grew all over the sink.") Then they're issuing orders in imperative mood. ("Load the dishwasher. Stop whining. Don't think your allowance is off limits!") Sometimes, a subjunctive mood pops up. ("If I were rich enough to hire a maid, I wouldn't ask for help. I'm not a millionaire, so get moving now!")

You don't need to know the grammatical terms; you just need to understand what mood is correct in a particular sentence. Never fear. In this section, I take you through all three moods, with a little extra attention on the subjunctive, which is the one most likely to trip you up and also to appear on standardized exams.

Indicating facts: Indicative mood

Just about everything I *say* about verbs in this book actually *applies* to indicative verbs, which, as the name implies, *indicate* facts. Indicative mood *is* the one you *use* automatically, stating action or being in any tense and for any person. *Do* you *want* to see some samples of indicative verbs? No problem. Every verb in this paragraph *is* in indicative mood. I *have placed* all the verbs in italics so you *can locate* them easily.

Indicative verbs change according to the time period you're talking about (the *tense*) and, at times, according to the person doing the action. I cover the basics of verb use in Chapters 4 and 5.

EXAMPLE

If you're in the mood, circle the indicative verb that works best in each of the following sentences. The verb choices are in parentheses.

Q. Mr. Adams (holds/held) a performance review every June.

A. **holds.** Both choices are indicative, but the present tense works better. The clue is the expression *every June*.

21 Each employee (is/was) summoned annually to Adams' office for what he calls "a little chat."

22 All the workers (know/will know) that the "chat" is all on Adams' side.

23 Adams (likes/like) to discuss baseball, the economy, and the reasons no one (will/would) receive a raise.

24 "(Is/Was) business good these days?" he always says.

25 He always (mentions/will mention) that he may have to make personal sacrifices to save the company.

26 Sacrifices! He (means/meant) that he (earns/will earn) only a million instead of two million next year!

Issuing commands: Imperative mood

The command, also known as the imperative mood, is fairly easy to work with because an imperative verb is the same whether you're talking to one person or 20, to a peasant or to a queen. The command form is simply the infinitive minus the *to*. In other words, the unchanged, plain form of the verb. ("*Stop* sniveling, Henry. *Pull* yourself together and *meet* your new in-laws." The command-form verbs are *stop, pull,* and *meet.*) Negative commands are slightly different. They take the infinitive-minus-*to* and add *do not*. ("*Do not mention* our engagement. *Do not let them find* out we're getting married!" *Do not mention* and *do not let* are negative commands.)

EXAMPLE

Fill in the blanks with commands for poor Henry, who is meeting his prospective in-laws. The base verb you're working with appears in parentheses at the end of each sentence.

Q. _____ quietly on the couch, Henry, while I fetch Daddy. *(to sit)*

A. **Sit.** The command is formed by dropping the *to* from the infinitive.

27 Henry, _____ my lead during the conversation. *(to follow)*

28 If Mom talks about Paris, _____ your head and _____ _____ interested. *(to nod, to look)*

29 Dad hates fake accents, so _____ French. *(to speak, negative command)*

30 _____ them to show you slides of last year's trip to Normandy. *(to ask)*

31 _____ asleep during the slide show, if you can help it! *(to fall, negative command)*

32 _____ some of Mom's potato salad, even if it's warm. *(to eat)*

33 _____ about unrefrigerated mayonnaise and the risk of food poisoning. *(to talk, negative command)*

34 When she ignores you and serves the potato salad anyway, just _____ an appointment with your doctor and _____ quiet. *(to make, to keep)*

Telling lies: Subjunctive mood

The subjunctive is a very big deal in some languages; whole months were devoted to it in my college Spanish class. Fortunately for you, in English the subjunctive pops up only rarely, mostly in "condition-contrary-to-fact" sentences. *Condition-contrary-to-fact* means that you're talking about something that isn't true. ("If I *were* famous, I would wear sunglasses to hide my identity." The verb *were* is subjunctive. "*Had* I *known* the secret password, I would have passed the bouncer's test and entered the club." The verb *had known* is subjunctive.)

Notice that the subjunctive changes some of the usual forms. In indicative, the pronoun *I* is paired with *was*. The switch to *were* in the first sample sentence tells you that you're in contrary-to-fact land. In the second sample sentence, the *had* doesn't do its usual indicative job, which is to place events earlier in the past than other past-tense events. (See Chapter 4 for more details on this use of *had*.) Instead, in a subjunctive sentence the *had* means that I didn't know the secret password, and I didn't socialize with sports stars and supermodels.

TIP Condition-contrary-to-fact sentences always feature a *would* form of the verb. In Standard English, the *would* form never appears in the part of the sentence that is untrue. Don't say, "If I would have known . . ." when you didn't know. Say, "If I had known, I would have . . ."

EXAMPLE Write the correct verb in the blank for each exercise in this section. The verb you're working with appears in parentheses after each sentence. Just to keep you honest, I tucked in a few sentences that don't require subjunctive. Keep your eyes open.

Q. If Ellen _____ for her turn at the wheel, she wouldn't have wrapped her car around that telephone pole. *(to prepare)*

A. **had prepared.** The *had* creates a subjunctive here, because Ellen didn't prepare for her road test. Instead, she went to a drive-in movie, as a passenger.

35 If the examiner _____ an appointment available in late afternoon, Ellen would have signed up for that slot immediately. *(to make)*

36 The test would have gone better if Ellen _____ a morning person. *(to be)*

37 "If it _____," explained the instructor, "you will be required to take the test as soon as the roads are plowed." *(to snow)*

38 If the snow plow _____ the entire route, Ellen would have passed. *(to cover)*

39 Unfortunately, the supervisor of the snow-removal crew _____ the highways cleaned first. *(to want)*

40 Terrified of ice, Ellen _____ to postpone her test. *(to try)*

41 If he _____, Ellen would have taken the test on a sunny, dry day. *(to refuse, negative form)*

42 If Ellen _____ about the examiner, the motor vehicle department would have investigated. *(to complain)*

43 If an examiner _____ unfair, the motor vehicle department schedules another test. *(to be)*

44 The department policy is that if there _____ a valid complaint, they dismiss the examiner promptly. *(to be)*

45 If Ellen _____ the test five times already, she would have been more cheerful about her grade. *(to take, negative form)*

Spicing Up Sentences by Adding Interesting Verbs

Say, walk, be, have — nothing is wrong with these verbs except that (excuse me for a moment while I yawn) they're a bit boring. So are many other, used-all-the-time verbs. Wouldn't it be more fun to spice up a sentence occasionally with a more specific or unusual verb? Take a look:

> BORING VERSION: Nina said, "I walked out when the argument started."

> INTERESTING VERSION 1: Nina sighed, "I stomped out when the argument started."

> INTERESTING VERSION 2: Nina confided, "I slipped out when the argument started."

As you see, the new verbs (*sighed* and *stomped* in 1, *confided* and *slipped* in 2) add shades of meaning to the original.

EXAMPLE

Try adding a little spice to these sentences. After each sentence, a number of verbs appear. Choose any that could substitute for the underlined verb in the original. Be sure that your choice fits the context of the sentence.

Q. Max was angry when he <u>walked</u> into the store.

 I. strolled

 II. ambled

 III. charged

A. **III.** If Max is angry, he's not going to "move slowly without purpose," the definition of *stroll* and *amble*. *Charge* (to move quickly and agressively) fits here.

46 "I want my money back," <u>said</u> Max, his temper rising by the minute.

 I. screamed

 II. declared

 III. whispered

47 He defiantly <u>sat in</u> the chair in front of the information desk.

 I. plopped on

 II. eased into

 III. sank into

48 With menace in his eyes, Max <u>looked</u> at the clerk.

 I. glanced

 II. glared

 III. smiled

49 The clerk <u>was nervous</u>.

    I. trembled

    II. contemplated

    III. quivered

50 Max <u>looked at</u> the clerk for two minutes.

    I. examined

    II. visualized

    III. scrutinized

51 Ashamed at his tantrum, Max <u>said</u>, "I'm sorry I scared you."

    I. mentioned

    II. commented

    III. whispered

52 "That's all right, sir," the clerk <u>said to</u> Max.

    I. commanded

    II. directed

    III. reassured

Calling All Overachievers: Extra Practice with Voice and Mood

If you're a master at voice (not opera or yodeling, but passive or active) and mood (not cranky or ready to drop an atomic bomb but indicative, imperative, and subjunctive), this memo will be easy to correct. Check the underlined portions of the following memo. If they're correct, write "C." If they're incorrect, reword them. *Note:* You may have to change more than the underlined words, or rearrange some words, when you make a correction.

From: Ms. Bell, Coffee-Break Coordinator

To: Ms. Schwartz, Department Head

Re: Coffee-Break Control

1 As **was known by you**, I **were** now in charge of implementing the new **2** directive about coffee breaks. A coffee-residue test **will be given** by me **3** once a week at a time when coffee-sipping **were not authorized.** **4** According to the policy, if a worker **were to test** positive, the worker will **5** "donate" a pound of coffee to the break room.

The negative reaction of the workers **has been reported** to me by the **6** union representative. If they **were** happy, they would have written a **7** letter expressing support. Unfortunately, the letter **sent from** the union **8** was somewhat nasty. **Would you have known** about the reaction before **9** creating the new policy, you would have reconsidered. If the stains resulting from the workers' throwing hot beverages at me remain, I hope **to have the dry-cleaning bill covered by you**. **10**

Answers to Voice and Mood Problems

Feeling active? Moody? However you feel, it's time to check your answers.

1. **was posted (PV).** The *job opening* didn't do the posting. It received the action of the verb, *was posted,* so it's passive.

2. **were emailed (PV).** The *resumes* (subject) didn't do the emailing. Whoever sent them did. *Were emailed* is a passive-voice verb.

3. **heard (AV), was announced (PV), was (AV).** The subject of *heard* is *Pete,* who performs the action. *Heard* is in active voice. *It* is the subject of *was announced,* but *it* didn't do any announcing. *It* receives the action and is a passive-voice verb. *He* is the subject of *was,* an active-voice verb.

4. **had been given (PV).** The subject is *job,* which didn't perform the action of giving. The verb is in passive voice.

5. **set (AV), are requested (PV), is informed (PV).** *Pete* is the subject in the first sentence, and *Pete set.* Therefore, *set* is an active-voice verb. In the second sentence, the subject is *resumes* and the verb is *are requested.* The resumes don't perform the action, so the verb is passive. Next up, in the same sentence, is the subject-verb combo *Pete is informed.* Because the action happens to the subject, the verb *is informed* is passive too.

6. **have (AV), must apply (AV), can find (AV).** The first subject-verb pair is *Philosophers have.* *Philosophers* are the ones who *have,* so this is an active-voice verb. Next you have *Pete must apply.* *Pete* is doing the applying, so the verb is in active voice. Finally, *he can find* creates another active-voice situation because *he* does the action expressed by *can find.*

7. **can be flipped (PV), sets(AV), explained (AV).** Three subject-verb pairs appear here: *burgers can be flipped, boredom sets,* and *explained Pete.* The first is passive because the flipping happens to the *burgers.* The next pair contains an active-voice verb because the *boredom* does the setting. The last pair reverses the usual subject-verb order, but that doesn't matter. This is an active-voice verb because the subject, *Pete,* does the action, *explained.*

8. **has been given (PV), are losing (AV).** The subject, *Pete,* isn't giving. Instead, he's receiving, so *has been given* is in passive voice. The second pair has an active-voice verb because *they* are doing the action (*losing*).

9. **offered (AV), refused (AV).** Two active-voice verbs here, because Lola did the offering and Pete did the refusing.

10. **think (AV), declared (AV).** You may have a had time thinking that *think* is in active voice, but it is because the subject, *I,* does the thinking. The subject of *declared, he,* also does the action, so *declared* is also an active-voice verb.

11. **The home team hit the ball out of the park 562 times.** Instead of the passive verb *was hit,* this revised sentence has an active-voice verb, *hit.*

12. **Fans retrieved and kept most balls as cherished souvenirs.** Instead of the passive verbs *were retrieved* and [*were*] *kept,* you have the active verbs *retrieved* and *kept.*

13. **No change.** You don't know who found the baseball, and the identity of the finder isn't important. Nor do you know who hit the ball. The passive verbs *wasn't found* and *was hit* work fine here.

14 The team groundskeeper placed it in a glass case in the locker room and labeled it "the one that almost got away." The groundskeeper did the work (*placed, labeled*), and this active-voice sentence gives him the credit.

15 Joe Smokey, the owner, allows fans to see the display only during the off-season. Instead of the passive *are allowed*, you have the active *Joe Smokey allows*.

16 When the owner first invited outsiders to the locker room, players filed objections with their union. Strictly speaking, the original sentence doesn't tell you who invited outsiders, but *the owner* is a good guess. (You could also write *Joe first invited.*) If you left that part of the sentence unchanged, though, count yourself right. The second part is easier because who else would file an objection with the players' union but the players? The active-voice verbs in the new sentence are *invited* and *filed*.

17 After the owner read the union's complaint, he strictly limited visits. Passive verbs (*was read, were limited*) change to active (*read, limited*). *Joe* could easily substitute for *the owner,* if you wish.

18 No change. The verbs *told* and *were* are in active voice already.

19 The new policy did not please some players. The passive *were pleased* changes to the active *policy did not please*. Notice that the helping verb *did* helps create this negative statement. For more on helping verbs, turn to Chapter 2.

20 The policy barred their friends and family also! I wrote *the policy*, but if you substituted *Joe* or *the owner,* count yourself correct.

21 is. The sentence speaks of an ongoing situation, so present tense is best.

22 know. The workers have been through this "chat" many times, so the act of knowing isn't in the future but in the present.

23 likes, will. The present-tense form for talking about someone (*Adams,* in this sentence) is *likes*. The future-tense verb *will* explains that in the coming year, as always, employees will be shopping for bargains.

24 Is. The expression *these days* is a clue that you want a present-tense verb that talks about something or someone.

25 mentions. If an action *always* occurs, present tense is the best choice.

26 means, will earn. The boss is talking about the future (the clue is *next year*). The talking takes place in the present (so you want *means*), but the earning is in the future (hence, *will earn*).

27 follow. The command is formed by stripping the *to* from the infinitive.

28 nod, look. Drop the *to* and you're in charge, commanding poor Henry to act interested even if he's ready to call off the engagement rather than listen to one more story about French wine.

29 don't speak or do not speak. The negative command relies on *do* and *not*, as two words or as the contraction *don't*.

30 Ask. Poor Henry! He has to request boredom by dropping the *to* from the infinitive *to ask*.

31 Do not fall. Take *to* from the infinitive and add one *do* and *not* and you have a negative command.

32 Eat. Henry's in for a long evening, given the command *eat*, which is created by dropping *to* from the infinitive.

(33) **Don't talk** or **Do not talk.** The negative command needs *do* or it dies. You also have to add *not*, either separately or as part of *don't*.

(34) **make, keep.** Drop the *to* from each infinitive and you're in imperative mood.

(35) **had made.** The subjunctive *had made* is needed for this statement about available time slots because it's contrary to fact. No time slot was available in the afternoon.

(36) **were.** Ellen likes to sleep until midafternoon. As she's not a morning person, the subjunctive verb *were* expresses condition-contrary-to-fact. The verb *were* is better than *had been* because Ellen still *is* not a morning person, and *had been* implies that her grouchiness is in the past.

(37) **snows.** Surprise! This one isn't subjunctive. The instructor is talking about a possibility, not a condition that didn't occur. The normal indicative form, *snows,* is what you want.

(38) **had covered.** The plow didn't finish (the clue here is *would have passed*), so subjunctive is needed.

(39) **wanted.** No subjunctive is needed here. This is a factual statement that I threw in to see whether you were paying attention.

(40) **tried.** The indicative (the normal, everyday form) of *to try* in the past tense is *tried,* and is right for this simple statement.

(41) **had not refused.** The examiner stood firm: Take the test or die. Thus the first part of this sentence is condition-contrary-to-fact and calls for the subjunctive.

(42) **had complained.** Ellen said nothing, as revealed by the conditional *would have investigated* in the second part of the sentence. Subjunctive is the way to go!

(43) **is.** Did I get you here? The possibility expressed in the *if* portion of the sentence calls for a normal, indicative verb *(is)*. Stay away from subjunctive if the statement may be true.

(44) **is.** The first part of this sentence is not condition-contrary-to-fact. It expresses a possibility and thus calls for the normal, indicative verb *(is)*.

(45) **had not taken.** She has taken it five times, so the statement isn't true and needs a subjunctive verb.

(46) **I, II.** You know Max is angry, so *whispered,* option III, doesn't fit. The other two choices add an edge to Max's voice. The first *(screamed)* is more angry. The second, *declared,* is firm and powerful but less aggressive.

(47) **I.** If there's defiance, you don't want options II or III, which are somewhat timid synonyms for *sat. Plopped* can show physical exhaustion, but it also has an element of force in it, so it's a good fit.

(48) **II.** You've got *menace,* so *glared* works well here. *Smiled* is the opposite of what you want, and *glimpsed* is too casual.

(49) **I, III.** To show fear, you can select *trembled* or *quivered,* because both indicate that the clerk is shaking. *Contemplated* (looked thoughtfully) doesn't fit.

(50) **I, III.** Max doesn't have to *visualize* (see with his imagination) the clerk because he's actually looking at the clerk for two minutes. That's a long time, so options I and III, which both mean "analyze," are good substitutes.

51. **III.** Max is ashamed, so *whispered* is the best choice. *Mentioned* is too casual, as is *commented*.

52. **III.** The clerk has just told Max not to worry about the tantrum, so option III works best here.

Here are the answers to the "Overachievers" section:

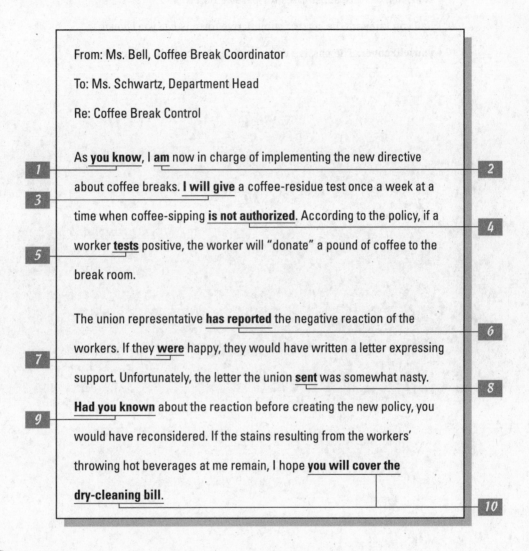

From: Ms. Bell, Coffee Break Coordinator

To: Ms. Schwartz, Department Head

Re: Coffee Break Control

As **you know**, I **am** now in charge of implementing the new directive about coffee breaks. **I will give** a coffee-residue test once a week at a time when coffee-sipping **is not authorized**. According to the policy, if a worker **tests** positive, the worker will "donate" a pound of coffee to the break room.

The union representative **has reported** the negative reaction of the workers. If they **were** happy, they would have written a letter expressing support. Unfortunately, the letter the union **sent** was somewhat nasty.

Had you known about the reaction before creating the new policy, you would have reconsidered. If the stains resulting from the workers' throwing hot beverages at me remain, I hope **you will cover the dry-cleaning bill**.

1 **you know.** The passive verb in the original becomes active in the revised memo.

2 **am.** No need for subjunctive here. The indicative works fine for a statement of fact.

3 **will give.** The passive verb changes to active.

4 **is not authorized.** No need for subjunctive mood here, because there's no condition contrary to fact. Nor can you easily change this passive verb to active. If you tried with something like "you did not authorize," that's fine.

5 **tests.** A positive test is a real possibility, not a condition contrary to fact, so plain indicative mood works here.

(6) **has reported.** Here, with a little rewording, the sentence becomes active, not passive.

(7) **correct.** They clearly aren't happy, so a condition contrary to fact exists, and a subjunctive verb is appropriate.

(8) **sent.** Active voice substitutes for passive here.

(9) **had you known.** The correct subjunctive form is *had you known.*

(10) **you will cover.** The passive voice changes to active in this correction.

Chapter 16

Identifying Clauses and Their Effects

C lauses are everywhere, and none of them wear red suits and travel with reindeer and a sled. A *clause* is a basic unit of expression, the fundamental structure that carries meaning in a sentence. Unless you rely on emoticons, you can't write without clauses. This chapter deals with clauses and their effect on a sentence: what makes sense alone, what needs a little extra help to express meaning, and how various types of clauses and their placement affect the meaning you convey. By the time you've completed this chapter, you'll be an expert in every type of clause.

Locating Clauses

Clauses are easy to find. Look for a matching subject-verb pair, and you have a clause. When I say "matching," I mean that the pair makes sense together in Standard English. *Bill is watching* makes a pair (*Bill* = subject, *is watching* = verb). *Bill watching* isn't a proper pair. Why? The verb is incomplete. To sum up: Where a matching subject-verb pair appears, so does a clause. Where one doesn't appear, no clause exists. (For more on matching subject-verb pairs, turn to Chapter 3.)

TIP

Occasionally a subject or a verb is understood to be part of the sentence but isn't actually present. For example:

> Go home. (The understood subject of the verb *go* is *you*.)

> While sleeping, I dreamed I was an astronaut. *(I* is the understood subject, *was* is an understood part of the verb *sleeping*.)

WARNING

Not every clause is a complete sentence. Check Chapter 3 for more information on complete sentences.

EXAMPLE

Before you can do anything with clauses, you have to know what they look like. Examine the underlined words. Some are clauses and some aren't. Identify the clauses with the letter "C."

Q. <u>Oh boy.</u> <u>Ella agreed to attend her fifteenth high-school reunion!</u> She resolved <u>to get a promotion</u>, a new wardrobe, and at least one new impressive hobby <u>before the class dinner</u>.

A. **Ella agreed to attend her fifteenth high-school reunion!** You've got a subject-verb pair here *(Ella agreed)*, so this one is a clause. The first underlined section *(Oh boy)* has neither a subject nor a verb. *To get a promotion* has no subject, and strictly speaking, the infinitive *to get* isn't a verb in this sentence. *Before the class dinner* lacks a subject verb pair. *Dinner* is a noun, and *class* is a description of the noun (an adjective, to be precise).

1. <u>Was the reunion scheduled for Labor Day weekend?</u> <u>Seriously?</u> <u>Meeting on a holiday!</u>

2. <u>Last week</u>, Ella, <u>who is very interested in gossip</u>, decided <u>to attend</u>.

3. <u>Coming from the other coast</u>, <u>Ella needs a hotel</u>, preferably <u>one with a pool</u>.

4. <u>If she were honest</u>, Ella would admit <u>that she's nervous</u>.

5. <u>To calm her nerves</u>, <u>Ella has begun yoga lessons</u>.

6. Her <u>downward-facing-reunion</u> posture is her best move, <u>which she practices for an hour a day</u>.

7. <u>Ella has also hired a dance instructor</u>, who promises to make Ella look <u>cool or, at a minimum, less nerdy</u>.

8. <u>Having studied ballet</u>, Ella believes <u>that today's dance moves will be easy to learn</u>.

9. <u>Wrong!</u> <u>Ella has two left feet</u>, <u>as her ballet teacher remarked</u>.

10. <u>To make a good impression on her former classmates</u>, <u>Ella will do almost anything</u>, but <u>she draws the line at dieting</u>. More to love, <u>she says</u>.

Sorting Independent and Subordinate Clauses

You can sort clauses into two categories: *independent* (it can stand on its own, making sense and forming a complete sentence) and *subordinate* (a clause that must rely on an independent clause in order to form a complete thought). Subordinate clauses are sometimes referred to as *dependent clauses.* Either term is correct. Check out these examples:

> Betsy checked her email. (independent clause)
>
> After she had read every tweet (subordinate clause)

Did you notice that the independent clause makes sense all by itself? It's a sentence. The subordinate clause just hangs there. A subordinate clause may give you more information about a noun or a verb, acting as a description. A subordinate clause may also play the role of a noun in the sentence, acting as a subject or object. No matter what job they do, subordinate clauses never sound complete. Only when you put a subordinate clause with an independent clause do you have a complete sentence:

> After she had read every tweet, Betsy checked her email.

TEST ALERT Does it matter whether a clause is independent or subordinate? Yes! Standardized tests often ask whether a sentence is complete or not, and at lease one independent clause must be present to fulfill this requirement. Pronoun case and punctuation also change at times depending upon the type of clause you're writing, and these topics are also popular with test writers. (For more information about case, check Chapter 6. To learn more about punctuation, see Chapter 11.) Also important — and popular with testers — is the proper use of subordinate clauses to tuck information into a sentence. For more on this topic, check out the next section, "Making Clauses Work Together."

EXAMPLE Independent or subordinate? Read the underlined words and label each "I" for independent or "S" for subordinate.

Q. Betsy stares at her phone <u>whenever she has a free moment</u>.

A. **Subordinate.** The underlined words don't form a complete thought, so this clause is subordinate. In case you're wondering, clauses that give information about time are often subordinate. This one explain when *Betsy stares.*

11. <u>The pocket for Betsy's phone has never been used</u> because Betsy never puts her phone away.

12. The last time <u>that Betsy left the house without her phone</u> was traumatic for her.

13. Sal, <u>who is Betsy's best friend</u>, told her that she must face her phone addiction.

14. <u>Betsy strongly denies having phone problems</u>, but Sal is not convinced.

15. <u>While Betsy was looking at her phone</u>, Sal removed Betsy's shoes.

(16) When Betsy stood up, <u>she finally noticed that her feet were bare</u>.

(17) Furious, Betsy grabbed Sal's phone, <u>which he had left on the table</u>.

(18) <u>Will Betsy and Sal's fight be resolved</u>, or will the phone feud continue?

Making Clauses Work Together

In grammar, the term *subordinate* or *dependent* doesn't refer to the poor slob who has to make coffee for the boss. Instead, this type of clause is the part of the sentence that, while still containing a subject and a verb, occupies a position of lesser importance in relation to the rest of the sentence. Subordinate clauses may fall at the beginning, middle, or end of the sentence. Here are some examples, with the subordinate clause in italics:

> The box, *which Jack was told never to open,* practically screamed, "Look inside!"

> *After he had pried up the lid,* Jack ran screaming down the hall.

> Jack is planning to repair *whatever was damaged.*

As you see, a subordinate clause embeds one idea in another, making your writing less choppy by eliminating a series of short sentences.

TIP

Generally, less important ideas belong in the subordinate clause, unless you're trying to be funny or to illuminate character by emphasizing something unimportant. Take a look at these two sentences:

> George, who was convicted of treason and is facing the death penalty, giggles a lot.

> George, who giggles a lot, was convicted of treason and is facing the death penalty.

I think everyone agrees that the conviction and punishment are more important than George's laughter. In the first example sentence, those ideas appear in a subordinate clause. Furthermore, the subordinate clause is surrounded by commas — punctuation that implies the information isn't necessary. (Chapter 11 explains this point.) The second example makes more sense because the crucial information appears in the independent clause. You can do without the giggling and still grasp the main idea.

EXAMPLE

Take a shot at using subordinate clauses to insert ideas. First you see two separate sentences and then three combinations. Which choices use subordinate clauses to combine ideas properly? Consider punctuation and grammar, as well as the placement of important ideas.

Q. Nadia's boss held a press conference. The boss issued a statement about "the incident."

    I.   Nadia's boss held a press conference, where he apologized for "the incident."

    II. Nadia's boss, who held a press conference, apologized for "the incident."

    III. Nadia's boss held a press conference, with "the incident" being apologized for.

A. **I, II.** Both I and II contain all the information of the original. In option I, *where he issued a statement about "the incident"* is a subordinate clause. In option II, *who held a press conference* is a subordinate clause. Both choices work in different circumstances. Option I emphasizes the press conference. You'd write this way if the boss's willingness to face the press is the main idea. Option II emphasizes the apology, not where it was issued. Option III doesn't have a subordinate clause, just a rather clumsy prepositional phrase, *with "the incident" being apologized for.*

19 Joseph Schmo is a prize-winning reporter. He discovered the scheme to hack every social media account in the Midwest.

   I. Joe Schmo, who is a prize-winning reporter, discovered the scheme to hack every social media account in the Midwest.

   II. Joe Schmo, who discovered the scheme to hack every social media account in the Midwest, is a prize-winning reporter.

   III. Joe Schmo discovered the scheme to hack every social media account in the Midwest, and he is a prize-winning reporter.

20 The boss asked Joe to sit down and be quiet. Joe refused. He was still looking for information about "the incident."

   I. Joe is still looking for information about "the incident," and he refused the boss, who asked him to sit down and be quiet.

   II. Joe refused the boss, asking him to sit down and be quiet, because he is still looking for information about "the incident."

   III. Although the boss asked Joe to sit down and be quiet, Joe refused, as he is still looking for information about "the incident."

21 The CIA became interested in the case. The agency sent several agents to investigate.

   I. The CIA, being interested, sent several agents to investigate the case.

   II. The CIA, which became interested in the case, sent several agents to investigate.

   III. Sending several agents, the CIA became interested and investigated.

22 Nadia didn't want to talk to the agents. Her boss said that her job was in jeopardy.

   I. Nadia, who didn't want to talk to the agents, her job was in jeopardy the boss said.

   II. Nadia didn't want to talk to the agents because her boss said her job was in jeopardy.

   III. Because her boss said her job was in jeopardy, Nadia didn't want to talk to the agents.

23 Nadia bought a bus ticket. She slipped out of the office.

   I. Nadia bought a bus ticket, then she slipped out of the office.

   II. Because Nadia slipped out of the office, she bought a bus ticket.

   III. When she slipped out of the office, Nadia bought a bus ticket.

24. The CIA may track her down. They will deal with her harshly.

    I.   If the CIA tracks her down, they will deal with her harshly.

    II. When the CIA will deal with her harshly, they will track her down.

    III. That the CIA will track her down and that they will deal with her harshly.

25. Nadia is away. The boss is trying to manage the news media.

    I.   Although Nadia is away, the boss is trying to manage the news media.

    II. While Nadia is away, the boss is trying to manage the news media.

    III. The boss is trying to manage the news media while Nadia is away.

26. Nadia has offered her story to an independent film company. The film company is tentatively interested.

    I.   Nadia has offered her story to an independent film company, which is tentatively interested.

    II. An independent film company, which is tentatively interested, was offered Nadia's story by her.

    III. Tentatively interested, Nadia offered her story to an independent film company.

27. She wrote a complete account of "the incident." Nadia put her manuscript in a box.

    I.   After she wrote a complete account of "the incident," Nadia put her manuscript in a box.

    II. Nadia put her manuscript in a box after she wrote a complete account of "the incident."

    III. She wrote a complete account of "the incident," Nadia put it in a box.

28. The box has been placed in a bank vault. The vault has a titanium door.

    I.   A bank vault with a titanium door has the box, which was placed in it.

    II. The box, which has been placed in a bank vault that has a titanium door.

    III. The box has been placed in a bank vault that has a titanium door.

29. Nadia's closest friends know the location of the box. Those people are in danger.

    I.   Nadia's closest friends, who know the location of the box, are in danger.

    II. That Nadia's closest friends know the location of the box puts them in danger.

    III. Nadia's closest friends, who are in danger, know the location of the box.

30. The film will come out next summer. Then the whole world will know about "the incident."

    I.   When the film comes out next summer, the whole world will know about "the incident."

    II. Because the film comes out next summer, the whole world will know about "the incident."

    III. The film will come out next summer, when the whole world will know about "the incident."

Answers to Clause Problems

Do clauses cause you problems? Check your answers to find out how well you understand clause-and-effect.

(1) **Was the reunion scheduled for Labor Day weekend?** This is a clause because it has a matching subject–verb pair, *reunion was scheduled.*

TIP

To understand the structure of a question, try turning it into a statement. The original becomes "The reunion was scheduled for Labor Day weekend." Now you can more easily pick out the subject–verb pair and see that you have a clause. The other underlined material lacks this essential pair.

(2) **who is very interested in gossip.** The subject is *who,* which matches the verb *is. Last week* has neither a subject nor a verb. *To attend* is an infinitive, not a verb in the sentence, and has no subject.

(3) **Ella needs a hotel.** The subject–verb pair is *Ella needs.* They match, so this is a clause. Did I catch you with *Coming from the other coast?* This one has no subject, either stated or implied, so it's not a clause.

(4) **If she were honest, that she's nervous.** This sentence actually has three clauses, but *Ella would admit* isn't underlined. Are you wondering where the verb is in the second answer? *She's* is short for *she is.*

(5) **Ella has begun yoga lessons.** The subject–verb pair is *Ella has begun.* The introductory statement in this sentence, *to calm her nerves,* isn't a clause because *to calm* is an infinitive, not a verb, and there's no subject.

(6) **which she practices for an hour a day.** Yup, this one has the pair *(she practices),* so this one's the clause.

(7) **Ella has also hired a dance instructor.** The pair here is *Ella has hired.* The second underlined potion lacks a subject–verb pair.

(8) **that today's dance moves will be easy to learn.** Did you find the pair? It's *moves* (subject) and *will be* (verb). The other underlined words have no subject–verb pair.

(9) **Ella has two left feet**, **as her ballet teacher remarked.** The pairs are *Ella has* and *teacher remarked.*

(10) **Ella will do almost anything, she draws the line at dieting, she says.** Three subject–verb pairs *(Ella will do, she draws, she says* = three clauses). Did you select the first underlined portion? The infinitive doesn't function as a verb, and it has no subject. Hence, it's not a clause.

(11) **Independent.** If you chop off the rest of the sentence, you still have a complete thought. The reason Betsy has an untouched pocket is interesting, but it doesn't have to appear in that sentence in order for the underlined words to make sense.

(12) **Subordinate.** When you start a clause with *that,* it's often subordinate, which is the case here. Say the underlined words. They're incomplete without the support of the rest of the sentence.

13) **Subordinate.** The underlined words would form an independent clause if they were asking a question, but they aren't. They're making a statement — an incomplete one. Therefore, you're looking at a subordinate clause.

14) **Independent.** Read the underlined words aloud. Do you hear the complete thought? This is an independent clause.

15) **Subordinate.** You have a time statement beginning with *while,* but that statement, all by itself, leaves you wondering. No doubt about it: This is a subordinate clause.

16) **Independent.** The underlined words make sense, so you have an independent clause.

17) **Subordinate.** The word *which,* when it isn't part of a question, generally signals a subordinate clause.

18) **Independent.** This one is a little tricky. You have only one question mark, but bring out your reading comprehension skills. Do you see that the sentence asks two separate questions? Question one is *Will Betsy and Sal's fight be resolved?* Question two is *will the phone feud continue?* Both parts of the sentence are independent clauses.

19) **I.** The subordinate clause in option I lies between the commas. Unless you're defending the integrity and competence of the reporter, this is where the information about prize-winning belongs. Option III has no subordinate clause.

20) **III.** This sentence relies on two subordinate clauses to convey information that's less important than the main idea, which is that *Joe refused.* The clauses beginning with *Although* and *as he was* are subordinate.

21) **II.** The pronoun *which* stands in for *the CIA* and introduces relatively unimportant information.

22) **II, III.** Both II and III create a cause-and-effect sentence structure with the subordinate clause beginning with *because.* The location of the subordinate clause doesn't matter, just the fact that it's subordinate.

23) **III.** Your reading comprehension skills should tell you that option III makes sense, and options I and II don't. Option I is also a grammatical felony — a run-on sentence.

24) **I.** Option I links the ideas in a logical way, beginning with the subordinate clause *If the CIA tracks her down.* Option II includes a subordinate clause, *When the CIA will deal with her harshly,* but the full statement doesn't quite make sense. Option III contains two subordinate clauses but no independent clause. Penalty box!

25) **II, III.** The subordinate clause beginning with *while* makes more sense than *although.* Because placement at the beginning and the end of the sentence yields the same meaning, both II and III are fine.

26) **I.** Option I places the subordinate clause, *which is tentatively interested,* in the correct spot. Option II is awkward, changing the verb to *was offered.* Option III says that Nadia is tentatively interested — not the meaning you want.

27) **I, II.** The subordinate clause beginning with *after* works fine at the beginning or the end of the sentence. Did you notice that a comma appears in option I but not in II? Traditionally, an introductory subordinate clause is set off from the independent clause with a comma, unless the clause functions as the subject of the sentence. If the same clause shows up at the end of the sentence, it's not usually separated with a comma. Option III, by the way, is a run-on sentence. (For more on run-ons, see Chapter 3.)

28 **III.** Read the three options aloud and you see that only III makes sense, is true to the original meaning, and flows smoothly.

29 **I, II.** Options I and II emphasize the danger, something I personally would want to know if I were one of Nadia's closest friends. The third option emphasizes that these friends know the location of the box. It's not wrong, precisely, but it shifts the emphasis to an odd place. Did I fool you with option II? This one uses a subordinate clause *(That Nadia's closest friends know the location of the box)* as the subject of the verb *puts.* The whole sentence is an independent clause, with a subordinate clause as subject.

30 **I. III.** The first and third options set up a time situation as well as a cause/effect relationship: The film informs the world about "the incident." These options both work. Option II deals only with cause and effect, making timing part of the cause. This option is less logical than the other two.

Chapter **17**

Adding Style to Sentences

Many television shows feature aspiring designers who cut patterns and sew, glue, or staple fashion-forward clothing. Why do so many people, including me, watch? To see something new, a jolt out of the "same old, same old" pattern. Writing is no different. Chances are you've got some basic sentence patterns that serve you well. But if you've ever longed for a change of pace, this chapter is for you. Here you practice adding variety and style to your sentences by employing verbals, combining ideas, and changing word order.

Speaking Verbally

Every family has some interesting members who can add zing to a boring day. *Verbals* are the grammatical equivalent of those relatives. As the name implies, verbals have a connection with verbs, but they also have a link with other parts of speech (nouns, adjectives, and adverbs). Verbals never act as the verb in a sentence, but they do influence the sense of time that the sentence conveys. This section gives you practice in identifying verbals and selecting the correct tense for each.

Identifying verbals

Time to meet the verbal family. Here's the lowdown on *infinitives*, *participles*, and *gerunds* — the three types of verbals.

>> **Infinitives** are what you get when you tack *to* in front of the most basic form of the verb. Infinitives may take a descriptive role or function as a noun, but they never act as the verb in a sentence.

- *To be* safe, Alice packed a few hundred rolls of breath mints. *(to be = infinitive describing packed)*

- *To win* was Roger's goal. *(to win = subject of the verb was)*

>> **Participles** are the *-ing* or *-ed* or *-en* form of verbs, plus a few irregulars. Sometimes participles function as part of the verb in a sentence, attached to *has, have, had* or *is, are, was,* or *were.* In this situation, participles aren't verbals. When participles act as descriptions, they're verbals.

- *Inhaling* sharply, Elaine stepped away from the blast of peppermint that escaped from Alice's mouth. *(inhaling = participle giving information about Elaine)*

- The *dancing* statue is famous. Everyone *seeing* it takes a selfie. *(dancing = participle describing the noun statue, seeing = participle describing the pronoun everyone.)*

>> **Gerunds** are the *-ing* form of verbs, used as nouns.

- *Going* to the beach is fun. *(Going = gerund functioning as the subject of the verb is)*

TIP

Many verbals show up in phrases, which may include objects or descriptions. In the infinitive phrase *to learn algebra immediately*, for example, *algebra* is the object of the infinitive *to learn* and *immediately* is a description.

EXAMPLE

Check out the underlined portions of each sentence and label them "I" for *infinitive*, "P" for *participle*, or "G" for *gerund*. If none of these labels fit, write "N" for *none*.

Q. Sam flew <u>to Phoenix</u> for a conference on "<u>Rebuilding</u> Your Company's Image."

A. **N, G.** *Phoenix* is not a verb, so *to Phoenix* is not a verbal. *Rebuilding* is a gerund. In case you were wondering, *rebuilding* is the object of the preposition *on. Rebuilding Your Company's Image* is the entire gerund phrase.

1. <u>Arriving</u> in Arizona, Sam was eager <u>to settle</u> in at his hotel.

2. The hotel room, newly <u>redecorated</u>, was on the same floor as an <u>overflowing</u> ice machine.

3. <u>To reach</u> his room, Sam had <u>to skate</u> across a miniature glacier.

4. <u>Sliding</u> across a slippery floor <u>to his room</u> was not one of Sam's happiest moments.

5. Sam, <u>easygoing</u> by nature, nevertheless decided <u>to complain</u>.

6   "I want <u>to relax</u>, not <u>to practice</u> winter sports!" Sam stated <u>firmly</u>.

7   The manager, not <u>knowing</u> about the ice machine, found Sam's comment <u>confusing</u>.

8   <u>Reaching</u> 100° is not unusual during summer in this part of the country.

9   <u>Choosing</u> his words carefully, the manager replied, "Of course, sir. I will cancel the bobsled <u>racing</u>."

10   Sam forgot about the ice machine and <u>protested</u>, because his lifelong dream was <u>to go</u> downhill on a fast sled.

Telling time with verbals

Verbals, like everything associated with verbs, give time information. The plain form (without *has, have, having,* or *had*) shows action happening at the same time as the action expressed by the main verb in the sentence. The perfect form (with *has, have, having,* or *had*) places the action expressed by the verbal before the action of the main verb.

TIP

Choosing either the plain or perfect form can be tricky. First, figure out how important the timeline is. If the events are so closely spaced so as not to matter, go for the plain form. If it matters to the reader/listener that one event followed or will follow another, select the perfect form for the earlier action.

TEST ALERT

Sequence of tenses — the combination of verbs and verbals to express the order of events — is a frequent flyer on college entrance tests.

EXAMPLE

In the example and the practice exercises that follow, get out your time machine and read about a fictional tooth whitener called "GreenTeeth." The content is strange, but all you need to worry about is locating and circling the correct verbal form.

Q.   (Perfecting/Having perfected) the new product, the chemists asked the boss to conduct some market research.

A.   **Having perfected.** The two events occurred in the past, with the chemists' request closer to the present moment. The event expressed by the verbal (a participle, as you may have guessed) attributes another action to the chemists. The perfect form (created by *having*) places the act of *perfecting* prior to the action expressed by the main verb in the sentence, *asked*.

11   (Peering/Having peered) at each interview subject, the researchers checked for discoloration.

12   One interview subject shrieked upon (hearing/having heard) the interviewer's comment about "teeth as yellow as sunflowers."

13   (Refusing/Having refused) to open her mouth, she glared silently at the interviewer.

14   With the market research on GreenTeeth (completed/having been completed), the team tabulated the results.

15 The tooth whitener (going/having gone) into production, no further market research is scheduled.

16 The researchers actually wanted (to interview/to have interviewed) 50 percent more subjects after GreenTeeth's debut, but the legal department objected.

17 Additional interviews will be scheduled if the legal department succeeds in (getting/having gotten) participants to sign a "will not sue" pledge.

18 "(Sending/Having sent) GreenTeeth to the stores means that I am sure it works," said the CEO.

19 (Deceived/Having been deceived) by this CEO several times, reporters were skeptical.

20 (Interviewing/Having interviewed) dissatisfied customers, one reporter was already planning an exposé.

21 (Weeping/Having wept), the marketing team applauded the boss's comment.

22 Next year's Product Placement Awards (being/having been) announced, the GreenTeeth team is celebrating its six nominations and looking for future dental discoveries.

Playing with Sentence Patterns

The spine of most English sentences is subject-verb: *Mary walks, Oliver opens,* and so forth. Most sentences also have some sort of completion, what grammarians call a complement or an object: *Mary walks the dog, Oliver opens the peanut butter jar.* Even when you throw in some descriptions, this basic skeleton is boring if it's the only structure you ever use. You can vary the sentence pattern (and wake up your readers) in several ways, all of which you practice in this section.

Introductory elements

An effective way to change the basic pattern is to add an introductory element, which is italicized in the following examples:

> *Sticking her finger in the jar,* Agnes stirred the peanut butter. (The introductory verb form, a *participle,* tells something Agnes did.)

> *Despite the new polish on her nails,* Agnes was willing to eat without a fork. (The introductory prepositional phrase gives information about Agnes's eating habits.)

> *When she was full,* Agnes closed the jar. (The introductory statement has a subject and a verb, *she was,* and in grammar terms is a clause. Once again, you get more information about Agnes.)

 As always in grammar, you don't need to clutter your mind with definitions. Simply try some of the patterns, but be sure to avoid a common error: The subject of the main part of the sentence must be the one doing the action or in the state of being described by the introductory verb form. Check out Chapter 19 for more information on this sort of error.

WARNING

TEST ALERT

The skills you practice in this section help you in paragraph- or sentence-revision questions on college entrance tests, such as the SAT and the ACT.

EXAMPLE

Put boredom behind you. Take a look at the original ideas and then choose an option that combines those ideas with an introductory element. Be sure the option you select is grammatically correct and expresses the same meaning as the original.

Q. The boss wants the memo immediately. Jesse stops cleaning his teeth and starts typing.

   I. Realizing that the boss wants the memo immediately, Jesse stops cleaning his teeth and starts typing.

   II. Having stopped cleaning his teeth and started typing, the memo Jesse was writing was what the boss wanted immediately.

   III. Having realized that the boss wanted the memo immediately, Jesse stops cleaning his teeth and starts typing.

A. **I.** Option I begins with a participle (*Realizing*) that properly explains what *Jesse* is doing. Option II is out because the introductory element — the participial phrase *Having stopped cleaning his teeth and started typing* — is attached to *memo*, the subject of the sentence. A *memo* has no teeth and can't type! Option III doesn't work because the participle is in the wrong tense. Jesse's realization and his subsequent actions happen more or less at the same time, so *having realized* makes no sense.

23 Jesse is considering retirement. Jesse's mortgage holder thinks that Jesse should work at least 100 more years.

   I. Although Jesse is considering retirement, his mortgage holder thinks that Jesse should work at least 100 more years.

   II. Despite the fact that Jesse is considering retirement, his mortgage holder thinks that Jesse should work at least 100 more years.

   III. Considering retirement, Jesse's mortgage holder thinks that Jesse should work at least 100 more years.

24 The bank official wants Jesse to work hard. Jesse's debt is quite large.

   I. Being quite large, the bank official wants Jesse to work hard to pay off his debt.

   II. Wanting Jesse to work hard, his debt is quite large.

   III. Because Jesse's debt is quite large, the bank wants him to work hard.

25 Jesse wants to drink martinis on a tropical island. Jesse also wants to keep his house.

   I. Even though Jesse wants to drink martinis on a tropical island, he also wants to keep his house.

   II. Having wanted to drink martinis on a tropical island, Jesse also wants to keep his house.

   III. In addition to his desire to drink martinis on a tropical island, Jesse wants to keep his house.

26 Jesse's entire plan is impractical. An especially unrealistic part lets Jesse drink martinis all day.

   I.   While it is impractical in every way, an especially unrealistic part lets Jesse drink martinis all day.

   II. Entirely impractical, an especially unrealistic part of Jesse's plan lets him drink martinis all day.

   III. Impractical in every way, the plan is especially unrealistic in letting Jesse drink martinis all day.

27 The bank manager speaks to Jesse in a loud voice. She points out that Jesse has $0.02 in his savings account.

   I.   Speaking to Jesse in a loud voice, the bank manager points out that Jesse has $.02 in his savings account.

   II. Although she speaks in a loud voice, the bank manager points out that Jesse has $.02 in his savings account.

   III. Having spoken in a loud voice, the bank manager points out that Jesse has $.02 in his savings account.

28 The bank manager angers easily. Jesse brings out the worst in her.

   I.   Angering easily, the bank manager admits that Jesse brings out the worst in her.

   II. Bringing out the worst, the bank manager was angered by Jesse.

   III. Because Jesse brings out the worst in her, the bank manager angers easily.

29 Jesse considered robbing the bank. Jesse is an honest man.

   I.   Robbing the bank, Jesse is an honest man.

   II. Even though he is an honest man, Jesse considered robbing the bank.

   III. Because he is an honest man, Jesse considered robbing the bank.

30 The bank manager eventually decided to rob the bank. She drank martinis on a tropical island.

   I.   With martinis on a tropical island in her future, the bank manager eventually decided to rob the bank.

   II. To drink martinis on a tropical island, the bank manager eventually decided to rob the bank.

   III. Having decided to rob the bank, martinis on a tropical island were the bank manager's future.

31 Jesse joined the FBI. He searched for the bank manager and arrested her.

   I.   Joining the FBI, Jesse searched for the bank manager and arrested her.

   II. Joined the FBI, he searched for and arrested the bank manager.

   III. When he joined the FBI, Jesse searched for the bank manager and arrested her.

32 Jesse received a $10 million reward. Jesse retired to the tropical island.

 I. To receive a $10 million reward, Jesse retired to a tropical island.

 II. After he received a $10 million reward, Jesse retired to a tropical island.

 III. Receiving a $10 million reward, Jesse retired to the tropical island.

Combining ideas and changing word order

When you have a bunch of ideas, you can state them one by one, each in a separate sentence. If you're like most people, that's what you usually do, and the result is fine. But *usually* is a short step from *boring,* so at times you may want to insert several ideas into a longer, complex sentence. Compare these two statements:

> The plant is covered with little purple bugs. The bugs are chewing the leaves. I am afraid. The bugs may tire of the plant. They may eat me.

> I'm afraid that the little purple bugs, which cover the plant and chew its leaves, may tire of the plant and eat me.

The second version sounds more mature, right? Notice that you have one long statement ("I'm afraid that the little purple bugs may tire of the plant and eat me") with another tucked inside ("which cover the plant and chew its leaves"). You can insert information with clauses (subject–verb expressions that I explain in Chapter 16), verbals, or other elements. Just be sure to do so properly.

Another simple way to add spice to your writing is to fiddle with the usual subject–verb–object/complement (S-V-O/C) pattern. You can try moving the subject to the end of the sentence (V-O/C-S) or leading with the object or complement (O/C-S-V). Take a look at the usual pattern and a possible variation:

> Everyone needs love. (S-V-O)

> Love, everyone needs. (O-S-V)

> Mark zoomed across the room on his skateboard. (S-V)

> Across the room on his skatedboard zoomed Mark. (V-S)

WARNING

When you play around with word order or sentence patterns, be careful not to repeat yourself. Adding variety to your writing does *not* entitle you to bore your reader with needless repetition.

EXAMPLE

Take a look at the original set of ideas. Which sentences insert ideas correctly? *Note:* Correctly rewritten sentences may rearrange, substitute, or add words.

Q. Ideas: Hollywood studios make many action films. Action scenes require less translation. For this reason action films are easy to market abroad.

    I. Hollywood studios make many action films, which require less translation, because they are easy to market abroad.

    II. Hollywood studios, making many action films, which require less translation and marketing abroad.

    III. Action films, which require less translation, are often made in Hollywood for markets abroad.

A. **I.** The first option tucks every idea into one grammatically correct sentence. Option II has grammar problems (not a complete sentence) and option III awkwardly shifts into passive voice (*are made*). To learn more about passive voice, see Chapter 15.

33 Ideas: Liars are untrustworthy. Marjorie lied.

    I. A liar, Marjorie is untrustworthy.

    II. That Marjorie lied makes her untrustworthy.

    III. Marjorie, who lies, making her untrustworthy.

34 Ideas: Jurors hear Marjorie's testimony. Some believe her. They think she looks honest.

    I. Some jurors, hearing Marjorie's testimony and thinking she looks honest, believe her.

    II. Thinking she looks honest, jurors hear Marjorie's testimony believing her.

    III. Looking honest, Marjorie's testimony is believed by some jurors.

35 Ideas: Marjorie went to prison. She committed perjury. She wrote a book about the trial. It was a bestseller.

    I. In prison Marjorie, who committed perjury, wrote a book about the trial, and it was a bestseller.

    II. Marjorie, who committed perjury, wrote a bestseller in prison about the trial.

    III. Marjorie, who wrote a bestseller about the trial, committed perjury in prison.

36 Ideas: George read Marjorie's book. George hoped to write a bestselling book. He searched for a crime to commit. Then he could write about that crime.

    I. Reading Marjorie's book, George wanted to write a bestseller too, so he searched for a crime and committed it so he could write about it.

    II. To write his own bestseller, George searched for a crime to commit and write about, just as Marjorie did.

    III. Having read Marjorie's book and hoping for a bestseller himself, George searched for a crime to commit and write about.

37 Ideas: George wanted to commit a crime!

   I.   A crime, George wanted to commit!

   II. George, a crime he wanted to commit!

   III. Wanted George a crime to commit!

38 Ideas: George wrote *Committing Crimes and Writing About Them For Dummies.* The book sold very few copies. Most buyers were convicted criminals.

   I.   *Committing Crimes and Writing About Them For Dummies*, which George wrote and sold to convicted criminals, but not many.

   II. George's book, *Committing Crimes and Writing About Them For Dummies*, sold poorly, mostly to convicted criminals.

   III. George's book was *Committing Crimes and Writing About Them For Dummies*, and it sold poorly to convicted criminals.

Calling All Overachievers: Extra Practice Honing Your Sentences

EXAMPLE

The following figure is a short story excerpt that could use some major help. Revise it as you see fit, paying attention to varied sentence patterns. *Note:* You can revise in a thousand different ways. In the answer section I provide some possible changes. Your revision may differ. In fact, it may be better than mine! Check for variety when you evaluate your work.

> Darla fainted. Darla was lying on the floor in a heap. Her legs were bent under her. She breathed in quick pants at a rapid rate. Henry came. He ran as fast as he could. He neared Darla and gasped. "My angel," he said. His heart was beating. His cardiologist would be worried about the fast rate. Henry did not care. Henry cared only about Darla. She was the love of his life. She was unconscious. He said, "Angel Pie, you don't have to pawn your engagement ring." He knelt next to her.

Answers to Sentence Improvement Problems

The best writing uses different sentence patterns and structures while still being grammatically correct. Check your answers here.

1. **P, I.** The participle *arriving* gives information about *Sam*, the subject of the sentence. The verb in the sentence is *was. To settle* is an infinitive.

TIP

Grammar rules require that a participle at the beginning of a sentence describe the subject of the sentence. This sentence is proper because *Sam* is the person *arriving*.

2. **P, P.** *Redecorated* (from the verb *redecorate)* describes *room. Overflowing* (from the verb *overflow)* describes *machine.*

3. **I, I.** These infinitives perform different jobs in the sentence. *To reach* describes the verb *had; to skate* is the object of the verb *had.*

4. **G, N.** *Sliding* is the subject of the verb *was. To his room* is a prepositional phrase, not a verb. (For more information on prepositional phrases, turn to Chapter 7.)

5. **N, I.** *Easygoing* isn't a verbal because the verb "easygo" doesn't exist. *To complain* is an infinitive acting as the object of the verb *decided.*

6. **I, I, N.** *To relax* and *to practice* are both infinitives acting as objects. *Firmly* is an adverb, not a verbal. (For more information on adverbs, read Chapter 8.)

7. **P, P.** Both *knowing* and *confusing* are participles. The first describes *manager,* and the second describes *comment.*

8. **G.** *Reaching* is a gerund acting as the subject of the verb *is.*

9. **P, G.** *Choosing* is something the manager is doing, but it's not the verb in the sentence. It's a description, what grammarians call an *introductory participle* because it sits at the beginning of the sentence. *Racing* is a gerund acting as an object.

10. **N, I.** *Protested* isn't a verbal; it's a verb. *To go* is an infinitive acting as an object.

11. **Peering.** Here the two actions take place at the same time. The researchers check out the subjects' teeth and check for trouble. The perfect form (with *having)* is for actions at different times.

12. **hearing.** Once again, two actions take place at the same time. Go for the plain form.

13. **Refusing.** The "not in this universe will I open my mouth" moment is simultaneous with an "if looks could kill" glare, so the plain form is best.

14. **having been completed.** The plain form *completed* would place two actions (the completing and the tabulating) at the same time. Yet common sense tells you that the tabulating follows the completion of the research. The perfect form (with *having)* places the completing before the tabulating.

15. **having gone.** The decision to stop market research is based on the fact that it's too late; the tooth whitener, in all its glory, is already being manufactured. Because the timeline matters here and one action is clearly earlier, the perfect form is needed.

16 **to interview.** The *have* form places the action of interviewing *before* the action expressed by the main verb in the sentence. With *have,* the timeline makes no sense.

17 **getting.** Three actions are mentioned in this sentence: scheduling, succeeding, and getting. The first action is placed in the future, so don't worry about it. The last two actions take place at the same time, because the minute somebody signs a legal paper, the attorneys are successful. As it expresses a simultaneous action, the plain form of the verbal (without *having*) is appropriate.

18 **Sending.** The CEO's statement places two things, sending and being sure, at the same time. Bingo: The plain form is best.

19 **Having been deceived.** The point of the sentence is that one action (deceiving the reporters) precedes another (being skeptical). You need the perfect form to make the timeline work.

20 **Interviewing.** The interviews and the planning of an exposé are simultaneous, so the plain form is best.

21 **Weeping.** The marketers are all choked up as they clap their hands and hope for a very big raise. Plain form works because the two things happen at the same time.

22 **having been.** The celebration and "time to get back to work" movement take place after the announcement, so you want the perfect tense.

23 **I, II.** Option I begins with a subordinate clause (see Chapter 16 for more information) that leads the reader into the independent clause, and perhaps another 100 years at the office. Verdict: Correct. Option II leads with a prepositional phrase that accomplishes the same goal. Option III is out because as written, the *mortgage holder* is *considering retirement* — clearly not the intended meaning.

24 **III.** The first time I show this sentence structure to my students, they often protest that "you can't begin a sentence with *because.*" Yes, you can, as long as you have a complete thought and an independent clause in the sentence. (Turn to Chapter 16 for more about independent clauses.) Option III fulfills both those requirements. The other options fail because they don't express the original meaning. In option I, the *bank official* is *quite large.* Option II omits the bank entirely.

25 **I, III.** Option I begins with a subordinate clause that explains Jesse's wish for martinis on the sand. The independent clause tackles the competing desire. Option I is grammatically correct. Not so option II, which starts with a participle in the wrong tense. The desire for martinis on the beach didn't take place before the desire to keep the house. Verdict: incorrect. Option III tucks the martini-wish into a prepositional phrase, flowing nicely (and properly) into the rest of the sentence.

26 **I, II, III.** Three winners here. Option I starts with a subordinate clause and moves on to an independent clause. Option II begins with two adjectives, both of which describe the implied noun *plan.* Option III begins with still another way to describe *plan,* the subject of the main part of the sentence.

27 **I.** In Option I, how the bank manager speaks is expressed by an introductory participle, which properly describes the subject of the sentence, *manager.* Option II starts with a subordinate clause, but *although* doesn't fit the meaning of the sentence. Option III employs the wrong tense, improperly placing the fact that the manager spoke in a loud voice before the clause stating what she said.

28 **I, III.** Option I adds a bit, but it expresses the same meaning and properly connects the introductory participle *(angering)* to *the bank manager*, the subject of the sentence. Option II has no one *bringing out the worst*, so you have to discard that choice. Option III begins with a subordinate clause and ends with an independent clause, a fine sentence.

29 **II.** In option II, the first part of the sentence is a clause because it has a subject and a verb, but it properly depends upon the statement in the second part of the sentence to complete the thought. Option I goes against the meaning of the original — Jesse didn't rob the bank — and makes little sense. Option III also defies logic, as this is not a cause-and-effect situation.

30 **I, II.** In option I, a set of prepositional phrases packs an opening punch and begins a grammatically correct sentence. Option II starts with an infinitive that accomplishes the same purpose. Option III has *martinis* making the decision, not a logical or grammatically correct choice.

31 **I, III.** Option I starts with a participle and option III with a subordinate clause. Both express the idea that two things happened more or less at the same time. Option II improperly uses a plain past-tense verb, *joined*, to introduce the rest of the sentence.

32 **II, III.** Option I has the cause and effect mixed up. The island was the result, not the cause, of the reward. Option II begins with a subordinate clause and segues into an independent clause. Option III starts with an introductory participle. Both II and III work well.

33 **II.** In option II a clause, *That Marjorie lied,* acts as subject of the sentence. Option I is grammatically correct, but it doesn't quite match the original, because being a *liar* implies that Marjorie lies all the time, not just on one occasion. Option III isn't a complete sentence.

34 **I.** The main idea is well said in option I: *Some jurors believe her.* The reasons for this opinion are tucked into the main statement as participles. Option I is correct. Option II begins well, but that last participle *(believing her)* just hangs there. The word it describes *(jurors)* is too far from the description. Option III has the *testimony* looking honest, not Marjorie.

35 **II.** Option II cuts the original 18 words to 12 but includes every idea. It's the winner here. Option I isn't wrong grammatically, but that last idea *(and it was a bestseller)* sounds tacked on. Option III misstates the facts (much like Marjorie) because it has her committing perjury in prison.

36 **III.** Option III establishes a timeline: two actions occur earlier in the past *(having read, hoping — both participles)* and then moves to the more recent past *(searched)* and into the future *(to commit and write — infinitives)*. This one is complete and correct. Option I is wordy, and option II repeats one idea *(to write* and *write about*, both infinitives).

37 **I.** The first option moves the object to the front of the sentence, with the subject-verb combination following. This one is interesting and grammatically correct. The second option incorrectly adds another subject *(he)*. The third option is technically correct but sounds strange — not exactly a technical reason, but a reason nevertheless.

38 **II.** Nice to think that crime doesn't pay, isn't it? Option II includes every idea but uses fewer words than the original. Option I inaccurately states the facts. He didn't sell to convicted criminals; he tried to sell to everyone and mostly criminals bought his book. Option III makes a similar error, stating that few criminals are buying the book.

Here are the answers to the "Overachievers" section:

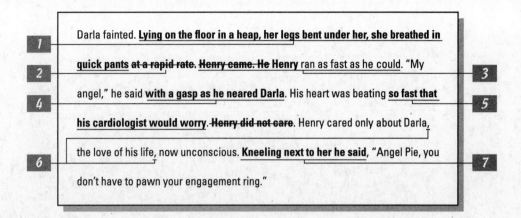

(1) Three sentences — *Darla was lying on the floor in a heap, Her legs were bent under her,* and *She breathed in quick pants* — may be easily combined. The ideas in the first two sentences are turned into introductory elements, with the last of the three sentences as the main idea. If you add an introductory element with a verb form, be sure that the subject of the main section of the sentence is the person or thing doing the action or in the state of being mentioned in the introduction. Another possible combination: *After Darla fainted, she was lying on the floor in a heap. With her legs under her, she breathed in quick pants.*

(2) The revision cuts repetition; *rapid* and *quick* are the same.

(3) Two sentences combine and retain *Henry* as the subject.

(4) Two sentences — *He neared Darla and gasped. "My angel," he said.* — have been combined. The new version is more concise and more interesting.

(5) A subordinate clause *(that his cardiologist would worry)* tucks an idea from one sentence into another.

(6) The original story ends with several short, choppy sentences. The revision combines all but the last sentence.

(7) The last two sentences of the original combine with an introductory verb form, *kneeling*. If you begin with *kneeling*, be sure that *he* or *Henry* is the subject of the main part of the sentence. You can also revise this section in this way: *"Angel Pie, you don't have to pawn your engagement ring," he said as he knelt next to her.*

Chapter **18**

Staying on Track: Parallel Writing

I n the world of grammar, parallelism refers to order and balance, the quality a sentence has when it flows smoothly. No parallel sentence starts out in one direction (toward, say, Grandma's house) only to veer suddenly off the road (perhaps to a tattoo parlor two states away). This chapter provides a road map and some practice drives to keep your sentences on track.

Geometry Meets English: Making Sentences Parallel

When a sentence is parallel, everything performing the same function in the sentence has the same grammatical identity. If you have two subjects, for example, and one is an infinitive *(to ski)*, the other one must be an infinitive also *(to fracture)*. You can't mix and match; *to ski* and *fracturing* shouldn't show up as paired (or part of tripled or quadrupled or whatever) subjects. Check out these sentences:

>> **Nonparallel:** Roberta didn't enjoy paying full price for a lift ticket and that the cashier treated her rudely.

>> **Parallel:** Roberta didn't enjoy paying full price for a lift ticket and being treated rudely by the cashier.

In checking for parallelism, don't worry about terminology. Just read the sentence aloud and listen: Parallel sentences sound balanced, but nonparallel sentences sound lopsided.

TEST ALERT You may see parallelism issues in error-recognition or sentence-revision questions on standardized tests. Let your ear be your guide as you listen to the voice inside your head, reading the sentence "aloud." (Of course, if you actually read the sentence aloud, you'll be thrown out of the exam room.)

EXAMPLE Keep your balance while you check out the following sentences. Decide which, if any, are parallel.

Q.

    I. Speeding down Thunder Mountain, spraying snow across his rival's face, and to get the best seat in the ski lodge were Robert's goals for the afternoon.

    II. To speed down Thunder Mountain, to spray snow across his rival's face, and to get the best seat in the ski lodge were Robert's goals for the afternoon.

A. **II.** Each sentence has three subjects. In option I the first two subjects are verb forms ending in *-ing* (*gerunds*, in official grammar terminology), but the third is an *infinitive* (the *to* form of a verb). Mismatch! Option II turns the subjects into infinitives *(to speed, to spray, to get)*. When the subjects match, the sentence is parallel.

1

    I. The ski pants that Robert favors are green, skintight, and stretchy.

    II. The ski pants that Robert favors are green, skintight, and made of stretch fabric.

2

    I. When he eases into those pants and zips up with force, Robert feels cool.

    II. When he eases into those pants and zipping up with force, Robert feels cool.

3

    I. In this ski outfit, Robert can breathe only with difficulty and forcefully.

    II. In this ski outfit, Robert can breathe only with difficulty and force.

4

    I. The sacrifice for the sake of fashion is worth the trouble and how he feels uncomfortable, Robert says.

    II. The sacrifice for the sake of fashion is worth the trouble and discomfort, Robert says.

5

    I. Besides, sliding down the mountain and coasting to a full stop is easier in clothing that resembles a second skin.

    II. Besides, to slide down the mountain and to coast to a full stop is easier in clothing that resembles a second skin.

6

I. Robert has often been known to object to secondhand clothing and used equipment.

II. Robert has often been known to object to secondhand clothing and how some equipment is used.

7

I. "With a good parka or wearing a warm face mask I'm ready for anything," he says.

II. "With a good parka or a warm face mask, I'm ready for anything," he says.

8

I. He adds, "The face mask is useful on the slopes and doing double duty in bank robberies."

II. He adds, "The face mask is useful on the slopes and does double duty in bank robberies."

9

I. The ski pants can also be recycled, if they are rip-free and clean.

II. The ski pants can also be recycled, if they are rip-free and without stains.

10

I. However, robbing a bank and to mug someone is more difficult in ski pants.

II. However, bank robbery and mugging are more difficult in ski pants.

11

I. Robbers need speed and to be private, but they also need pockets.

II. Robbers need speed and privacy, but they also need pockets.

12

I. How to stash stolen money and where to put an incriminating ski mask are important issues.

II. Stashing stolen money and where to put an incriminating ski mask are important issues.

13

I. Robert, who is actually quite honest and not having the inclination to rob anyone, nevertheless thinks about crime and fashion.

II. Robert, who is actually quite honest and not inclined to rob anyone, nevertheless thinks about crime and fashion.

14

    I. He once wrote and had even edited a newsletter called *Crimes of Fashion.*

    II. He once wrote and even edited a newsletter called *Crimes of Fashion.*

15

    I. To ski and to pursue a career in law enforcement are Robert's dreams.

    II. Skiing and pursuing a career in law enforcement are Robert's dreams.

Staying in Gear: Avoiding Unnecessary Shifts

My driving instructor explained to me at least a thousand times that shifting at the wrong time was bad for (a) the engine and (b) his nerves. I did my best, though the grinding noise echoing through the car wasn't always my teeth. Sentences should stay in gear also, unless the meaning requires a shift. Every sentence has *tense* (the time of the action or state of being), *person* (who's talking or being talked about), and *voice* (active or passive). A sentence has a parallelism problem when one of those qualities shifts unnecessarily from, say, present to past tense, or from first person (the *I* form) to third (the *he* or *they* form). Nor should a sentence drift from singular to plural without good reason. For help with verb tense, check out Chapters 4 and 15. Pronoun tips appear in Chapter 5.

Some shifts are crucial to the meaning of the sentence. If "I hit you" and then "he hits me," the shift from one person to another is part of what I'm trying to say. That sort of sentence is fine. What's not parallel is a statement like "I hit him because you always want to be aggressive in tight situations," where the *you* is a stand-in for *I* or *everyone*.

WARNING

Singular and plural pronouns — along with pronouns that do double duty as both singular and plural — have often been the source of controversy. For hundreds of years, the pronouns *they*, *their*, and *them* paired with pronouns such as *everyone, somebody, anyone* and the like without causing problems. The same pronouns also properly referred to nouns with no obvious gender (*professor, cop, mayor*, and so forth). Then some grammarians objected, viewing *they/their/them* as solely plural. But that usage caused a different problem, because English has no singular, nongendered pronoun to refer to a human being. Nowadays, more and more grammarians accept *they/their/them* as either singular or plural. With that standard, a sentence like "everybody bought their own wine" has no shift. For more information on pronouns and gender, see Chapter 5.)

TEST ALERT

Standardized tests often ask you to recognize or correct an illegal shift.

Hop in for a test ride. Check out the following sentences. Which, if any, are correct?

 Q.

EXAMPLE

    I. Miranda read her introduction, and then the slides of our trip to Morocco were shown by me.

    II. Miranda read her introduction, and then I showed the slides of our trip to Morocco.

A. **II.** The first sentence unwisely shifts from active voice (*Miranda read*) to passive (*slides . . . were shown*). Verdict: Stripped gears, caused by a shift from active to passive. The second option changes *were shown by me* to *I showed.* Now both verbs are active, and the sentence is parallel.

16

I. If you've studied biology, you know that a person must learn the names of hundreds, if not thousands, of organisms.

II. If anyone has studied biology, you know that a person must learn the names of hundreds, if not thousands, of organisms.

17

I. Who gave those names, and why?

II. Why were those names given, and by whom?

18

I. The Amoeba Family provides a good example of the process, so its name will be explained by me.

II. The Amoeba Family provides a good example of the process, so I will explain its name.

19

I. You may not know that the first example of this single-celled organism was named Amy.

II. You may not know that the first example of this single-celled organism would have the name Amy.

20

I. When they split, the new organisms name themselves.

II. When a split has been made, the new organisms name themselves.

21

I. The right half of Amy was still called Amy by herself, but the left half now called herself Bea.

II. The right half of Amy still called herself Amy, but the left half now called herself Bea.

22

I. The next time Amy and Bea split, they formed four new organisms.

II. The next time Amy and Bea split, you have four new organisms.

23

I. Amy Right Half favored a name that people will notice.

II. Amy Right Half favored a name that people would notice.

24

I. Amy Left Half thought about the choice for so long that she neglected her swimming.

II. Amy Left Half thought about the choice for so long that her swimming was neglected.

25

I. Bea Right Half opted for "Amy-Bea," because she wants to honor both her parents.

II. Bea Right Half opted for "Amy-Bea," because she wanted to honor both her parents.

26

I. Everyone always pronounced "Amy-Bea" very fast, and soon "Amoeba" was our preferred spelling.

II. Everyone always pronounced "Amy-Bea" very fast, and soon "Amoeba" was the preferred spelling.

27

I. Single-celled organisms should have simple names that biology students can remember.

II. Single-celled organisms should have simple names that can be remembered by biology students.

28

I. Bea Left Half, by the way, will change her name to Amy-Bea when she becomes an adult at the age of seventeen days.

II. Bea Left Half, by the way, will change her name to Amy-Bea when she became an adult at the age of seventeen days.

29

I. You know what a teenager is like; we always have to assert our identities.

II. You know what teenagers are like; they always have to assert their identities.

30

I. For amoebas, identity-building experiences include sitting under a microscope or having a chance to swim in a large pond.

II. For amoebas, identity-building experiences include sitting under a microscope or having had a chance to swim in a large pond.

Following Special Rules for VIPs: Very Important Pairs

Some words that join ideas (*conjunctions*, in grammar-speak) arrive in pairs. Specifically, *either/or, neither/nor, not only/but also,* and *both/and* work as teams. Your job is to check that the elements linked by these words have the same grammatical identity (two nouns, two noun-verb combos, two adjectives, or two whatevers). If they don't, your sentence has a parallelism problem. Check out the following examples, in which the linked elements are underlined and the conjunctions are italicized:

> » **Nonparallel:** Gertrude was *not only* <u>anxious</u> to achieve fame *but also* <u>she wanted</u> to make a lot of money. *Either* <u>by going to the moon</u> *or* <u>to swim across the Pacific Ocean</u> will make Gertrude famous.

> » **Parallel:** Gertrude was *not only* <u>anxious to achieve fame</u> *but also* <u>eager to make a lot of money</u>. *Either* <u>going to the moon</u> *or* <u>swimming the Pacific Ocean</u> will make Gertrude famous.

The linked elements in the first parallel example are both adjectives and infinitives. In the second parallel example, the linked elements are nouns created from the *-ing* form of a verb — in grammar terminology, a gerund. (You don't really need to know the grammatical terms.) If you say the underlined sections aloud, your ear tells you that they match. In the first nonparallel sentence, the first element is just a description, but the second contains a subject/verb combo (a clause). Nope! Grammar crime! In the second nonparallel sentence, the first element is a gerund and the second an infinitive (*to* plus a verb). Grammar jail for you!

TEST ALERT If you see a conjunction pair on a standardized test, check the joined elements. Parallelism is a big deal on these exams. A good tactic is to underline the elements, as I did in the examples. Then you can see whether or not they match. Keep your eye out for *not only . . . but also.* That construction is especially popular with test writers.

EXAMPLE Parallel or nonparallel? Take a look at the following sentences. Identify which, if any, are parallel.

Q.

    I. The bird both swooping over my head and the surprise in the garbage pail startled me.

    II. Both the bird swooping over my head and the surprise awaiting me in the garbage pail startled me.

    III. Both the bird that swooped over my head and the surprise that I found in the garbage pail startled me.

A.   **II, III.** In option I, *swooping over my head* and *surprise in the garbage pail* don't match. The first element has a verb form *(swooping)*, and the second doesn't. Option II pairs *the bird swooping over my head* and *the surprise awaiting me in the garbage pail.* They match, so this sentence is correct. Option III correctly matches *bird that swooped* to *surprise that I found.*

31

    I. When she traveled to the biker convention, Lola intended both to show off her new Harley and to display her new tattoo.

    II. When she traveled to the biker convention, Lola intended to show off both her new Harley and to display her new tattoo.

    III. When she traveled to the biker convention, Lola both intended to show off her new Harley and to display her new tattoo.

32

    I. Lulu would accompany either Lola or stay home to work on a screenplay about bikers.

    II. Either Lulu would accompany Lola or stay home to work on a screenplay about bikers.

    III. Lulu would either accompany Lola or stay home to work on a screenplay about bikers.

33

    I. Lulu plans neither ahead, nor does her friend Lola.

    II. Neither Lulu nor Lola plans ahead.

    III. Neither Lulu plans ahead nor Lola.

34

    I. Lola writes not only screenplays but about bikers and alien invasions also.

    II. Lola not only writes screenplays about bikers but about alien invasions also.

    III. Lola writes screenplays not only about bikers but also about alien invasions.

35

    I. Lulu is jealous of both Lola's writing talent and the award for "best cycle" on Lola's trophy wall.

    II. Lulu both is jealous of Lola's writing talent and the award for "best cycle" on Lola's trophy wall.

    III. Lulu is both jealous of Lola's writing talent and the award for "best cycle" on Lola's trophy wall.

36

    I. Not only Lola scorns awards but also refuses to enter most contests.

    II. Lola scorns not only awards but also refuses to enter most contests.

    III. Lola not only scorns awards but also refuses to enter most contests.

37

    I. Neither the cycling award nor the trophy for largest tattoo has significance for Lola.

    II. Neither the cycling award has, nor the trophy for largest tattoo, significance for Lola.

    III. The cycling award neither has significance for Lola nor the largest tattoo.

Drawing Parallel Comparisons

Did you ever hear someone dismiss an argument by saying that it's comparing "apples and oranges"? The implication is that you can't compare things that don't fall into the same category. Grammar frowns on comparisons of "apples and oranges," too, and insists that the grammatical identity of whatever you're comparing be the same. Three sets of words — *more/than*, *but not*, and *as well as* — sometimes create comparisons. When you see these words, check for parallel structure. Take a look at these examples:

> Bob was more *annoyed* than *hungry* when he snatched the sandwich from Fred's hand. (*annoyed* and *hungry* = adjectives)
>
> Fred protested Bob's *attitude* but not his *right* to seize the sandwich. (*attitude* and *right* = nouns)
>
> Bob had bought the *sandwiches* as well as the *dessert*. (*sandwiches* and *dessert* = nouns)

EXAMPLE

Read these sentences. Which, if any, are parallel?

Q.

    I. Fred, as well as Monica, often snacked before dinner.

    II. Before dinner, Fred, as well as Monica, often snacked.

A. **I, II.** Surprised? Moving *before dinner* doesn't affect the fact that Fred and Monica are both nouns and therefore make a parallel comparison with the connector *as well as*.

38

    I. To whip up a great pie but not to clean the kitchen is Monica's favorite pastime.

    II. Whipping up a great pie but not cleaning the kitchen is Monica's favorite pastime.

39

    I. Monica believes that cooking is creative but not cleaning.

    II. Monica believes that cooking is creative but that cleaning is not.

40

    I. Bob is more interested in justice than in revenge.

    II. Bob is more interested in justice than he is in revenge.

41

    I. Bob, who is capable as well as responsible, heads the picnic committee.

    II. Bob, who is capable as well as he is responsible, heads the picnic committee.

42

    I. Fred, who loves to eat more than liking paperwork, was never a candidate for committee head.

    II. Fred, who loves to eat more than he likes paperwork, was never a candidate for committee head.

Calling All Overachievers: Extra Practice with Parallels

Look for any parallelism problems in the following letter to an elected official from an unfortunate citizen. You should find ten mistakes in parallelism, various shifts, and conjunction or comparison pairs. When you find a mistake, correct it.

EXAMPLE

Dear Mr. Mayor:

I do not like complaining or to be a nuisance, but if people are persecuted, he should be heard. As you know, the proposed new highway not only runs through my living room but also into my swimming pool. When I spoke to the Department of Highways, the clerk was more rude than respectful, and that he took my complaint lightly. He said I should either be glad the road didn't touch the breakfast nook or the kitchen. I demand that the issue be taken seriously by you, as well as your employees. I have written to you three times already, and you will say that you were "working on the problem." I am angry and in the mood to take legal action. Moving the highway or to cancel the project entirely is the only solution. I expect you not to delay but firing the clerk immediately.

Sincerely,

Joshua Hickman.

Answers to Parallelism Problems

Writing parallel sentences doesn't require the stars to be aligned; it just takes some practice. See how you did on the questions in this chapter by checking your answers here.

(1) **I.** Option I relies on three adjectives (*green, skintight,* and *stretchy*) to describe Robert's favorite pants. Option II isn't parallel because the original sentence links two adjectives (*green* and *skintight*) with a verb form (*made of stretch fabric*). Two adjectives + one verb form = penalty box.

(2) **I.** Option II isn't parallel because the *and* joins two verbs (*eases* and *zipping*) that don't match. In option I, *and* links *eases* and *zips,* so option I is parallel.

(3) **II.** Option I matches up *with difficulty* (a prepositional phrase) and *forcefully* (a description). These two are headed for the divorce court. Option II pairs two nouns (*difficulty* and *force*).

(4) **II.** Option I joins a noun, *trouble,* and a whole clause (that's the grammar term for a statement with a subject/verb combo), *how he feels uncomfortable.* Not parallel! Option II links two nouns, *trouble* and *discomfort.*

(5) **I, II.** Option I yokes two *-ing* forms (*sliding* and *coasting*). Verdict: legal. Option II links two infinitives (*to slide* and *to coast*): also legal.

(6) **I.** You're okay with two nouns (*clothing* and *equipment*), the combo you see in Option I. You're not okay with a noun (*clothing*) and a clause (*how some equipment is used*), which is what you have in option II.

(7) **II.** The *or* in Option I links *with a good parka* and *wearing a warm face mask.* The second term includes a verb form (*wearing*), and the first doesn't, so you know that the parallelism is off. In option II, *parka* and *face mask* are linked. Because they're both nouns, the parallelism works.

(8) **II.** The first option isn't parallel because *is useful* and *doing* don't match. The second option pairs *is* and *does,* two verbs.

(9) **I.** *Rip-free* is an adjective, but *without stains* is a phrase, so option II doesn't work. Option I has two adjectives (*rip-free* and *clean*).

(10) **II.** Option II matches two nouns (*robbery* and *mugging*). It's parallel. Option I mistakenly pairs *robbing* and *to mug* (a gerund and an infinitive), resulting in a sentence that isn't parallel.

(11) **II.** Option I falls off the parallel tracks because *speed* is a noun and *to be private* is an infinitive. Option II joins two nouns, *speed* and *privacy.*

(12) **I.** In option I, the subjects are both clauses; that is, they're both expressions containing subjects and verbs. (Think of a clause as a mini-sentence that can sometimes, but not always, stand alone.) Two clauses = legal pairing. Option II derails because the first subject (*stashing stolen money*) is a gerund, and the second is based on an infinitive (*to put*).

(13) **II.** The first option links a plain-vanilla-no-sprinkles description (*honest*) with an *-ing* verb form (*not having the inclination to rob anyone*). No sale. The second option matches two descriptions, *honest* and *inclined.*

(14) **II.** Option II matches two past tense verbs, *wrote* and *edited.* Option I matches a past (*wrote*) and a past perfect (*had edited*) without any valid reason for a different tense, so it isn't parallel.

15 **I, II.** Pair two infinitives (*to ski* and *to pursue*) and you're fine. You can also pair the gerunds *skiing* and *pursuing* for an alternate correct answer. Both options are correct.

16 **I.** The first option stays with *you,* the second person. It's correct. Option II fails because it shifts from *anyone* (third person) to *you* (second person).

17 **I, II.** Two questions appear in each sentence. In option I, the questions are active. In option II, the questions are passive. No shifts, no problem.

18 **II.** Option I sentence shifts unnecessarily from active (*provides*) to passive (*will be explained*). Option II stays in active voice. True, option II contains a shift from third person (talking about the Amoeba Family) to first, but that shift is justified by meaning.

19 **I.** The tenses in option I change, but the changes make sense. The first part is present and the second is past, because you *may not know* right now about something that happened previously. The meaning justifies the shift. Option I also has another shift, also justified, from active (*may not know*) to passive (*was named*). Because the person giving the name is unknown, the passive is correct. The problem with option II is that the sentence shifts inappropriately from present tense (*may not know*) to conditional (*would have*) for no logical purpose.

20 **I.** The first sentence is parallel because it stays in active voice (*they split, organisms name*). Option II moves passive (*split has been made*) to active (*they name*). The shift isn't justified by meaning, so II doesn't work.

21 **II.** Option II is all active voice, so it's correct. In option I, you have a shift from passive (*was called*) to active (*called*).

22 **I.** Option I is parallel because it stays in third person, talking about *Amy, Bea,* and *they.* Option II shifts from third (*Amy Bea*) to second (*you*).

23 **II.** The first verb in option I is past, but the second shifts illogically to the future. Penalty box! In option II, the past tense *favored* is matched with a conditional (*would notice*), but that change is logical because Amy is attaching a condition to her choice of name.

24 **I.** Two active verbs (*thought, neglected*) make option I parallel. Option II improperly shifts from active (*thought*) to passive (*was neglected*).

25 **II.** The first sentence has a meaningless tense shift, from past (*opted*) to present (*wants*). The second stays in past tense (*opted, wanted*).

26 **II.** Option II has no pronouns and therefore no pronoun problems. Option I shifts from third person (*everyone*) to first (*our*). Nope. Not parallel!

27 **I.** The verbs in option I (*should have, can remember*) stay active, jogging at least an hour a day. The shift from active in option II (*should have*) to passive (*can be remembered*) isn't a good idea.

28 **I.** In option I, both actions are in the future (*will change, when she becomes*). Option II contains an illogical tense shift. The first verb is future (*will change*) and the second is past (*became*), placing the sentence in some sort of time warp and out of the realm of parallel structure.

29 **II.** Option II stays in plural (*teenagers, they*), but Option I improperly shifts from third person (*a teenager*) to first (*we, our*).

30 **I.** *Sitting* is parallel to *having,* so option I is correct. Option II pairs *sitting* with *having had* — an unnecessary change in tense.

31 **I.** The paired conjunction here is *both/and*. The first option correctly matches two infinitives *(to show and to display)*. Contrast the correct sentence to option II, which joins a noun *(Harley)* and an infinitive *(to display)*. Option III fails because *both* precedes *intended* (a verb) and the second part of the conjunction, *and*, precedes an infinitive, *to display*.

32 **III.** Option III links two verbs *(accompany and stay)*. The elements joined by *either/or* in the other options don't match. Option I tries to pair a noun *(Lola)* with a verb *(stay)*. Option II links a subject-verb combo *(Lulu would accompany)* to a verb *(stay)*.

33 **II.** In option I, *neither* precedes a description *(ahead)*, and *nor* precedes a subject-verb combo, presented with the verb first *(does Lola)*. Regardless of the order, the sentence isn't parallel. Option II correctly links two nouns *(Lulu, Lola)* with the *neither/nor* conjunction pair. The last sentence fails the parallelism test because it links a subject-verb *(Lulu plans)* with a noun *(Lola)*.

34 **III.** The first option links a noun, *screenplays*, with a prepositional phrase, *about bikers and alien invasions*. Nope. The second option isn't parallel because the first element joined by *not only/but also* includes a verb *(writes)* but the second doesn't. Option III correctly joins two prepositional phrases.

35 **I.** Here you're working with *both/and*. In option I, each half of the conjunction pair precedes a noun *(talent, award)*. In option II *both* precedes *is*, a verb, but no verb follows the *and*. In option III, *both* precedes *is* (a verb), and *and* precedes *award* (a noun). Options II and III aren't parallel.

36 **III.** The conjunction pair, *not only/but also*, links two verbs *(scorns, refuses)* in the correct sentence, option III. Option I places *not only* in front of *Lola scorns* (a subject-verb pair), and the *but also* in front of a verb *(scorns)*. Nope. The second sentence joins a noun, *awards*, to a verb, *scorns*. Mismatch!

37 **I.** The *neither/nor* combo in option I precedes two nouns in the sentence *(award, trophy)*. Verdict: parallel. The second option joins a subject-verb combo *(award has)* and a noun *(tattoo)*. Option II is not parallel. Option III places *neither* in front of a verb, *has*, and *nor* in front of a noun, *tattoo*.

38 **I, II.** *But not* joins two infinitives *(to whip, to clean)* and two gerunds *(whipping, cleaning)* in these sentences. Because they match, they're parallel.

39 **II.** Option I links a subject-verb statement *(that cooking is creative)* with a noun *(cleaning)*. Penalty box! Option II joins two subject-verb statements *(that cooking is creative* and *that cleaning is not)*. Option II is parallel.

40 **I.** Option I links two prepositional phrases *(in justice* and *in revenge)* to make a parallel comparison. Option II pairs *interested in justice* and *he is in revenge*. The first element lacks a subject-verb combo, which the second element has. Therefore, option II isn't parallel.

41 **I.** Two adjectives, *capable* and *responsible*, make option I parallel. Option II pairs an adjective *(capable)* with a subject-verb statement *(he is responsible)*. Nope. Option II isn't parallel.

42 **II.** The expression *more than* joins *who loves to eat* with *liking paperwork*. Option I is a mismatch. Option II correctly links *who loves to eat* and *he likes paperwork*, two subject-verb statements. Option II is correct.

Here are the answers to the "Overachievers" section:

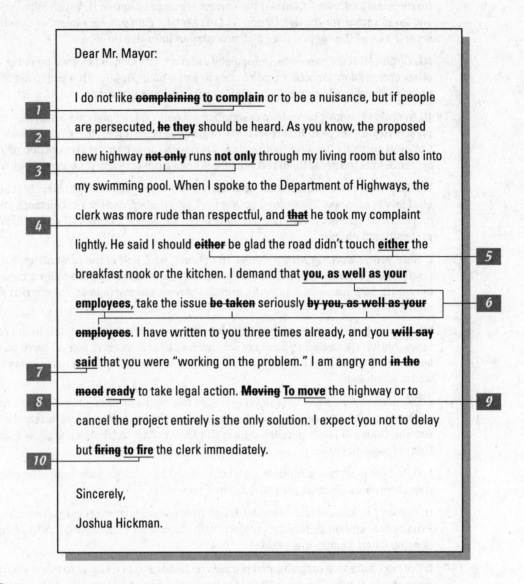

Dear Mr. Mayor:

1. I do not like ~~complaining~~ **to complain** or to be a nuisance, but if people
2. are persecuted, ~~he~~ **they** should be heard. As you know, the proposed
3. new highway ~~not only~~ runs **not only** through my living room but also into
my swimming pool. When I spoke to the Department of Highways, the
4. clerk was more rude than respectful, and ~~that~~ he took my complaint
lightly. He said I should ~~either~~ be glad the road didn't touch **either** the
5. breakfast nook or the kitchen. I demand that **you, as well as your**
6. **employees**, take the issue ~~be taken~~ seriously ~~by you, as well as your~~
~~employees~~. I have written to you three times already, and you ~~will say~~
7. **said** that you were "working on the problem." I am angry and ~~in the~~
8. ~~mood~~ **ready** to take legal action. ~~Moving~~ **To move** the highway or to
9. cancel the project entirely is the only solution. I expect you not to delay
10. but ~~firing~~ **to fire** the clerk immediately.

Sincerely,

Joshua Hickman.

1. You may change *complaining* to *to complain*, as I did, or you may change *to be* to *being*. Either change makes a parallel sentence.

2. *People* is plural, but *he* is singular. Change *he* to *they* and you've got a parallel sentence.

3. Each part of the *not only/but also* pair should precede the same grammatical element — in this case, prepositional phrases.

4. The *and* may link *was* and *took*, two verbs, but not a verb (*was*) and a subordinate clause (*that he took*). Did I catch you with *more rude than respectful*? The expression *more than* is correctly employed here, linking two adjectives.

(5) After the correction, each half of the conjunction pair *either/or* precedes a noun. In the original, the *either* comes before a verb (be) and the *or* before a noun.

(6) The original sentence switches from active (I demand) to passive (be taken . . . by you). The corrected version avoids the shift.

(7) The original shifts from present perfect tense (have written) to future (will say) for no good reason. The correction is in past tense, but that tense is justified by the meaning of the sentence.

(8) *Angry* is an adjective, but *in the mood* is a phrase. *Ready*, an adjective, makes the sentence parallel. Other adjectives, such as *willing*, would also work here.

(9) Either two infinitives (my correction) or two -ing forms (Moving and canceling) are acceptable here, but not one of each.

(10) Two infinitives (to delay, to fire) are legal, but not *to delay* and a gerund (firing).

Chapter **19**

Steering Clear of Confusion: Clarity

The most important principle of writing or speaking is simple:

Be clear!

Every other rule in this book takes second place to this one, because if your audience doesn't understand what you're trying to communicate, you've failed. Never fear: In this chapter you practice placing descriptions where they belong, dealing with understood subjects (so they're never *mis*understood), creating proper comparisons, and fine-tuning vague pronouns. Then every sentence you write will express exactly what you want to say.

Putting Descriptive Words in Their Proper Place

An inch to the left, an inch to the right . . . who cares? You should, because placing descriptive words in the wrong spot may dramatically change the meaning of a sentence. In this section, you practice inserting descriptions where they belong and anchoring free-floating, vague descriptions.

Inserting single-word descriptions

Single-word descriptions — *even, almost, just, nearly,* and *only,* for example — cause a ton of problems. Consider a T-shirt declaring that "Grandma went to New York City and only bought me one lousy T-shirt." The sentence as written means that Grandma did nothing at all in my hometown except buy one T-shirt. Why? Because one-word descriptions should precede the word being described. The correct shirt should read, "Grandma went to New York City and bought me only one lousy T-shirt." Take a look at these examples:

Even Mary knows that song. (Mary generally sticks to talk radio, but the song is so popular that she recognizes it.)

Mary knows *even* that song. (Mary has downloaded 56,098 songs. She knows every musical work ever written, including the one that the sentence is referring to.)

Got the idea? Now take a look at the following sentences. If you find a misplaced single-word description, rewrite the sentence. If everything is fine and dandy, write "correct" in the blank.

EXAMPLE

Q. My Uncle Fred only pays taxes when he's in the mood or when the IRS serves an arrest warrant.

_____

_____

A. **My Uncle Fred pays taxes only when he's in the mood or when the IRS serves an arrest warrant.** The *only* has to move because it makes a comment on the conditions that make Fred pay up (his mood and the times when the IRS puts him in the mood). This description should precede the conditions it talks about. The *only* is not a comment on *pays,* so it's out of place in the original.

1 Because she was celebrating an important birthday, Ms. Jonge only gave us ten hours of homework.

_____

_____

2 The first task nearly seemed impossible: to write an essay about the benefits of homework.

_____

_____

3 After I'd almost written two pages, my instant messenger beeped, and I put my pen down.

_____

_____

4   I even figured that Ms. Jonge, the meanest teacher on the planet, would understand the need to take a break.

_____

5   I made a cup of coffee, but because I care about nutrition, I only ate one doughnut and ignored the other three.

_____

_____

6   My friend Eloise's cholesterol level nearly doubled last week just from eating glazed doughnuts.

_____

_____

7   Eloise, my brother, and I love doughnuts, but all of us do not eat them; Eloise can't resist.

_____

_____

8   Eloise even draws the line somewhere, and she seldom munches more than three jelly doughnuts a day.

_____

_____

9   After I had sent a text message to Eloise, I returned to my homework and found I only had five tasks left.

_____

_____

10   Not all the work was boring, and I actually liked the history assignment.

_____

_____

Relocating longer descriptions

If you're at a car dealership and want to buy a new car from a sales associate with snow tires, you're in the right place. Unfortunately, the description — _with snow tires_ — is not, because its current placement attaches it to _sales associate_ and thus indicates a car guy whose feet have been replaced by big round rubber things, not a vehicle you can drive confidently through a storm.

This section deals with long descriptions (for the grammar obsessed: prepositional phrases, verbals, and clauses) that sometimes stray from their appointed place. To keep your descriptions legal, be sure that they're very close to the word they describe.

Except for a few place or time descriptions, nearly every multiword description directly follows the word it describes. The example in the first paragraph of this section should be "I want to buy a car *with snow tires* from a sales associate." In this version, the description *with snow tires* describes *car.*

WARNING

When you move a misplaced description, take care not to make another error. For example, if I change "I placed a stone in my pocket that I found in the playground" to "I placed a stone that I found in the playground in my pocket," I have a problem. In the original sentence I found the *pocket* in the *playground.* In the changed sentence, I have a *playground* in my *pocket.* The solution is to place a description at the beginning of the sentence: "In my pocket I placed a stone that I found in the playground."

EXAMPLE

Check out the following sentences. Identify the sentence(s) with correctly placed descriptions.

Q.

   I. Even before she passed the road test, Julie bought a leather license holder that was given only twice a month.

   II. Even before she passed the road test that was given only twice a month, Julie bought a leather license holder.

A. **II.** The license holder is available all the time in a leather goods store, but the test shows up only twice a month. Move the description closer to *test* and you're all set.

   I. Julie passed the eye examination administered by a very near-sighted clerk with flying colors.

   II. With flying colors, Julie passed the eye examination administered by a very near-sighted clerk.

   I. The written test inquired about maneuvers for cars skidding on ice.

   II. The written test for cars skidding on ice inquired about maneuvers.

   I. Another question, which required an essay rather than a multiple-choice response, inquired about defensive driving.

   II. Another question inquired about defensive driving, which required an essay rather than a multiple-choice response.

14.

I. About a week after the written portion of the exam, the Department of Motor Vehicles sent a letter giving Julie an appointment for the road test lacking sufficient postage.

II. About a week after the written portion of the exam, the Department of Motor Vehicles sent a letter lacking sufficient postage and giving Julie an appointment for the road test.

15.

I. Before the letter arrived, Julie asked her sister to drive her to the testing site.

II. Julie asked her sister to drive her to the testing site before the letter arrived.

16.

I. Julie's examiner, a nervous man whose foot kept slamming onto an imaginary brake pedal, constantly wrote notes on an official form.

II. A nervous man whose foot kept slamming onto an imaginary brake pedal, Julie's examiner constantly wrote notes on an official form.

17.

I. The first page, which was single-spaced, contained details about Julie's turning technique.

II. The first page contained details about Julie's turning technique, which was single-spaced.

18.

I. Julie hit only two pedestrians and one tree in the middle of a crosswalk.

II. Julie hit only two pedestrians in the middle of a crosswalk and one tree.

19.

I. The examiner relaxed in his aunt's house in Florida soon after Julie's road test.

II. The examiner relaxed soon after Julie's road test in his aunt's house in Florida.

20.

I. Because the examiner had fainted when the speedometer hit 80, Julie wasn't surprised to hear that she had failed her first road test, but the pedestrians' lawsuit was a shock.

II. Julie wasn't surprised to hear that she had failed her first road test, but the pedestrians' lawsuit was a shock because the examiner had fainted when the speedometer hit 80.

Dangling descriptions

To spice up your writing, you may begin some sentences with introductory descriptions that resemble verbs but aren't actually verbs. (In official grammar terminology, they're *verbals*. Verbals can show up elsewhere in the sentence; in this section I'm just dealing with those that introduce sentences.) Usually a comma separates these introductory statements from the main portion of the sentence. When you begin a sentence this way, the introductory description must refer to the subject — the person or thing you're talking about in the sentence. In these examples, the introductory description is italicized:

Dazzled by Tiffany's new diamond ring, Lulu reached for her sunglasses. (The introductory description gives more information about *Lulu,* the subject.)

To block out all visible light, Lulu's glasses have been coated with a special plastic film. (The introductory description gives more information about the subject, *glasses.*)

A variation of this sort of introduction is a statement with an implied subject. Here you must be certain that the implied subject matches the stated subject in the main portion of the sentence:

While wearing these glasses, Lulu can see nothing at all and thus constantly walks into walls. (The implied statement is *While Lulu is wearing these glasses.*)

TEST ALERT

A common error is to detach the introduction from the subject, resulting in a sentence with flawed logic, what grammarians call a *dangling modifier.* Standardized tests frequently include these errors for you to identify or correct. For example, you may see a sentence like this one: "Before buying them, the glasses carried a clear warning, which Lulu ignored." In this incorrect sentence, the meaning is "Before the glasses were buying them, the glasses carried a clear warning, which Lulu ignored." Illogical! To correct this sort of error, you often have to rewrite the sentence: "Before buying the glasses, Lulu read a warning about them and chose to ignore it."

Check out these sentences for danglers. Identify the correct sentence(s).

EXAMPLE

Q.

    I. After waiting for a green light, the crosswalk filled with people rushing to avoid Lulu and her speeding skateboard.

    II. After waiting for a green light, people rushed into the crosswalk to avoid Lulu and her speeding skateboard.

A. **II.** In the first sentence, the *crosswalk* is *waiting for a green light,* because *crosswalk* is the subject and an introductory verb form describes the subject. The second sentence has the people escaping from the sidewalk, where Lulu is riding blind, thanks to her non–see-through sunglasses.

21

    I. To skateboard safely, kneepads help.

    II. To skateboard safely, skaters need kneepads.

22

    I. Sliding swiftly across the sidewalk, Lulu smashed into a tree.

    II. Sliding swiftly across the sidewalk, a tree was smashed into by Lulu.

23

I. Although Lulu was bleeding from a cut near her nose ring, a change of sunglasses was out of the question.

II. Although bleeding from a cut near her nose ring, a change of sunglasses was out of the question.

24

I. To look fashionable, a certain amount of sacrifice is necessary.

II. To look fashionable, one must sacrifice a certain amount.

25

I. While designing her latest tattoo, Lulu thought it would be a good idea to attach a small camera to the frames of her glasses.

II. While designing her latest tattoo, a small camera attached to the frames of her glasses seemed like a good idea.

26

I. Covered in rhinestones, Lulu's glasses made a fashion statement.

II. Covered in rhinestones, Lulu made a fashion statement with her glasses.

27

I. Discussed in the fashion press, many articles criticized Lulu's choice of eyewear.

II. Discussed in the fashion press, Lulu's choice of eyewear was criticized in many articles.

28

I. Coming to the rescue, Tiffany swiped the offending glasses and lectured Lulu on the irrelevance of such fashion statements.

II. Coming to the rescue, the offending glasses were swiped by Tiffany, who lectured Lulu on the irrelevance of such fashion statements.

29

I. To pacify Tiffany and the pedestrians' lawyers, Lulu eventually threw the glasses into the trash can.

II. To pacify Tiffany and the pedestrians' lawyers, the glasses eventually went into the trash can.

30

I. Lulu, being reasonable, opted for a wraparound stainless steel helmet with UV protection.

II. Being reasonable, Lulu opted for a wraparound stainless steel helmet with UV protection.

Getting caught in the middle: Vague descriptions

If you've read the previous sections in this chapter, you already know that the general rule governing descriptions is that they should be near the word they're describing. If you place a description an equal distance from two words it may describe, however, you present a puzzle to your reader. Not a good idea! Consider this sentence: "Protesting successfully scares politicians." Which word does *successfully* describe? *Protesting* or *scares*? You can't tell. The writer may be saying, "Successful protests scare politicians." Or the meaning may be that "protests scare politicians successfully." The moral of the story: Clarity is crucial.

Exam writers prize clarity, so take care to place your descriptions where they belong when you face a standardized test.

Check out the following sentences and decide which, if any, are clear.

Q.

    I. The senator speaking last week voted against the Clarity Bill.

    II. The senator speaking voted against the Clarity Bill last week.

    III. The senator who spoke last week is the one who voted against the Clarity Bill.

A. **II, III.** What does *last week* refer to — when the senator spoke or when the senator voted? Because *last week* is in the middle in option I, the sentence is unclear. By moving the description, as options II and III do, you have a clear statement.

31

    I. A single run through a red light earned a stiff fine.

    II. Running a red light once earned a stiff fine.

    III. Running a red light earned a stiff fine at one time.

32

    I. Backing away from the traffic cop swiftly caused a reaction.

    II. Backing swiftly away from the traffic cop caused a reaction.

    III. Backing away from the traffic cop caused a swift reaction.

33

    I. Last summer's ticket was a blot on his otherwise spotless driving record.

    II. The ticket he got last summer was a blot on his otherwise spotless driving record.

    III. The ticket he got was a blot on his otherwise spotless driving record last summer.

34

    I. The judge said when the case came to trial he would punish the drivers severely.

    II. The judge said that he would punish the drivers severely when the case came to trial.

    III. When the case came to trial, the judge said that he would punish the drivers severely.

I. The punishment the judge imposed quickly drew criticism from the press.

II. The quick punishment the judge imposed drew criticism from the press.

III. The punishment the judge imposed drew criticism from the press quickly.

Avoiding Illogical Comparisons

Comparison (and competition) seem to be hard-wired into the human mind. Who's got more "likes" on social media — Jean or John? Which player has the highest batting average? Is today's stock price higher than yesterday's? Comparisons are everywhere. So, unfortunately, are faulty comparisons. In this section you practice creating complete and logical comparisons.

Completing half-finished comparisons

By definition, a comparison discusses two elements in relation to each other or singles out the extreme in a group and explains exactly what form the extremism takes. For example, "She throws more pies than I do" or "Of all the clowns, she throws the most pies." A comparison may also examine something in relation to a standard, as in "Her comment was so sugary that I had to take an extra shot of insulin." A comparison may be any of these things, but what it may not be is partially absent. If someone says, "The snapper is not *as* fresh" or "The sea bass is *most* musical," you're at sea. *As fresh* as what? *Most musical* in comparison to whom? You have no way of knowing.

Of course, in context these sentences may be perfectly all right. If I say, "I considered the snapper but in the end went with the flounder. The snapper is not as fresh," you know that the second sentence is a continuation of the first. Also, some words in a comparison may be implied, without loss of meaning. I may write, "The snapper makes fewer snotty comments than a large-mouth bass *does.*" The italicized word in the preceding sentence may be left out — and frequently is — without confusing anyone. And that's the key: The reader must have enough information to understand the comparison.

 Incomplete comparisons appear on many standardized tests. Watch for them!

TEST ALERT Take a trip underwater to a crazy world of comparisons. In each group of three, identify the incomplete comparison.

 Q.

EXAMPLE

I. "There are more fish in the sea," commented the grouper as she searched for her posse.

II. "There are more fish in the sea than you know," commented the grouper as she searched for her posse.

III. "There are more fish in the sea than on a restaurant menu," commented the grouper as she searched for her posse.

A. **I.** The key here is to define the term *more*. *More than* what? Option I doesn't answer that question, so it's incomplete. Options II and III add *than you know* or *than on a restaurant menu* to complete the comparison.

I. The trout, who is wealthier than a tech titan, spends a lot of money on waterproof smartphones.

II. The trout, who is wealthier than the president of a Swiss bank, spends a lot of money on waterproof smartphones.

III. The trout, who is wealthier, spends a lot of money on waterproof smartphones.

I. The octopus plays more video games than the shark, often opposing himself with different arms.

II. The octopus plays more video games, often opposing himself with different arms.

III. The octopus plays more video games than any land animal, often opposing himself with different arms.

I. Mermaids are the most adept at financial planning, in my experience.

II. Mermaids are the most adept at financial planning of all marine mammals, in my experience.

III. Of all marine mammals, mermaids are the most adept at financial planning, in my experience.

I. On the other hand, mermaids are less competent at purchasing shoes than other mammals.

II. On the other hand, mermaids are less competent at purchasing shoes.

III. On the other hand, mermaids are less competent at purchasing shoes than sea lions.

I. Not many people realize that mermaid tail fins are so sensitive that special tail-protection is a must.

II. Not many people realize that mermaid tail fins are so sensitive that shoes are extremely painful.

III. Not many people realize that mermaid tail fins are so sensitive.

I. Whales are as fashion-challenged at shoe and accessory selection as mermaids.

II. Whales are as fashion-challenged at shoe and accessory selection.

III. Whales are as fashion-challenged at shoe and accessory selection as the average octopus.

I. This whole under-the-sea theme has become more boring.

II. This whole under-the-sea theme has become more boring than a lecture on the physics of toenail clippers.

III. This whole under-the-sea theme has become more boring than watching paint dry.

I. The marine jokes are so uninteresting that I may volunteer to be shark bait.

II. The marine jokes are so uninteresting that I may never go to the beach again.

III. The marine jokes are so uninteresting.

I. You can always boycott this chapter if you find it less than satisfying.

II. You can always boycott this chapter if you find another chapter more satisfying.

III. You can always boycott this chapter if you find it less satisfying.

I. Compared to here, in Chapter 16 the jokes are better.

II. The jokes are better in Chapter 16 than they are here.

III. The jokes are better in Chapter 16.

Being smarter than yourself: Illogical comparisons

If I say that Babe Ruth was a better slugger than any Yankee, I'm making an error that's almost as bad as a wild throw into the stands. Why? Because the Babe was a Yankee. According to the logic of my original statement, the Babe would have to outslug himself. I don't think so! The solution is simple. Insert *other* or *else* or a similar expression into the sentence. Then the Babe becomes "a better slugger than any other Yankee" or "better than anyone else who has ever played for the Yankees."

Don't insert *other* or *else* if the comparison is between someone in the group and someone outside the group. I can correctly say, for example, that "the current Yankee shortstop is faster than all the Mets" — in terms of grammar, at least. You can time their sprints to first base to see if that statement is true.

TEST ALERT

Standardized-test writers love to test your powers of logic, so carefully check every comparison you encounter.

EXAMPLE

Time for some comparison shopping. Check out the following sentence pairs. Which one (if any) is logical? Note: Just to keep you on your toes, occasionally I throw in two correct, logical comparisons.

Q.

    I. The average pigeon is smarter than any animal in New York City.

    II. The average pigeon is smarter than any other animal in New York City.

A. **II.** Pigeons are *animals,* and pigeons flap all over New York. (I've even seen them on subway cars, where they wait politely for the next stop before waddling onto the plat-form.) Without the word *other* (as in option I), pigeons are smarter than themselves. Penalty box! Option II, which includes *other,* is logical.

    I. Except for the fact that they don't pay the fare, subway pigeons are no worse than any human rider.

    II. Except for the fact that they don't pay the fare, subway pigeons are no worse than any rider.

    I. Spotting a pigeon waiting for the subway door to open is no odder than anything else you see on an average day in New York.

    II. Spotting a pigeon waiting for the subway door to open is no odder than anything you see on an average day in New York.

    I. I once saw a woman on a New York street shampooing her hair in the rain, an experience that was weirder than anything I've seen in New York City.

    II. On a New York street, I once saw a woman shampooing her hair in the rain, an experience that was weirder than anything else I've seen in New York City.

    I. Singing a shower song with a thick New York accent, she appeared saner than city residents.

    II. Singing a shower song with a thick New York accent, she appeared saner than other city residents

    I. A tourist gawking through the window of a sightseeing bus was more surprised than New Yorkers on the street.

    II. A tourist gawking through the window of a sightseeing bus was more surprised than other New Yorkers on the street.

    I. Is this story less believable than what you read in this book?

    II. Is this story less believable than the rest of what you read in this book?

52

I. You may be surprised to know that it is more firmly fact-based than the material in this chapter.

II. You may be surprised to know that it is more firmly fact-based than the other material in this chapter.

53

I. Tourists to New York probably go home with stranger stories than visitors to other big cities.

II. Tourists to New York probably go home with stranger stories than visitors to big cities.

Making Sure Your Pronouns Are Meaningful

Unless you're a politician bent on hiding the fact that you've just increased taxes on everything but bubble gum, you probably want the meaning of every pronoun to be obvious. And you should, because vague pronouns lead to misunderstandings.

Standardized tests often hit you with a double-meaning sentence. Keep your eye out for vague pronouns.

TEST ALERT

To avoid confusing pronouns, keep these points in mind:

>> **Every pronoun needs one clear antecedent.** An *antecedent* is the word(s) the pronoun refers to. Problems occur when you have more than one possible antecedent in the sentence: "My aunt and her mother-in-law were happy about her success in the Scrabble tournament." Who had success, the aunt, the mother-in-law, or some other woman? To clear up any confusion, rewrite: "My aunt and her mother-in-law were happy with my aunt's success in the Scrabble tournament" or something similar.

>> **The pronoun must match its antecedent.** When I say match, I mean that the antecedent and the pronoun could be interchanged without changing the meaning. In this sentence, they can't: "Jane's an architect, and I want to study it too." The pronoun *it* refers to *architect,* but you can't write "I want to study *architect* too." Many corrections are possible, including this one: "Jane's an architect, and I'd like to learn more about her profession."

>> **Pronouns shouldn't refer to whole sentences or paragraphs.** A singular pronoun refers to one noun or one pronoun. A plural pronoun may stand in for more than one noun (for example, *they* may refer to *Nancy* and *Joe*). But you run into problems when you try to refer to an entire sentence or even more with *which, this,* or *that.* Take a look at this sentence: "Joe was a day late and a dollar short when he paid his rent, which annoyed his landlady." What bothered the landlady — the lateness or the dollar or both? *Which* doesn't work here. Try this version (or something like it) instead: "That Joe was a day late and a dollar short when he paid his rent annoyed his landlady." Or this one: "Joe's landlady didn't mind receiving the rent a day late, but the fact that Joe was a dollar short annoyed her."

Often, the best way to clear up a pronoun problem is to rewrite the sentence with no pronoun at all.

TIP

Clear or unclear? Check out the underlined pronoun and decide.

EXAMPLE **Q.** Stacy and Alice photographed <u>her</u> tattoos.

A. **Unclear.** Did Stacy and Alice photograph Alice's tattoos? Or perhaps they photographed Stacy's tattoos? Because you can't tell, the pronoun is unclear. To be clear, rewrite without the pronoun: *Stacy and Alice photographed Alice's (or Stacy's) tattoos.*

54 Chad and his sister are campaigning for an Oscar nomination, but only <u>she</u> is expected to get one.

55 Chad sent a donation to Mr. Hobson in hopes of furthering <u>his</u> cause.

56 If Chad wins an Oscar, he will place the statue on his desk, next to his Emmy, Tony, Obie, and Best-of-the-Bunch awards. <u>It</u> is his favorite honor.

57 Chad's sister has already won one Oscar for <u>her</u> portrayal of a kind but slightly crazy artist who can't seem to stay in one place without extensive support.

58 In the film, Rachel, who played a model for Chad's sister, thought <u>her</u> interpretation of the role was the best.

59 Rachel worked hard to prepare for the modeling part by attending art classes and posing in front of a mirror, <u>which</u> made her portrayal more realistic.

60 Rachel's interest in modeling dates from childhood; ever since she saw a fashion show, she wanted to be <u>one</u>.

61 "I see you as a poet, not a model," commented Chad as he smiled and gave Rachel a romantic look; she wasn't impressed by <u>this</u> at all.

62 In the film, the artist creates giant sculptures out of discarded hubcaps, although museum curators seldom appreciate <u>them</u>.

63 When filming was completed, Rachel was allowed to keep the leftover chair cushions and hubcaps because she liked <u>them</u>.

64 After seeing the set, Chad's sister kept <u>one</u> for a souvenir.

65 Rachel, Chad, and Chad's sister went out for a cup of coffee after the awards show, but <u>he</u> refused to drink <u>his</u> because the cafe was out of fresh cream.

66 Rachel remarked to Chad's sister that Chad could drink <u>her</u> iced tea if he was thirsty.

67 Chad called his brother and asked him to bring the cream from <u>his</u> refrigerator.

68 Chad's sister took a straw and a packet of sugar, stirred her coffee, and then placed <u>it</u> on the table.

69 Chad hit the coffee cup with his elbow, <u>which</u> was broken.

70 "No, I did not see the cup break when I moved my arm," explained Jeffrey, "but <u>that</u> isn't the issue. The cup was unsteady."

Calling All Overachievers: Extra Practice in Writing Clear Sentences

As you breathe deeply, check out this yoga instruction manual, which, my lawyer begs me to mention, does *not* describe real postures that a normal human body can achieve. Do *not* try these positions at home, but *do* look for unclear or misplaced descriptions, comparisons, and pronouns. You should find 15. Correct the mistakes. *Note:* Precisely because the poorly written expressions are vague, you may rewrite them in more than one way. When you check the answer key, you may find that my corrections differ from yours. As long as your revisions are clear, count yourself correct.

An Excerpt from *Yoga and You*

Deciding which yoga posture to learn, the "Greeting Turtle" and the "One-Legged Grammar Cross" should be considered. If you only learn one yoga posture, "Greeting Turtle" should be it. Beginners can even do it and not pull a muscle, which is an advantage. In fact, "Greeting Turtle" is the easiest. To form the "Greeting Turtle," the mat should extend from knees to armpits freshly laundered and dried to fluffiness. While bending the right knee up to the nose, the left ankle relaxes. You should almost bend the knee sharply for a minute before straightening it again. That may be a problem if your watch or phone is in the locker room. When my sister learned "Greeting Turtle," her teacher, Ms. Jones, told her that she didn't have to worry about timing. Ms. Jones also said that in a survey of her yoga students, they voted her yoga class better than any class they took.

Once the ankle is straight, throw your head back and extend each muscle to its fullest, only breathing two or three times before returning your head to its original position. Tucking your chin close to your collarbone, the nose should wiggle. Finally, raise both arms to the sky and bless the yoga posture that is blue.

Answers to Clarity Problems

Now that you've had a chance to practice making your writing clear and comprehensible, check your work with the following answers.

(1) **Because she was celebrating an important birthday, Ms. Jonge gave us only ten hours of homework.** The implication of this sentence is that she could have given twenty hours. Because the number of hours is the issue, the *only* belongs in front of *ten hours*, not in front of *gave.*

(2) **The first task seemed nearly impossible: to write an essay about the benefits of homework.** If it *nearly seemed,* it did not *seem* — just approached that state. But that's not what you're trying to say here. Instead, the task approached *impossible* but stopped just short, still in the realm of possibility. Thus the *nearly* describes *impossible* and should precede that word.

(3) **After I'd written almost two pages, my instant messenger beeped, and I put my pen down.** How many pages did you write? That's what the sentence discusses. When the *almost* is in the right place, you have about a page and a half or a bit more. In the original sentence you have nothing at all on paper because the sentence says that the speaker *had almost written* (had approached the action of writing but then stopped).

(4) **I figured that even Ms. Jonge, the meanest teacher on the planet, would understand the need to take a break.** Clearly the sentence compares this particular teacher with all others, so the *even* belongs in front of her name.

(5) **I made a cup of coffee, but because I care about nutrition, I ate only one doughnut and ignored the other three.** This sentence compares the number of doughnuts eaten (*one*) with the number available (*four*). The *only* belongs in front of the number, not in front of the action (*ate*).

(6) **Correct.** The *nearly* tells you that the increase was a bit less than double. The *just* tells you the reason (snarfing down doughnuts). Both descriptive words are in the correct spot.

(7) **Eloise, my brother, and I love doughnuts, but not all of us eat them; Eloise can't resist.** To correct this sentence you have to play around with the verb a little, because you don't need the *do* in the new sentence. Here's the logic: If Eloise eats the doughnuts and the rest keep their lips zipped, *not all* but *some* eat doughnuts. The original sentence illogically states that no one eats and then goes on to discuss Eloise's gobbling.

(8) **Even Eloise draws the line somewhere, and she seldom munches more than three jelly doughnuts a day.** The *even* shouldn't precede *draws* because two actions aren't being compared. Instead, *Eloise* is being singled out.

(9) **After I had sent a text message to Eloise, I returned to my homework and found I had only five tasks left.** The sentence comments on the amount of remaining homework (*only five tasks,* not six or seven). Hence the *only* properly precedes *five tasks.*

(10) **Correct.** Some work made you yawn and some didn't. Logic tells you that *not all* is what you want.

(11) **II.** You can easily see what's wrong with option I. You don't want a clerk *with flying colors.* Option II places *with flying colors* at the beginning of the sentence, where it's close enough to the verb to tell you how *Julie passed,* the meaning you want.

12 **I.** In option I, the two descriptions — *written* and *for cars skidding on ice* — are close to the words they describe. *Written* describes *test* and *for cars skidding on ice* describes *maneuvers*. Option II places *for cars skidding on ice* after *test*, so exam is for cars. If self-drive cars ever actually enter the market, this may be a correct option, but for now, it's wrong.

13 **I.** Defensive-driving techniques don't include essays, but test questions do. The description *which required an essay rather than a multiple-choice response* belongs after *question*, its location in option I. Option II incorrectly places the description after *driving*.

14 **II.** The *letter* is described by *lacking sufficient postage*, so that description must follow *letter*, as it does in option II. Option I places the description after *test* — which doesn't lack postage!

15 **I.** Both sentences mention two actions: *asked* and *drive*. The time element, *before the letter arrived*, tells you when Julie asked, not when she wanted her sister to drive. The description should be closer to *asked* than to *drive*, as it is in option I, because *asked* is the word it describes.

16 **I, II.** In both options the description (which, in grammar terms, is actually an appositive or equivalent) is where it should be. In option I, *a nervous man whose foot kept slamming onto an imaginary brake pedal* attaches to *examiner*. In option II, the same information also attaches to *examiner*. Flipping the order doesn't matter.

17 **I.** The *page* is described by *single-spaced*, not Julie's three-point turn, so option I, which places the information about spacing after *page*, is correct.

18 **II.** Common sense tells you that the tree isn't in the crosswalk, but the pedestrians are. The description *in the middle of a crosswalk* should follow the word it describes, in this case, *pedestrians*, as it does in option II. Option I mistakenly places the tree in the crosswalk.

19 **I.** The relaxing took place *in his aunt's house in Florida*. The road test took place on a road. Option I places the description close to the word it describes. Option II has the road test taking place inside a house — not the most likely meaning.

20 **I, II.** Both options work, but they have different meanings. The *because* statement explains why Julie wasn't surprised about her failure. In option I, the *because* statement is close to *was not surprised*. The meaning of option I is that the examiner's fainting indicates that the test wasn't successful. Option II links the fainting to the surprise about the *lawsuit* and implies that the condition of Julie's examiner exonerates her and she shouldn't be sued.

21 **II.** In option I, no one is skateboarding. Option II includes *skaters*, so it's correct.

22 **I.** Lulu should be the one doing the *sliding*, not the tree. Option I puts Lulu where she should be, as the subject of the sentence. Option II has the tree sliding across the sidewalk.

23 **I.** When you begin a sentence with an implied subject, the subject that is present does double duty, acting as subject for both parts of the sentence. Option II has *a change of sunglasses* doing the *bleeding*. The easiest way to correct a sentence with the wrong implied subject is to insert the real subject, which is *Lulu*, as option I does.

24 **II.** Who is looking fashionable? In the first sentence, no one. Option II adds *one*, a person, and is correct.

25 **I.** Someone has to be doing the designing, but in option II, *a small camera* is *designing her latest tattoo*. Option I correctly places *Lulu* in the subject spot, so she's doing the *designing*.

26. **I.** Lulu's glasses are covered in rhinestones, not Lulu herself. *Lulu's glasses* must be the subject of the sentence, as it is in option I. Option II has Lulu covered in rhinestones. Nope!

27. **II.** What was discussed? The *eyewear,* not the *articles.* That's what option II says, making it the correct answer. Option I has the *articles* doing the discussing.

28. **I.** Tiffany's *coming to the rescue* in option I, so the sentence is fine. In option II, the *glasses* are doing the rescuing, so that sentence is incorrect.

29. **I.** Check the subject of the main portion of the sentence. In option I, the subject is *Lulu* and in option II, *glasses.* The *glasses* can't pacify, but *Lulu* can, so option I is correct and option II falls short.

30. **I, II.** Okay, it's a stretch to see *Lulu* as *reasonable,* not to mention the discomfort of a *stainless steel helmet,* but grammatically both sentences are correct because in both, *being reasonable* is attached to *Lulu.*

31. **I, III.** In option I, the *stiff fine* comes from one mistake. In option III, the penalty *at one time* was harsh, but is different now. Option II is confusing — and therefore wrong — because *once* could attach to either *running* or *earned.*

32. **II, III.** In option I, *swiftly* causes problems because it could describe either *backing* or *caused.* The problem goes away if you place this description closer to *backing* (option II) or change it to *swift* to describe *reaction* (option III).

33. **I, II.** The first two are clear, each saying in different ways that he got the ticket last summer. The third choice presents a problem. Is last summer's ticket a blemish on the summer driving record or on the entire record (from the first driving moment through the present time)? Because two possible interpretations exist, III doesn't work.

34. **II, III.** The problem with the first sentence is subtle but nevertheless worthy of attention. The expression *when the case came to trial* may be when the judge made his statement or when the judge intended to penalize the drivers. Option II has the punishment (perhaps the collection of a large fine) occurring at the trial. Option III has the judge speaking about the punishment at the trial. Options II and III are clear, but option I isn't.

35. **II, III.** Option I is unclear because *quickly* may describe either how fast the judge *imposed* the punishment or how fast the press reacted. Option II clearly expresses the first meaning and option III the second meaning.

36. **III.** The problem with the option III is that you can't tell what or who is being compared to the trout. The missing element of the comparison must be supplied, as it is in options I and II (*tech titan, Swiss bank*).

37. **II.** The second sentence begins the comparison nicely (*more video games than*) and then flubs the ending (*than what? than who?*). Options I and III supply an ending — *than the shark, than any land animal* — so they're complete.

38. **I.** The first comparison doesn't specify the group in which mermaids excel. Options II and III provide context by inserting *of all marine mammals.* The position of that phrase doesn't matter, but its presence does.

39 **II.** Option II leaves the reader wondering about the basis of comparison. Option I adds *than other mammals* and option III inserts *than sea lions.* Both comparisons I and III are complete because the context is clear.

40 **III.** In common speech, *so* is often used as an intensifier, the equivalent of *very.* In proper English, however, *so* begins a comparison. Option III contains an incomplete comparison. *So sensitive* that what? Options I and II finish the comparison by supplying another idea *(that special tail protection is a must* and *that shoes are extremely painful).*

41 **II.** *As fashion challenged as who or what?* Option II doesn't say. Option I plugs in *mermaids,* and option III goes for *the average octopus.* Both I and III are complete, but II isn't.

42 **I.** To finish the comparison, you need an example of excruciating boredom. Options II and III supply those examples *(lecture on the physics of toenail clippers, watching paint dry).* Option I doesn't, so it's incomplete.

43 **III.** The *so* statement must be completed by some sort of *that* statement, and option III isn't. Options I and II include the *that statement (that I may volunteer to be shark bait, that I may never go to the beach again).* Options I and II are complete, but III isn't.

44 **III.** The phrase *less than satisfying* compares the comedy to an ideal state (satisfying), so option I is fine. Option II, which introduces the idea of *another chapter,* is fine as well. The comparison in option III is incomplete because it doesn't say *less satisfying* in comparison to something else.

45 **III.** Two locations, the chapter you're reading (19) and Chapter 16, are compared in the first two sentences, giving you complete and correct comparisons. The third option has no context, so it's incomplete.

46 **I.** Option I adds *human,* therefore correctly comparing *pigeons* to another group, *humans.* Verdict: logical. Option II fails because it presents pigeons as no worse than themselves, an impossible situation.

47 **I.** In option I, the *else* serves an important purpose: It shows the reader that the pigeon waiting for the subway is being compared to *other* events in New York City. Without the *else,* as in option II, the sentence is irrational because then the sentence means that seeing pigeons in New York is no odder than what you see in New York.

48 **II.** The *else* in option II creates a logical comparison between this event (also true!) and other strange things I've seen in New York City. Because option I lacks *else,* it's illogical.

49 **II.** If she's got a New York accent, she's a city resident. Without the word *other,* as in option I, you're saying that she's saner than herself. Not possible! Option II repairs the logic by inserting *other.*

50 **I.** The tourist isn't a city resident, so he or she may be compared to *New Yorkers on the street* without the word *other.* Option I is fine. Option II veers away from logic by introducing the word *other.* A tourist isn't a New Yorker, so that word is unnecessary and illogical.

51 **II.** The story is in the book, and it can't be compared to itself, as option I does. The phrase *the rest of,* which appears in option II, differentiates the story but preserves the logic.

52 **II.** The story is in this chapter, so you need *other* or a similar word to create a logical comparison, which option II does.

53 **I.** New York is a big city, but the second sentence implies otherwise. The word *other* in the first sentence solves the problem.

54 **Clear.** Chad is male and his sister is female, so *she* may refer only to one person, Chad's sister.

55 **Unclear.** Does *his* mean Chad's or Mr. Hobson's? The way the sentence reads, either answer is possible.

56 **Unclear.** Maybe the Tony is his favorite honor, or maybe the Obie. The sentence is so unclear that almost any award may be plugged into the favorite.

57 **Clear.** The pronoun *her* can refer only to Chad's sister. Everything is clear.

58 **Unclear.** You can't tell what *her* means — *Rachel's* or *Chad's sister's*, so the pronoun is unclear.

59 **Unclear.** What does *which* refer to, the art classes or the mirror posing? The pronoun should clearly refer to another pronoun or noun, and in this sentence, *which* doesn't.

60 **Unclear.** *One* what? *One fashion show?* Okay, you probably guessed that *one* means *model*, but that word isn't in the sentence. Penalty box!

61 **Unclear.** What does *this* refer to? Chad's statement, his smile, or the romantic look? *This* doesn't clearly refer to any of these, so the pronoun is vague.

62 **Unclear.** You have two groups of objects in the sentence: the *sculptures* and the *hubcaps. Them* could refer to either. To eliminate the uncertainty, replace *them* with a more specific statement.

63 **Unclear.** What does *them* mean? *Cushions? Hubcaps?* Because you can't tell, the pronoun is vague and the sentence is unclear.

64 **Unclear.** *One* is vague because you don't know what *one* refers to. One artwork? One hubcap? One art lover? Who knows?

65 **Clear.** The sentence refers to two females (Rachel and Chad's sister) and one male. Because only one male is in the sentence, the masculine pronouns *he* and *his* are clear.

66 **Unclear.** The pronoun is unclear because you can't tell whether *her* refers to Rachel or to Chad's sister.

67 **Unclear.** Is Chad a cheapo who is always mooching someone else's stuff? In other words, is Chad asking for his brother's cream? Or does Chad want his brother to bring Chad's cream? You don't know, so the pronoun is unclear.

68 **Unclear.** The sentence contains a pronoun (*it*) with several possible meanings (the straw, the sugar packet, or the coffee).

69 **Unclear.** What was broken, the *cup* or the *elbow*? The pronoun *which* is unclear.

70 **Unclear.** What does *that* refer to? The sentence presents two possibilities, not seeing the cup break and moving the arm. Verdict: vague pronoun.

Here are the answers to the "Overachievers" section:

An Excerpt from *Yoga and Y'All*

~~Deciding which yoga posture to learn,~~ **When you decide which yoga posture to learn,** the "Greeting Turtle" and the "One-Legged Grammar Cross" should be considered. If you ~~only~~ learn **only** one yoga posture, "Greeting Turtle" should be it. **One advantage is that even** beginners can ~~even~~ do it and not pull a muscle, ~~which is an advantage~~. In fact, "Greeting Turtle" is the easiest **of all the postures**. To form the "Greeting Turtle," ~~the mat should~~ **you should** extend **yourself** from knees to armpits **on a mat that is** freshly laundered and dried to fluffiness. While **you are** bending the right knee up to the nose, the left ankle relaxes. You should ~~almost~~ bend the knee sharply for **almost** a minute before straightening it again. ~~That~~ **Timing** may be a problem if your watch or phone is in the locker room. When my sister learned "Greeting Turtle," her teacher, Ms. Jones, told her that ~~she~~ **my sister** didn't have to worry about timing. Ms. Jones also said that in a survey of yoga students, they voted her yoga class better than any **other** class they took.

Once the ankle is straight, throw your head back and extend each muscle to its fullest, ~~only~~ breathing **only** two or three times before returning your head to its original position. Tucking your chin close to your collarbone, ~~the nose should wiggle~~ **wiggle your nose**. Finally, raise both arms to the sky ~~that is blue~~ and bless the yoga posture **that is blue**.

1

2

3

4

5

6

7

8

9

10

11

12

13

14

15

1. An introductory verb form must describe the subject. In the original sentence, *Deciding which posture to learn* describes "Greeting Turtle" or the "One-Legged Grammar Cross," the subjects of the sentence. Postures can't decide. To correct the error, you can change the introductory verb form to a clause *(When you are deciding . . .)*, which has its own subject *(you)*.

2. The *only* applies to the number *(one)*, not to the act of learning.

3. The description *even* should be attached to *beginners* to show how easy this posture is.

4. In the original, *which* may apply to doing the posture or to not pulling a muscle or to both. The reworded version clarifies that both are advantages.

5. *Easiest*, in the original, is presented with no context. I supplied one possible context, but you can insert something else (for example, *easiest of all the postures in this chapter*).

6. In the original, the mat has *knees* and *armpits*. Nope. *You* do.

7. The laundry description belongs to *mat*, not to *armpits*, though I do think that fluffy armpits are nice.

8. In the original sentence, the *ankle* is bending the *knee*. Nope.

9. The *almost* applies to *minute*, not to *bend*.

10. What does *That* refer to? The original is unclear. Changing *that* to *timing* solves the problem.

11. Who didn't have to worry about timing, *Ms. Jones* or *my sister*? The original is vague, but inserting a noun solves the problem.

12. The original comparison is illogical, because the students are in the class, which can't be better than classes they took. Insert "other" and the logic works.

13. *Only* applies to the number of times the person should breathe, not to the action of breathing itself.

14. The introductory verb form must apply to an action done by the subject, but *the nose* can't *tuck the chin.* The understood subject *you* can.

15. The color description belongs to the *sky*, not to the *yoga posture*.

Chapter **20**

Dealing with Grammar Demons

In folk tales and myths, demons are supernatural creatures that cause trouble everywhere they go. Grammar has demons, too, and there's nothing supernatural about them. In fact, grammar demons are the mistakes that writers fall into naturally — and avoid easily with just a little practice. In this chapter, you sharpen your demon-slaying skills.

Dropping Double Negatives

In some languages, the more negatives you pile into a sentence, the more strongly you're saying no. In English, though, two negative words make a positive statement. For example, "Henry did not want no vegetables" means that Henry wanted some vegetables (perhaps just not the one that was on his plate). Unless you're trying to say something positive, steer clear of these double negatives, presented here with examples:

WRONG: Lucette cannot help but dance when the salsa band plays. (*not* and *but* = negatives)

RIGHT: Lucette cannot help dancing when the salsa band plays.

WRONG: Elizabeth can't hardly wait until the music starts. (*can't* and *hardly* = negatives)

RIGHT: Elizabeth can hardly wait until the music starts.

WRONG: Tom, the guitarist, hadn't but ten minutes until showtime. *(not,* which appears in the contraction *hadn't,* and *but* = negatives)

RIGHT: Tom, the guitarist, had only ten minutes until showtime.

Identify the double negatives. Rewrite the sentence correctly.

EXAMPLE

Q. I can't help but think that your questions about the final exam are extremely annoying.

_____

_____

A. **I can't help thinking that your questions about the final exam are extremely annoying.** The expressions *can't help but* and *cannot help but* are double negatives. English, not always the most logical language in the universe, is logical in this instance: The two negatives *(not* and *but)* cancel each other and express a positive meaning. Thus the original sentence means that you can stop thinking this way if you want to do so.

1 Vincent is humming so loud that I can't hardly think.

_____

_____

2 Candice ain't got no problem with Vincent's noisy behavior.

_____

_____

3 The teacher looked at Vincent and declared, "I do not allow no singing here."

_____

_____

4 Vincent hadn't but five minutes to finish the math section of the test.

_____

_____

5 "I can't help but think that your rule is unfair to musicians," said Benny.

_____

_____

Telling Word-Twins Apart

Do you know any twins who resemble each other but have completely different personalities? If so, you already understand that each half of a similar-sounding pair may function differently, and woe to the writer who sends one to do the other's job. This section helps you employ word-twins (and some triplets) properly. Take a look:

>> **Your and you're.** *Your* shows possession: *Your* foot is on my seat. *You're* is short for "you are": *You're* very rude.

>> **Its and it's.** *Its* shows possession: The table fell when *its* legs snapped. *It's* is short for "it is": *It's* at the repair shop now and should be ready in time for the party.

>> **Whose and who's.** *Whose* shows possession: The clerk *whose* line is longest is the slowest worker in the office. *Who's* is short for "who is" or "who has": *Who's* going to fire that clerk and hire someone faster?

>> **Their, they're, and there.** *Their* shows possession: The clients took *their* business elsewhere. *They're* is short for "they are": *They're* tired of waiting. *There* is a place: The clients found a more efficient office and went *there*.

>> **Two, to, and too.** *Two* is a number: You have *two* hands. *To* may attach to a verb to form an infinitive (*to* show, *to* dream, *to* be) or show movement toward something or someone (*to* the store, *to* you): Go *to* the kitchen and use those hands *to* wash the dishes. *Too* means "also" or "more than enough": Michael will wash *too*, because there is *too* much work for one person."

 Choose the correct word and write it in the blank.

EXAMPLE

Q. Don't judge a book by _____ (its, it's) cover unless _____ (your, you're) buying a text for art class.

A. **its, you're.** In the first blank, you want a possessive form. In the second, *you are buying* is the meaning you need.

6 "_____ (Whose, Who's) _____ (your, you're) professor?" asked Mandy.

7 "I don't know," Mark replied. "_____ (Its, It's) a new class. I'll find out when I go _____ (their, they're, there)."

8 Mark was hoping the workload wouldn't be _____ (two, to, too) intense because he had _____ (two, to, too) find a job _____ (two, to, too) help his parents pay _____ (their, they're, there) bills.

9 "Smithson, _____ (whose, who's) assignments look hard, is the best teacher. Plus, _____ (your, you're) in class only _____ (two, to, too) hours a week," said Mandy.

10 "Regardless of the teacher, _____ (its, it's) a tough class, with _____ (two, to, too) many facts," added Jonathan. "I often send letters of complaint _____ (two, to, too) the deans, but _____ (their, they're) not sympathetic."

Distinguishing Between Commonly Confused Words

What a difference a letter (or a few letters) make! The word pairs in this section are commonly confused, with one word appearing where the other is more appropriate. Take note of the difference, and use them wisely:

TIP

>> **Affect and Effect.** *Affect* is a verb meaning "to influence": Mallory's tantrum did not *affect* her mother's decision to leave the candy aisle. *Effect* is most often used as a noun meaning "result": One *effect* of Mallory's sweet tooth was a truly impressive dental bill.

Both *affect* and *effect* may be used in other ways, though much less frequently. *Affect* as a noun means "the way someone displays emotions." *Effect* as a verb means "to bring about a change in the face of opposition." In this chapter, though, I concentrate on the more common usage for each.

>> **Farther and Further.** *Farther* refers to distance: Mallory runs *farther* than anyone else when a candy bar is at stake. *Further* refers to just about everything but distance (intensity, degree, time, and so forth): When Mallory thought *further* about the matter, she decided that artificial sweetener was not a good choice.

>> **Continually and Continuously.** *Continually* (and its close relative, *continual*) refer to actions that happen again and again, with little breaks between: Joe *continually* opened the oven to check on the cake baking inside. With *continual* drafts of cold air, the oven cooled down. *Continuously* (and its relative, *continuous*) refer a constant action that has no gaps: Without *continuous* heat, the cake took forever to bake. Margie scolded him *continuously* until he ordered a cake from the corner bakery.

>> **Accept and Except.** *Accept* is "to say yes to, to agree, to receive": Margie, who loves sweets, *accepts* every dessert offered to her. *Except* means "everything but": Joe eats every type of dessert *except* pie, which he doesn't like.

>> **Hanged and Hung.** *To hang* is "to suspend." In the present tense, *hang* works in every situation. In the past tense, though, two very different forms appear, *hanged* and *hung.* A person being executed for a crime is *hanged,* but a picture is *hung* on a wall.

Circle the best word or phrase in each set of parentheses.

EXAMPLE

Q. Fueled by the caffeine in two double lattes, Jake drove (farther/further) than anyone else.

A. **Farther.** If you're dealing with distance, *farther* is the one you want.

11 The judge insisted on (farther/further) proof that the cop's speed gun was broken.

12 I gave the judge tons of proof, which he refused to (accept/except).

13 Waving my wallet vigorously at the judge, I tried to (affect/effect) the verdict by hinting at a large bribe.

14. Judge Crater stubbornly refused to hear my side of the story and (continually/continuously) interrupted me.

15. "Don't go any (farther/further) with your testimony," he snarled.

16. I shut up because I didn't want to be (hanged/hung).

17. The judge's words, unfortunately, were drowned out by the (continual/continuous) hammering from the construction next door, which never stopped.

18. The (affect/effect) of this noise was disastrous.

19. Nothing I said, when I started talking again, (affected/effected) the judge's ruling.

20. A portrait of the judge (hanged/hung) on the wall behind the bench.

21. I can't convince my romantic partner to spend (farther/further) time with me if the judge imposes a large fine.

22. High-priced food, in my experience, (affects/effects) the way a potential date reacts; if I don't offer an expensive restaurant, my date will not (accept/except) me.

Counting and Measuring Grammatically

Lost in the fog of the history of English is the reason why different words are used to describe singulars and plurals when you're counting or measuring:

WARNING

More than, many, and **fewer** work for plurals: *more than* 19 witnesses, *many* problems, *fewer* than 50 coffee cups. These words work well with things you can count. **Less, much,** and **over** take you into singular territory: *less* interest in the sport, *much* unrest, *over* an hour. These words are best with things you can measure but not count.

The word *over* is frequently misused in place of *more* or *more than*.

Amount is appropriate when the item you're discussing is singular: the *amount* of enthusiasm. **Number** applies to plurals: the *number* of bowties.

Between is the word you want when you're talking about two people or things: I'm having trouble choosing *between* pistachio and chocolate chip. **Among** is for groups of three or more: *Among* the twelve candidates for mayor, Shirley stands out.

EXAMPLE

Uncover your toes (in case you need to count higher than ten) and take a stab at these sentences. Circle the correct word in each set of parentheses.

Q. Just (between/among) you and me, do you think he needs a dye job?

A. **between.** *You* plus *me* equals two, and *between* is the word for couples. *Among* comes into play for three or more, as in *among the five of us.*

23. The boss sent (more than/over) 300 memos describing when and how we can order paper for the copy machine.

24. We employees, all 4,546 of us, discussed the memo (between/among) ourselves, and despite (many/much) difference of opinion, we eventually agreed on one thing.

25. We decided that email uses (fewer/less) paper and is easier to ignore.

26. The boss's (many/much) memos scold us for the (number/amount) of paper we waste.

27. Recently, the boss's secretary collected (more than/over) 5,000 sheets of paper from our desks, all of them memos sent by the boss.

28. Surely it takes (fewer/less) energy to shelve the issue altogether.

29. (More than/over) a year ago the boss caught "shredding fever."

30. The (number/amount) of important material he shredded is impossible to determine.

31. Personally, I believe that in a contest (between/among) him and his dog, the dog would win the award for "Best Boss."

32. The dog would fire (fewer/less) employees.

33. With the dog in charge, the (amount/number) of barking would also decrease.

34. (Among/between) the other candidates for a replacement boss that I would consider are all the inhabitants of New York City.

Taming Tricky Verbs

Sit (not *set*) yourself down for some practice with six headache-inducing verbs. Afterward you can *lie* (not *lay*) down for a rest. You have nothing to *lose* (not *loose*) if you let your inner grammarian *loose* (not *lose*).

>> **Lie and Lay.** One meaning of *lie* is "rest or recline the body." (Yes, it also means that you aren't telling the truth, but that definition isn't a problem.) The past tense of *lie* is *lay*. The form of the verb *lie* that combines with *has, have,* or *had* is *lain.* To **lay** is "to place something" or "to put." The past tense of *lay* is *laid.* For *lay,* the form that combines with *has, have,* or *had* is *laid.*

>> **Sit and Set.** To **sit** is "to bend your knees and put your bottom on some sort of surface." The past tense and the combo form are both *sat.* To **set** is "to place, to put something somewhere." The past tense and combo forms are also *set.*

>> **Lose and Loose.** To *lose* is "to be unable to find" or to "come up short in a contest." To *loose* is "to set free," or, as a description, "roomy, unleashed."

TIP

To help you remember the difference between the first two pairs of verbs, think of *lie* and *sit* as actions that a person does to himself or herself: I *lie* down, I *sit* in the chair. *Lay* and *set*, on the other hand, are actions that a person does to something else: I *lay* the check on the desk, I *set* the vase down on the piano.

EXAMPLE

Don't set down your pen until you try the following questions. Circle the correct form of the verb in the parentheses.

Q. Yesterday Alice was so tired that she (lie/lay/lied/laid/lain) down for a nap even though her favorite soap opera was on television.

A. **lay.** The meaning in this sentence is "to rest or to recline," so the verb you want is *to lie*, and the past tense of *to lie* is *lay*.

35. The main character in Alice's favorite show (lies/lays) in bed, comatose.

36. In the world of soaps, the rule is that the doctor must (sit/set) by the bed every day with a look of concern and love on his or her face.

37. In yesterday's episode, the doctor (sit/sat/set) a bouquet of flowers on the nightstand. By the end of the show, she would (lose, loose) her temper and smash the vase.

38. When the nurse told the doctor to go home and (lie/lay) down, the doctor replied that she would "(sit/set) down for a while."

39. Last week the doctor (lay/laid) a wreath on a mysterious tomb. A dog got (lose, loose) and snatched the wreath.

40. The viewers think the wreath that (lies/lays) there is a sign that the tomb contains the body of the doctor's long lost lover.

41. During sweeps week, the long lost lover will show up and (sit/set) next to the doctor in the cafeteria, but she will eventually (lose, loose) her lover again.

42. The final show will reveal that the long lost lover has (lain/laid) in a bed, comatose too.

43. While the doctor (sits/sets) there gobbling tuna salad, the lover will explain what happened to the evil twin.

Banishing Bogus Expressions

English *should of* been easier. *Being that* English is difficult to learn, I'm going to *try and* spend more time studying it. *Irregardless*, I *gotta* have time for origami, a hobby I can't resist. *Alright*, I admit that this hobby has *alot* of relaxing qualities. So does eating *grill* cheese. My brother and *myself* plan to have some for lunch.

By now I'm sure you've figured out that the italicized words in the preceding paragraph are all problematic in proper English. Check out Table 20-1 to see some acceptable substitutes.

Table 20-1   Correcting Made-Up Words

Wrong	Right
should of	should have, should've
would of	would have, would've
could of	could have, could've
myself, himself, herself, themselves, and similar -self pronouns	Unless the action doubles back on the subject (I told myself to be brave) or unless you want emphasis (I myself will do it), stay away from -self pronouns.
gotta	got to, have to
being that	because, as
try and	try to
alot	a lot
alright	all right
irregardless	regardless (Note: *Irregardless* has become more acceptable in casual conversation, but it's still not considered Standard English.)

Here's your challenge: Check out the following sentences, identifying those using Standard English. You may find one, more than one, or none.

EXAMPLE

Q.

I. When you're in trouble, remember that you have a friend.

II. When you're in trouble, remember that you gotta friend.

III. When you're in trouble, remember that you've gotta friend.

A. I. *Gotta* is not Standard English. Only option II eliminates that expression and substitutes *have*.

 44

I. Irregardless of the teacher's views on having a lot of technology in the classroom, Mark sends an instant message to his brother.

II. Regardless of the teacher's views on having a lot of technology in the classroom, Mark sends an instant message to his brother.

III. Irregardless of the teacher's views on having alot of technology in the classroom, Mark sends an instant message to his brother.

 45

I. Kevin doesn't answer immediately, because he is in the middle of the sandbox and feels that everything is all right.

II. Kevin doesn't answer immediately, being that he's in the middle of the sandbox and feels that everything is alright.

III. Kevin doesn't answer immediately, as he's in the middle of the sandbox and feels that everything is all right.

I. "I'll try to answer Mark after snack," he thinks.

II. "I'll try and answer Mark after snack," he thinks.

III. "I myself will try and answer Mark after snack," he thinks.

I. The teacher will try and avoid distractions from the lesson she prepared, but she should of confiscated Kevin's smartphone, too, to prevent Kevin's tweeting a lot during class.

II. The teacher will try to avoid distractions from the lesson she prepared, but she should have confiscated Kevin's smartphone, too, to prevent Kevin's tweeting a lot during class.

III. The teacher will try and avoid distractions from the lesson she prepared, but she should've confiscated Kevin's smartphone, too, to prevent Kevin's tweeting a lot during class.

I. Kevin should have hidden his smartphone until nap time, but he thought it would be all right to use it openly.

II. Kevin would of hidden his smartphone until nap time, but he thought it would be all right to use it openly.

III. Kevin could have hidden his smartphone until nap time, but he thought it would be all right to use it openly.

I. Because Mark can hardly believe some of the stories Kevin tells about kindergarten, his wife and himself ask many questions.

II. Being that Mark can hardly believe some of the stories Kevin tells about kindergarten, his wife and himself ask many questions.

III. Because Mark can hardly believe some of the stories Kevin tells about kindergarten, his wife and he ask many questions.

I. Mark remembers his own days in finger-paint land, which he should've treasured.

II. Mark remembers his own days in finger-paint land, which he should have treasured.

III. Mark remembers his own days in finger-paint land, which he should of treasured.

51

   I.   While the third-grade room is near the kindergarten, Mark could've walked out of the classroom and spoken directly to Kevin.

   II. Because the third-grade room is near the kindergarten, Mark could have walked out of the classroom and spoken directly to Kevin.

   III. Being that the third-grade room is near the kindergarten, Mark could have walked out of the classroom and spoken directly to Kevin.

52

   I.   Kevin tries not to think about his smartphone, which he says he's gotta have, but he fails.

   II. Kevin tries and fails not to think about his smartphone, which he says he has to have.

   III. Kevin tries not to think about his smartphone, which he says he must have, but he fails.

53

   I.   Because the day is almost over, Kevin asks the teacher to return the phone.

   II. Being that the day is almost over, Kevin asks the teacher to return the phone.

   III. As the day is almost over, Kevin asks the teacher to return the phone.

54

   I.   Kevin told himself that being in kindergarten is really annoying sometimes.

   II. "Being that I'm in kindergarten is really annoying sometimes," Kevin told himself.

   III. "Being in kindergarten is really annoying sometimes," Kevin told himself.

55

   I.   "Myself and Gina should skip first grade and go right to second," Kevin remarked.

   II. "Gina and myself should skip first grade and go right to second," Kevin remarked.

   III. "Gina and I should skip first grade and go right to second," Kevin remarked.

Calling All Overachievers: Extra Practice with Tricky Words

EXAMPLE

In the following figure, check out an obituary that (never, I assure you) appeared in a local paper. Whenever you encounter a misused word, correct the clunker. You should find 15 mistakes.

Lloyd Demos Dies at 81: Historian Who Specialized in Ancient Egypt

Lloyd Demos died yesterday as he was pursuing farther study in ancient Egyptian culture. Demos, who effected the lives of many residents of our town, had alot of varied interests. Demos should of been famous, but he was shy and couldn't hardly stand talking to reporters. The historian, who's curiosity continuously led him to attend lectures from experts in every field, knew 12 languages. Being that he spent much time studying ancient Egyptian grammar, its not surprising that his writing was always alright. Demos had just set down to lunch when he felt ill. Irregardless, Demos insisted on finishing his grill cheese. After eating he said, "I am tired and would like to lay down." Demos, who wrote over 50 books, will be fondly remembered.

Answers to Grammar Demon Problems

Keeping tricky words straight takes a lot of effort. Use the answers below to check your work on the practice exercises.

(1) **Vincent is humming so loud that I can hardly think.** The double negative *can't hardly* should be *can hardly.*

(2) **Candice has no problem with Vincent's noisy behavior.** *Ain't* isn't standard, and pairing it with *no* creates an additional problem.

(3) **The teacher looked at Vincent and declared, "I do not allow singing here."** If you place *not* and *no* together, you have a double negative. Get rid of *no*, as I did, or *do not*: I allow no singing.

(4) **Vincent had but five minutes to finish the math section of the test.** The contraction *hadn't* contains *not*, a negative, and *but* is also negative. Change *hadn't* to *had* and the sentence is fine. You can also substitute *only* for *but.*

(5) **"I can't help thinking that your rule is unfair to musicians," said Benny.** Inside *can't* is the negative word *not. But* is also negative. Change *but think* to *thinking* and the sentence is correct.

(6) **Who's, your.** In the first blank, you need "Who is." In the second, a possessive form is required.

(7) **It's, there.** In the first blank, "it is" (it's) makes sense. The second blank needs a place, *there.*

(8) **too, to, to, their.** In the first blank you want a word to show "overly," *too.* The next two blanks are part of infinitives, so *to* is appropriate. In the last blank, a possessive form is what you want.

(9) **whose, you're, two.** The first blank requires a possessive. The second needs "you are," which is *you're.* Finally, you want a number (*two*).

(10) **it's, too, to, they're.** *It is*, or *it's* fits the first blank. In the second blank, you want a sense of "more than enough," or *too.* Next up is movement, so you want *to.* Last, "they are," or *they're*, is needed.

(11) **further.** Once you're talking about extra information, *farther* isn't an option, because *farther* refers to distance. Go for *further.*

(12) **accept.** Substitute "receive" and you see that *accept* is the word you want here, not *except*, which means "everything but."

(13) **affect.** In this sentence, you want a synonym for "have influence on," which is *affect.*

(14) **continually.** The judge interrupted from time to time, so *continually* fits best.

(15) **further.** You're not talking about distance, but rather about additional speech, so *further* is the word you need here.

(16) **hanged.** To have a rope around your neck is to be *hanged*, not *hung.*

(17) **continuous.** The hammering never stopped, so it was *continuous.*

(18) **effect.** Here you need a synonym for "result," which is *effect.*

(19) **affected.** Nothing influenced the judge's ruling, so *affected* is your answer.

(20) **hung.** The word *hung* is best when you refer to something suspended on a wall.

(21) **further.** *Further* refers to time, the context of the word in this sentence.

(22) **affects, accept.** In the first blank, you want a synonym for "influences," *so* affects is your answer. In the second blank, you need a synonym for "agree to," *or accept.*

(23) **more than.** *Memos,* a plural, calls for *more than.*

(24) **among, much.** Because more than two employees are talking, *among* is the one you want. *Between* works for couples, not mobs. In the second parentheses, *much* is the choice because *difference* is singular.

(25) **less.** The word *paper* is singular, so *less* is appropriate.

(26) **many, amount.** *Many* works for plurals, and *memos* is a plural word. In the second parentheses, the singular *paper* is the issue. *Number* works with plurals, but *amount* is for singular expressions.

(27) **more than.** When you're talking about *sheets,* you're in plural land. Use *more than.*

(28) **less.** It may take *fewer* employees to shelve the issue, but it takes *less* energy, because *energy* is singular.

(29) **over.** One year calls for *over,* the term for singulars.

(30) **amount.** The word *material* is singular, even though the term may refer to a ton of stuff, as in *the material in my file cabinet that I don't want to work on.* Singular takes *amount.*

(31) **between.** In comparing two potential candidates for leadership awards, *between* is best.

(32) **fewer.** *Employees* is a plural, so *fewer* does the job.

(33) **amount.** Here you're talking about *barking* (yes, the boss barks too), so *amount* is needed for the singular term.

(34) **Among.** If you're looking at *all the inhabitants of New York City,* you're talking about more than two people. Hence, *among.*

(35) **lies.** The character, in suitably pale makeup, rests in bed, so *lies* is correct.

(36) **sit.** The doctor isn't placing something else on the bed but instead is making a lap. Go for *sit.*

(37) **set, lose.** To place something somewhere calls for the verb *set.* To *lose* your temper is an idiom, an expression that doesn't always fit the dictionary definition of the words in it. "Temper" is a state of mind, especially in terms of anger or calmness. "To lose your temper" is "to become angry."

(38) **lie, sit.** Both of these spots call for personal body movements, not the placement of something else. *To lie* and *to sit* deal with plopping in bed, on the couch, or in a chair.

(39) **laid, loose.** Because the doctor placed the wreath, the verb of choice is *to lay,* and the past tense of *to lay* is *laid.* The dog got free, or *loose.*

(40) **lies.** This one is a bit tricky. The doctor *lays* the wreath, but the wreath itself just *lies* (rests) there.

(41) **sit, lose.** The lover will pull out a chair and *sit* in it, not place an object somewhere. Eventually the lover will depart, so the doctor will *lose* the lover.

(42) **lain.** The lover has been stretched out in a bed, in the traditional soapy coma, so the verb must be a form of *lie*. The combo form of *lie* is *lain*.

(43) **sits.** The doctor isn't placing something, just staying in a chair, eating. The verb is *to sit*, and the form that matches *doctor* is *sits*.

(44) **II.** *Irregardless* has gained acceptance in recent years, but Standard English still scoffs at this word. Substitute *regardless*. *A lot* is always written as two words. Option II makes both corrections. Option I correctly includes *a lot* but leaves *irregardless*. Option III has both errors.

(45) **I, III.** Another nonstandard expression is *being that*. Use *because* or *as*, which appear in options I and III. To express an A-OK situation, opt for *all right*. The single-word version *(alright)* is all wrong. Both errors appear in option II.

(46) **I.** The expression *try and* says that the speaker is going to do two things: *try* and *answer*. But the real meaning of the sentence is "try to answer." Option I changes *try and* to *try to*. Option III includes *myself* used for emphasis, a proper job for that sort of pronoun, but does not correct *try and*.

(47) **II.** *Try and* isn't Standard English because it refers to two separate actions. Substitute *try to*. The expression *should of* isn't standard; substitute *should have* (as in option II) or *should've* (as in option III). The two-word expression, *a lot*, is acceptable. The single-word *(alot)* is a no-no. Option II also fixes all three problems, but the other options don't.

(48) **I, III.** The expression *would of* isn't proper English, so option II is out. *Should have* (option I) and *could have* (option III) are fine. All the options properly write *all right* as two words.

(49) **III.** *Being that* isn't standard, so option II drops out. Option I incorrectly inserts *himself* where *he* should be. The *-self* pronouns provide emphasis or show that the action doubles back onto the subject. Only option III corrects both mistakes.

(50) **I, II.** The contraction *should've* is the short form of *should have*. The contraction appears in option I and the full version in option II. Option III incorrectly changes this expression to *should of*.

(51) **II.** *While,* a word that refers to time, doesn't fit the context of this sentence, so option I is wrong. *Being that* isn't standard, so option III drops out. Option II correctly substitutes *because* for *being that*. All three options correctly use *could've* or *could have*.

(52) **II, III.** Option I includes *gotta,* a nonstandard expression. The substitutes *has to* (option II) and *must have* (option III) are fine. Did I catch you with *tries and fails* in option II? *Tries and* implies two separate actions, and in option II two actions appears: Kevin *tries* (option I) and *fails* (option II).

(53) **I, III.** Delete *being that* wherever you find it (option II, for example); send in *because* or *as* instead, as options I and III do.

(54) **I, III.** The expression *being* is fine in options I and III because it's not used as a faulty substitute for *because*. Instead, it's a gerund — a fancy grammatical term for an *-ing* verb form functioning as a noun. Option II incorrectly includes *being that* as a reason, not as a gerund. In all the options, *himself* is properly used as a pronoun doubling back to refer to the subject

(55) **III.** *Myself* adds emphasis or may show action doubling back on the subject. Neither condition exists, so options I and II are wrong. Option III correctly substitutes *I*.

Here are the answers to the "Overachievers" section:

Lloyd Demos Dies at 81: Historian Who Specialized in Ancient Egypt

Lloyd Demos died yesterday as he was pursuing ~~farther~~ **further** study in ancient Egyptian culture. Demos, who ~~effected~~ **affected** the lives of many residents of our town, had ~~alot~~ **a lot** of varied interests. Demos ~~should of~~ **should have** been famous, but he was shy and ~~couldn't~~ **could** hardly stand talking to reporters. The historian, ~~who's~~ **whose** curiosity ~~continuously~~ **continually** led him to attend lectures from experts in every field, knew 12 languages. ~~Being that~~ **Because** he spent much time studying ancient Egyptian grammar, ~~its~~ **it's** not surprising that his writing was always ~~alright~~ **all right**. Demos had just ~~set~~ **sat** down to lunch when he felt ill. ~~Irregardless~~ **Regardless**, Demos insisted on finishing his ~~grill~~ **grilled** cheese. After eating he said, "I am tired and would like to ~~lay~~ **lie** down." Demos, who wrote ~~over~~ **more than** 50 books, will be fondly remembered.

1 2 3 4 5 6 7 8 9 10 11 12 13 14 15

---

(1) *Farther* refers to distance; *further* is for time, intensity, or duration.

(2) *Effected* can be a verb, but as such it means "to be the sole agent of change." In this sentence "influenced" is the more likely meaning, so *affected* is the one you want.

(3) *A lot* is always written as two words.

(4) *Should of* isn't proper English. Go for *should have* or *should've*.

(5) The double negative *couldn't hardly* should be replaced by *could hardly*.

(6) *Who's* is short for "who is," but here you want the possessive, *whose*.

(7) *Continuously* means there are no breaks, and the action never stops. Lectures occur from time to time, so *continually* is the word you need here.

8. *Being that* isn't proper English. Opt for *because*.

9. *Its* is a possessive form. Here you need the contraction *it's*, which is short for "it is."

10. *All right* is always two words, never one.

11. *Sat* is the past tense of *sit*, which is the verb you want for plopping your body in a chair. *Set* is to place something somewhere else.

12. Although some grammarians accept *irregardless* in informal conversation, this word isn't appropriate for a newspaper article or anywhere else you need formal language. *Regardless* expresses the same idea and is correct in Standard English.

13. The cheese sandwich is *grilled*, not *grill*.

14. *Lie* is "to rest or recline"; *lay* (in the present tense) is "to put something down somewhere." Demos wants to rest, so *lie* is appropriate.

15. Fifty books is plural, so *more than* comes into play. *Over* is for singular terms.

Appendix

Grabbing Grammar Goofs

How sharp are your eyes? This appendix is the grammatical equivalent of an optometrist's chart. If you can see it with 20/20 vision, you'll spot 30 mistakes in each of the first four exercises. Of course, after you spot the errors, your mission is to correct them. The errors may involve faulty structure or word choice, punctuation, capitalization, and anything else the *English Grammar Workbook For Dummies,* 3rd Edition covers.

Spotting and correcting errors prepares you for standardized writing tests. The last two exercises in this chapter go even further by mimicking a common format. If you're preparing for one of those tortures — sorry, *exams* — these exercises will help. Even if you aren't sharpening No. 2 pencils for the SAT, the ACT, or a similar challenge, you can still improve your grammar and writing style by working through exercises seven and eight.

Exercise One

Sneak a peek at the college catalogue (from a university that exists only in my mind) in Figure A-1. This course description has many faults — 30, by my count. Your count may differ slightly depending on how you group your answers. Don't worry about numbers — your mission is to search and destroy the mistakes.

6901 World Domination (3 credits): Professor Peck, Mr. Lapham, Ms. Austin. One two-hour lecture period every two weeks is required. Three periods of fieldwork per week is also required.

This course on world domination and dictatorship involve both lecture and that they put into practice what students will learn. A student will report to their faculty advisors once a month. Everyone must keep a journal of revolutions started, governments overthrown, and peasants' oppressed. Readings include Karl and Groucho Marx's masterful essay, "Laughing All The Way to The Throne", and Chairman Mayo's autobiography, *Hold the Bacon*. This is sure to interest students who's career plans are to be an emperor; tsar; dictator; or reality-show winner. By the time the course concludes, students have gathered all necessary information about what it takes to rule the world. We will be discussing topics such as propaganda, how you can manipulate the media, and telegenic coronation clothes (including crown-jewel selection). Working in the field, spy networks will be set up and students will recruit foreign agents, this will count as a quarter of the grade. The students's task is to outmaneuver everyone in the course by becoming the first to conquer a hostile country required for graduation. Exams also emphasizes real practical skills, and theoretical ideas. Students only write two papers.

Admission to this course and it's sequel (Universal Domination) are by permission of the Department of Politically Science Irregardless of age or class rank, applicants should be as motivated than the average freshman and should try and visit the departmental office for an interview.

FIGURE A-1: A scary sample course description that needs some work (in more ways than one).

Exercise Two

This letter from a made-up publisher, in Figure A-2, is full of errors. Try your hand at correcting all 30.

Higgen Publishing Company

459 elm Avenue

Bronxton, VT 05599

October 31, 2020

Mr. Chester Slonton

33 Warwickville Road

Alaistair, CA 90990

Dear Mr. Slonton:

Thank you for sending us your novel, "The Lily Droops at Dawn." To read over 1,000 pages about a love affair between plant's is a unique experience. In your talented hands, both of the plants becomes characters that are well rounded and of great interest to the reader. Before Mr. Higgen, whom you know is our founder, commits to publishing this masterpiece, I must ask for some real minor changes.

Most of the editors, including Mr. Higgen, was confused about the names. You are absolutely right in stating that each of the lovers are in the lily family, scientifically they have similar characteristics. Calling the lovers Lila and Lyle would not of been a problem if the characters were distinguished from one another in personality or habits or appearance. Unfortunately, your main characters resembles each other in petal color and height. True, one of the lilies is said to be smartest, but the reader doesnt know which.

A second problem are the love scenes. You mention in your cover letter that you can make them more lengthier. Mr. Higgen feels, and I agree, that you write vivid; nevertheless, we think you could cut them alot without losing the reader's attention. After all, once a person has read one flower proposal, he or she has essentially read them all.

Finally, the ending needs work. When the lily droops, the book ended. Are you comfortable with a tiny change. Market research shows that books with happy endings appeal to the readers, whoever he or she may be. These volumes sell good. Instead of drooping, perhaps the lily could spread it's petals and welcome the dawn. Or become a rose.

Higgen Publishing would like this novel for their fall list. I hope that you are open to the changes I had outlined in this letter. I cannot help but mention that Higgen Publishing is probably the only publisher with experience in plant romance volumes I look forward to having talked with you about the editing process.

Sincerely,

Cynthia Higgen

FIGURE A-2:
A sample letter from a publisher (with a lot of mistakes, so you know it must be fake).

Exercise Three

Try your hand at editing the newspaper article in Figure A-3. You should find 30 errors, including some in the quoted material. (If you're quoting someone who makes a grammar error, you may usually leave the error in the quotation in order to convey the speaker's style or personality. For the purposes of this exercise, however, correct every mistake.)

Hold the Tights: a Former Television Star Plays Shakespeare

Silver, the actor that played a talking horse on the Emmy-winning series *Mr. Said* is now starring in the Royal Theater production of "Hamlet." The handsome blond recently agreed to discuss his approach to acting. It were never about talking, in Silvers' view. As he had munched oats and sipped delicately from a water pail, the colt explained that he learned to talk at the age of one. Him talking was not fulfilling enough, only acting met his need for recognition.

"I started by reciting monologues for whomever would listen," he said. Then one day I got a call from a Hollywood agent offering me the part of Mr. Said." Tossing his mane in the air, Silver continued, "I plays that role for nine seasons. You get typecast. Nobody doesn't want to take a chance on your dramatic ability if someone else is available for the role." He added, "Sitting by the phone one day, it rang, and my agent tells me that I had a audition." That audition resulted in him getting the part. Silver is the only horse that have ever played Hamlet, as far as he knows.

The actor has all ready began rehearsals. His costume includes a traditionally velvet coat but no tights. "Between you and I," he whispered, "the tights snag on my fur." Director Ed Walketers asked Silver to consider shaving, and he also tried several types of material for the tights. Even Silver's wife got involved in this key costuming decision. "No one tried harder than her to find tights I could wear," Silver said. Nothing was suitable for this most rarest situation.

Silver is equally as involved with the role itself. "I relate to Hamlet's problems," he explained. "Us horses often find it hard to take action and being decisive." The role is also exhausting; Silver lays down for a quickly nap every day before having gone onstage as Hamlet.

FIGURE A-3: A sample newspaper article with a plethora of errors.

Exercise Four

Don't you hate computer manuals? The one in Figure A-4 is even worse than the usual techno-babble because it contains 30 mistakes. Correct them!

Installing You're New Worp Wheel

To install the worp wheel, a computer should first be turned off, then follow these simple steps.

Important: If you have an A4019 or a newest model, please discard this manual. You must have sent for manual number 218B, or, in the case of a computer that previously has a worp, for manual number 330B. Being that your computer is not covered in this manual, discard it. Faulty directions have been responsible for explosions and that software crashed.

1. Unpack the worp wheel which looks like a sharks tooth.

2. Unpack the two disk poles. Grasp the disk pole that is more flatter. Lining up the teeth with the teeth on the worp. *Note:* Teeth should be brushed alot with a WorpBrush. see the enclosed order form for more information.

3. After the teeth are tight clenched, a person should insert the worp disk into slot C. However, if the worp disk has a blue strip, in which case it should be inserted into slot D. Don't mix up the slots as the computer will catch fire. Neither of these slots are open when the computer is standing upright. Sit the computer on its side before beginning this step.

4. Turn on the computer. If the screen is blank call the service specialist at 914-555-5039. If the screen blinks rapid from red to green (or from blue to yellow in model 2W4T), run further from the screen. This means the worp was installed improper, the computer is altogether unusable.

5. You are almost ready to enjoy your new worp!! Tap a finger on the screen that is not wearing any rings, including wedding rings. Depending upon the model number, either press firmly or softly. Some worps can work good no matter what the pressure.

FIGURE A-4: The world's biggest headache inducer: A sample of a poorly written computer manual.

Exercise Five

If you're a high school student, sooner or later you're likely to encounter a reading passage that tests your grammar skills. Standardized tests, such as the SAT and the ACT, hit you with multiple-choice questions about a paragraph desperately in need of revision. If your school days are in the rear-view mirror, you can still sharpen your editing skills with this exercise, which resembles what you may encounter in standardized testing (but with a little humor thrown in).

Directions: Following this student essay are six questions. Choose the best answer.

[1]Being a teenager, a large part of my life takes place at school. [2]I love most of the academic experience. [3]But one aspect of school is frowned upon by me: tests. [4]Every year the school board, college admissions offices, and my personal teachers give more and more tests. [5]Sometimes I spend more time explaining what I know than I do having relaxed in the cafeteria.

[6]Last year the arts curriculum included a unit on technology. [7]Acquiring knowledge and relaxing with friends should be the primary reason for school. [8]I created a great movie script, cast the roles, and built the sets. [9]I only filmed one scene. [10]Why? [11]I was spending the days filling in little bubbles with a pencil. [12]When I offered my movie as an alternative to boring exams, the school board said no.

[13]Students should be able to skip their tests if they have another way to show how much they have learned. [14]The student will be happier, and the alternative assessment will be more valuable (Hollywood pays a lot), and exams create stress.

121 Which of the following is the best revision of Sentence 1?

(A) No change.

(B) Being a teenager, most of my life happens at school.

(C) Being a teenager, I spend a large part of my life at school.

(D) A large portion of every teenager's life takes place at school.

122 How may Sentences 2 and 3 be combined most effectively?

(A) No change.

(B) I love most of the academic experience, but tests are frowned upon by me.

(C) Accept for tests, I love most of the academic experience.

(D) I love most of the academic experience, but I frown upon tests.

123 How should Sentence 5 be revised?

(A) No change.

(B) Sometimes I spend more time explaining what I know, than I do relaxation in the cafeteria.

(C) Sometimes I spend more time explaining what I know than relaxing in the cafeteria.

(D) Sometimes I spend more time having explained what I know than I do having relaxed in the cafeteria.

124 Sentence 7 should

(A) remain where it is

(B) be deleted

(C) be moved to the end of the second paragraph

(D) be moved to the end of the third paragraph

125 Which of the following is the best revision of Sentence 9?

(A) No change.

(B) I filmed only one scene.

(C) Only I filmed one scene.

(D) I did film only one scene.

126 To improve this essay, what should be done with the third paragraph (Sentences 13 and 14)?

(A) No change.

(B) Delete Sentence 14.

(C) Add an additional example of a useless test.

(D) State that this essay represents the author's opinion.

Exercise Six

If you plan to fill little ovals with pencil lead anytime soon — or even if you don't — you can hone your writing skills with this exercise, which is set up in the same format you may meet on a standardized test. Read the essay and answer the questions that follow. *Note:* This essay is a little silly in terms of subject matter, but the questions are serious. And so are the SATs and ACTs and the rest of the "alphabet soup" of exams!

Directions: Following this student essay are six questions. Choose the best answer.

[1]A wise man once said that, "You may as well be yourself because being someone else requires too much makeup." [2]Being yourself isn't as easy as you may think. [3]First, you have to figure out who you are. [4]And who you are is defined in many ways. [5]Your family gives you one definition. [6]The society in which you lived in this current time also gives you a definition. [7]Really important are the choices you make because your experiences affect who you are.

[8]Once, when I was beginning a new school, I walked into the cafeteria of that school where I would be studying. [9]People were all over, and no one knew or cared who I was. [10]No one, except for the kid who threw his mashed potatoes at me, even saw me. [11]After I retaliated by slipping a slice of pizza into his backpack, I sat down to think. [12]Who would I be in my new school — a nerd, a jock, an activist? [13]I decided to devote all my energy to student government and nominated myself for office the very next day. [14]I gave free pizza to everyone who promised voting for me. [15]Society gave me a chance to prove myself by giving me a new school, even though I had burned down the old one. [16]My choices have led me to my true self. [17]Today I can proudly say that I am a successful politician and the owner of 2,592 pizzerias.

127 Which of the following, if any, is the best revision of Sentences 1 and 2?

(A) No change.

(B) Omit "that" from Sentence 1.

(C) Place Sentence 2 before Sentence 1.

(D) Delete Sentence 2.

128 In the context of this essay, which sentence, if any, would be a good addition to the first paragraph?

(A) No change.

(B) Self-definition is a lifelong task.

(C) No one really understands his or her own identity.

(D) Identity is a private matter.

129 What is the best revision, if any, of Sentence 6?

(A) No change.

(B) Your society which you had lived in also gives you a definition.

(C) The society, in which you will have lived, also gives you a definition.

(D) The society in which you live also defines you.

130 To improve Sentence 8, what should the writer do?

(A) No change.

(B) End the sentence after "cafeteria."

(C) Delete the words between the commas.

(D) Change "was beginning" to "had begun."

131 Which is the best revision, if any, of Sentence 14?

(A) No change.

(B) I gave free pizza to whoever will promise a vote for me.

(C) I gave free pizza to everyone who promised to vote for me.

(D) Giving free pizza, everyone promised to vote for me.

132 What change, if any, would you make to this essay?

(A) No change.

(B) Mention politics and pizza in the first paragraph.

(C) Insert additional examples of choices in the first paragraph.

(D) Place Sentences 16 and 17 in a concluding paragraph, expanding on the ideas they contain.

Answers to Exercise One

In the following figure the errors from the original course description are boldfaced and crossed out, with a possible correction following each one, as well as an occasional addition of a missing word or mark. All corrections are boldfaced and underlined. Check the corresponding numbered explanations that follow the revised course description.

6901 World Domination (3 credits): Professor Peck, Mr. Lapham, Ms. Austin. One two-hour lecture period per week is required. Three periods of fieldwork per week ~~is~~ **are** also required. [1]

This course on world domination and dictatorship ~~involve~~ **involves** both lecture and ~~that they put into practice~~ **practical application of** what students ~~will~~ **learn**. [2] [3] [4]

~~A student~~ **Students** will report to their faculty advisors once a month. Everyone must keep a journal of revolutions started, governments overthrown, and peasants**'** oppressed. Readings include Karl and Groucho Marx's masterful essay, "Laughing All ~~T~~**t**he Way to ~~T~~**t**he Throne**,**", and Chairman Mayo's autobiography, *Hold the Bacon*. This **reading list** is sure to interest students ~~who's~~ **whose** career plans are to be an emperor**,** tsar**,** dictator**,** or reality-show winner. By the time the course concludes, students **will have** gathered all necessary information about what it takes to rule the world. We will be discussing topics such as propaganda, ~~how you can manipulate the media~~ **media manipulation**, and telegenic coronation clothes (including crown-jewel selection). Working in the field, ~~spy networks will be set up~~ **students will set up spy networks,;** ~~this~~ **fieldwork** will count as a quarter of the grade. The ~~students's~~ **students'** task **that is required for graduation** is to outmaneuver everyone **else** in the course by becoming the first to conquer a hostile country ~~that is required for graduation~~. Exams also ~~emphasizes~~ **emphasize** ~~real~~ **really** practical skills**,** and theoretical ideas. Students ~~only~~ write **only** two papers. [5] [6] [7] [8] [9] [10] [11] [12] [13] [14] [15] [16] [17] [18] [19] [20] [21] [23]

Admission to this course and it**'**s sequel (Universal Domination) ~~are~~ **is** by permission of the Department of ~~Politically~~ **Political** Science. ~~Irregardless~~ **Regardless** of age or class rank, applicants should be as motivated ~~than~~ **as** the average freshman and should try ~~and~~ **to** visit the departmental office for an interview. [22] [24] [25] [26] [27] [28] [29] [30]

1. The subject is *three periods,* a plural, so the verb (are) must also be plural.

2. The subject *course* is singular, so the verb *(involves)* must also be singular.

3. To keep the sentence parallel, the noun *lecture* should be coupled with another noun, not with a subject/verb combo.

4. The *practical application* is simultaneous to the learning, so future tense isn't what you want. Go for present *(learn).*

5. The paragraph refers to *students* (plural), so a shift in one spot to singular is inappropriate. Also, in formal English, a singular noun (a student) doesn't pair with a plural pronoun (their). This rule is evolving, and "their" is increasingly accepted as a match for a singular noun. Changing "A student" to "Students" ensures that all readers see this sentence as correct in Standard English.

6. The original sentence includes the possessive *peasants'* for no valid reason. The possessive form should be linked to a noun, but here it precedes a verb form (oppressed).

7. In titles, articles (such as *the* in this title) shouldn't be capitalized.

8. When a comma follows quoted material, the comma is placed inside the closing quotation mark.

9. In the original sentence the pronoun *this* is vague. Insert the clarifying expression *reading list.*

10. The contraction *who's* means "who is," but the sentence calls for the possessive *whose.*

11. Items in a series are separated by semicolons only when one or more of the items contain a comma. In this series, no item contains a comma, so semicolons aren't necessary.

12. A future deadline (by the time the course concludes) calls for future perfect tense (will have gathered).

13. To make a list parallel, all items must have the same grammatical identity. In the original list, you have two nouns and one subject–verb combo. Change the subject–verb combo to another noun, "media manipulation," and the problem is solved.

14. The original sentence contains a dangler, *working in the field.* An introductory element containing a verb form must refer to the subject, and *spy networks* aren't *working in the field.* Reword the sentence so that the *students* are *working in the field.*

15. Two complete sentences may not be joined by a comma. Substitute a semicolon or make two sentences.

16. The pronoun *this* is too vague all by itself. In the original, *this* may refer to setting up spy networks or recruiting foreign agents. Change *this* to *fieldwork* and the sentence is clear.

17. To create a possessive form for a plural ending in the letter *s,* just add an apostrophe, not an extra *s.*

18. The student is *in* the course and so must be compared to everyone *else.*

(19) In the original, this misplaced description seems to say that *a country* is required for graduation, not the *task*. Descriptions should be close to the word they describe.

(20) The plural subject, *exams*, requires a plural verb, *emphasize*.

(21) The description *practical* should be intensified by an adverb (really), not by an adjective (real).

(22) If you unite two complete sentences with the word *and*, a comma precedes the *and*. If you unite two of anything else (in this sentence, two nouns — *skills* and *ideas*), no comma precedes the *and*.

(23) The descriptive word *only* should precede the word being compared — in this case, *only two* as compared to three or four or whatever the professor assigns.

(24) Possessive pronouns have no apostrophes.

(25) *Admission* is singular and takes a singular verb, *is*.

(26) The adjective *Political* describes the noun *Science*. *Politically* is an adverb and may describe only verbs (speaking politically) or other descriptions (politically inexperienced).

(27) A statement should end with a period, which is missing in the original.

(28) *Irregardless* isn't Standard English though it is increasingly popular in conversational English. Because this text appears in an official document (a course description), formal English is better. Substitute *regardless*.

(29) *As* and *than* don't belong in the same comparison. An *as* comparison is for equal items and a *than* comparison for unequal items.

(30) *Try and* implies two actions, but the sentence refers to one that should be attempted. The proper expression is *try to*.

Answers to Exercise Two

In the following figure the errors from the original letter are boldfaced and crossed out, with a possible correction following each one, as well as an occasional addition of a missing word or mark. All corrections are boldfaced and underlined. Check the corresponding numbered explanations that follow the revised letter.

Higgen Publishing Company

31 → 459 ~~elm~~ **Elm** Avenue

Bronxton, VT 05599

October 31, 2020

Mr. Chester Slonton

33 Warwickville Road

Alaistair, CA 90990

Dear Mr. Slonton:

Thank you for sending us your novel, ~~"The Lily Droops at Dawn."~~ ***The Lily Droops at Dawn.*** To read **32**

33 → ~~over~~ **more than** 1,000 pages about a love affair between plants is a unique experience. In your talented

34 → hands, both of the ~~plant's~~ **plants** ~~becomes~~ **become** characters that are well rounded and ~~of great interest~~ **35**

36 → **interesting** to the reader. Before Mr. Higgen, ~~whom~~ **who** you know is our founder, commits to publishing **37**

38 → this masterpiece, I must ask for some ~~real~~ **really** minor changes.

39 → Most of the editors, including Mr. Higgen, ~~was~~ **were** confused about the names. You are absolutely right

40 → in stating that each of the lovers ~~are~~ **is** in the lily family**;** scientifically they have similar characteristics. **41**

42 → Calling the lovers Lila and Lyle would not ~~of~~ **have** been a problem if the characters were distinguished

from one another in personality or habits or appearance. Unfortunately, your main characters ~~resembles~~

43 → **resemble** each other in petal color and height. True, one of the lilies is said to be ~~smartest~~ **smarter**, but the **44**

45 → reader doesn**'**t know which.

46 → A second problem ~~are~~ **is** the love scenes. You mention in your cover letter that you can make them ~~more~~ **47**

48 → lengthier. Mr. Higgen feels, and I agree, that you write ~~vivid~~ **vividly**; nevertheless, we think you could cut

49 → them ~~alot~~ **a lot** without losing the reader's attention. After all, once a person has read one flower proposal,

he or she has essentially read them all.

Finally, the ending needs work. When the lily droops, the book ~~ended~~ **ends**. Are you comfortable with a

50 → tiny change**.?** Market research shows that books with happy endings appeal to the readers, whoever

51 → ~~he or she~~ **they** may be. These volumes sell ~~good~~ **well**. Instead of drooping, perhaps the lily could spread **53**

52 → it**'**s petals and welcome the ~~dawn. Or~~ **dawn or** become a rose. **55**

54 →

56 → Higgen Publishing would like this novel for ~~their~~ **its** fall list. I hope that you are open to the changes I

57 → ~~had~~ outlined in this letter. I cannot help ~~but mention~~ **mentioning** that Higgen Publishing is probably the **58**

59 → only publisher with experience in plant romance volumes**.** I look forward to ~~having talked~~ **talking** with you **60**

about the editing process.

Sincerely,

Cynthia Higgen

(31) Proper names are capitalized.

(32) The title of a full-length work (in this case, a novel) is italicized or underlined, not enclosed in quotation marks.

(33) *Over* precedes a singular word, and *more than* precedes a plural.

(34) *Plants* is a plural, not a possessive, so no apostrophe should appear.

(35) *Both* is plural and should be matched with the plural verb *become*.

(36) The original sentence isn't parallel because it pairs the simple description *well rounded* with the phrase *of great interest*. The correction changes the phrase to a simple description, *interesting*.

(37) The pronoun *who* is needed to act as a subject for the verb *is*.

(38) *Real* is an adjective and appropriate for descriptions of people, places, things, or ideas. The adverb *really* intensifies the description *minor*.

(39) *Most of the editors* is a plural subject and requires a plural verb, *were*.

(40) *Each of the lovers* is a singular subject and requires a singular verb, *is*.

(41) A comma may not join two complete sentences. Use a semicolon instead.

(42) *Would of* doesn't exist in Standard English. The proper expression is *would have*, here changed to the negative *would not have*.

(43) The plural subject *characters* needs the plural verb *resemble*.

(44) *Smartest* is for the extreme in groups of three or more. Because only two lilies are compared, *smarter* is correct.

(45) The contraction *doesn't* contains an apostrophe.

(46) The singular subject *problem* takes the singular verb *is*.

(47) Double comparisons aren't correct. Use *lengthier* or *more lengthy*.

(48) The verb *write* may be described by the adverb *vividly* but not by the adjective *vivid*.

(49) The expression *a lot* is always written as two words.

(50) The present-tense verb *ends* works best with the rest of the sentence, which contains the present-tense verb *droops*.

(51) This sentence, a question, calls for a question mark instead of a period.

(52) The plural pronoun *they* refers to *readers*.

(53) *Good* is an adjective, but the sentence calls for the adverb *well* to describe the verb *sell*.

(54) A possessive pronoun, such as *its*, never includes an apostrophe.

(55) The expression *or become a rose* is a fragment and may not stand as a separate sentence.

(56) A company is singular, so the matching pronoun is *its*.

57 The helping verb *had* is used only to place one action in the past before another past action.

58 *Cannot help but mention* is a double negative.

59 Every sentence needs an endmark. This statement calls for a period.

60 *Having talked* implies a deadline, and the sentence doesn't support such a meaning.

Answers to Exercise Three

In the following figure the errors from the original article are boldfaced and crossed out, with a possible correction following each one, as well as an occasional addition of a missing word or mark. All corrections are boldfaced and underlined. Check the corresponding numbered explanations that follow the revised article.

---

61 Hold the Tights: ~~a~~ **A** Former Television Star Plays Shakespeare

Silver, the actor that played a talking horse on the Emmy-winning series *Mr. Said*, is now starring in the **62** Royal Theater production of ~~"Hamlet."~~ *Hamlet*. The handsome blond recently agreed to discuss his **63** approach to acting. It ~~were~~ **was** never about talking, in ~~Silvers'~~ **Silver's** view. As he ~~had~~ munched oats **65** and sipped delicately from a water pail, the colt explained that he learned to talk at the age of one. ~~Him~~ **66** **His** talking was not fulfilling enough~~,~~**;** only acting met his need for recognition. **68**

"I started by reciting monologues for ~~whomever~~ **whoever** would listen," he said. ~~"~~Then one day I got a **70** call from a Hollywood agent offering me the part of Mr. Said." Tossing his mane in the air, Silver continued, "I ~~plays~~ **played** that role for nine seasons. You get typecast. Nobody ~~doesn't want~~ **wants** to take a chance **72** on your dramatic ability if someone else is available for the role." He added, "Sitting by the phone one day, ~~it rang~~ **I heard the phone ring,** and my agent ~~tells~~ **told** me that I had ~~a~~ **an** audition." That audition resulted **75** in ~~him~~ **his** getting the part. Silver is the only horse that ~~have~~ **has** ever played Hamlet, as far as he knows. **77**

The actor has ~~all ready~~ **already** ~~began~~ **begun** rehearsals. His costume includes a ~~traditionally~~ **traditional** **80** velvet coat but no tights. "Between you and ~~I~~ **me**," he whispered, "the tights snag on my fur." Director Ed **81** Walketers asked Silver to consider shaving, and ~~he~~ **Silver** also tried several types of material for the tights. Even Silver's wife got involved in this key costuming decision. "No one tried harder than ~~her~~ **she** to **83** find tights I could wear," Silver said. Nothing was suitable for this ~~most rarest~~ **rare** situation. **84**

Silver is equally ~~as~~ involved with the role itself. "I relate to Hamlet's problems," he explained. "~~Us~~ **We** **86** horses often find it hard to take action and ~~being~~ **to be** decisive." The role is also exhausting; Silver ~~lays~~ **lies** down for a ~~quickly~~ **quick** nap every day before ~~having gone~~ **going** onstage as Hamlet. **90**

---

(61) The first word of a title and a subtitle should always be capitalized.

(62) *Silver* identifies the horse being discussed. The original sentence has a comma at the beginning of the long, descriptive expression (*the actor who played a talking horse on the Emmy-winning series* Mr. Said) but none at the end. The second comma is necessary because the information supplied is extra, not essential to the meaning of the sentence. It should be set off from the rest of the sentence by a pair of commas.

(63) The title of a full-length work (in this sentence, a play) should be in italics or underlined.

(64) The singular *it* pairs with the singular verb *was*.

(65) A singular possessive is formed by the addition of an apostrophe and the letter *s*.

(66) The helping verb *had* places one past action before another past action, but in this sentence the actions take place at the same time. Drop the *had*.

(67) The possessive pronoun *his* should precede an *-ing* form of a verb that is being used as a noun (in this sentence, *talking*).

(68) Two complete sentences shouldn't be joined by a comma. Use a semicolon instead.

(69) The subject pronoun *whoever* is needed as the subject of the verb *would listen*. The preposition *for* may have confused you because normally an object follows a preposition. However, in this sentence the entire expression (whoever would listen) is the object of the preposition, not just the pronoun.

(70) A quotation mark belongs at the beginning and the end of the quotation.

(71) The past tense verb matches the meaning of the sentence.

(72) The pronoun *nobody* is singular and requires a singular verb, *wants*.

(73) In summary of speech, past tense works best. *Tells* is present tense. *Told* is past tense.

(74) In the original sentence, *it* (the phone) is sitting by the phone — illogical! Reword in some way so that the speaker is sitting by the phone. Another possible correction: Add a subject/verb combo to the beginning of the sentence so that it begins "When I was sitting by the phone."

(75) Before a noun beginning with a vowel sound, *audition*, you need *an*, not *a*.

(76) The possessive pronoun *his* should precede the *-ing* form of a verb that is being used as a noun (in this sentence, *getting*).

(77) Because *only one horse* is the meaning of the pronoun *that*, the verb paired with *that* is singular. *Has* is singular, and *have* is plural.

(78) The single word *already* means "before this time," the meaning required by the sentence.

(79) *Begun* is the form of the verb *to begin* that is used with a helping verb. Here it's paired with *has*.

(80) The adjective *traditional* describes the noun *coat*.

(81) *Between* is a preposition and thus takes an object. The pronoun *me* is an object.

(82) Two males appear in the sentence *(Silver* and *Ed)*, so the pronoun *he* is unclear. Substitute a noun.

(83) The missing word in the original is *did*, as in *than she did. Her* is inappropriate as the subject of the implied verb *did*.

(84) Both *most* and *rarest* express the same meaning. You don't need both. Delete *most* and the error is fixed.

(85) The comparison *equally* should not be followed by *as*.

(86) *We* is the subject pronoun needed here. *Us* is for objects.

(87) To keep the sentence parallel, *to be* should be paired with *to take action*.

(88) *To lay* is "to place something else somewhere." *To lie* is "to rest or to recline," the meaning here.

(89) The noun *nap* must be described by an adjective *(quick)*, not an adverb *(quickly)*.

(90) The sentence is in present tense, and two actions are mentioned — *lies* and *having gone*. See the mismatch? Change *having gone* to *going* and you stay in the present, the best tense for habitual actions.

Answers to Exercise Four

In the following figure the errors from the original manual are boldfaced and crossed out, with a possible correction following each one, as well as an occasional addition of a missing word or mark. All corrections are boldfaced and underlined. Check the corresponding numbered explanations that follow the revised manual.

91 Installing ~~You're~~ **Your** New Worp Wheel

92 To install the worp wheel, ~~a computer should first be turned off~~ **first turn the computer off**, and then follow **93** these simple steps.

94 *Important:* If you have an A4019 or a ~~newest~~ **newer** model, please discard this manual. You must ~~have sent~~

95 **send** for manual number 218B, or, in the case of a computer that previously ~~has~~ **had** a worp, for manual **96**

97 number 330B. ~~Being that~~ **Because** your computer is not covered in this manual, discard ~~it~~ **the manual**. **98**

99 Faulty directions have been responsible for explosions and ~~that software crashed~~ **software crashes**.

1. Unpack the worp wheel, which looks like a shark**'**s tooth.
100 **101**

102 2. Unpack the two disk poles. Grasp the disk pole that is ~~more flatter~~ **flatter**. ~~Lining~~ **Line** up the teeth with **103**

104 the teeth on the worp. *Note:* Teeth should be brushed ~~alot~~ **a lot** with a WorpBrush. ~~s~~**See** the **105**

enclosed order form for more information.

106 3. After the teeth are ~~tight~~ **tightly** clenched, ~~a person should~~ insert the worp disk into slot C. However, if **107**

the worp disk has a blue strip, ~~in which case it should be inserted into slot D~~ **insert the worp into** **108**

slot D. Don't mix up the slots as the computer will catch fire. Neither of these slots ~~are~~ **is** open when **109**

110 the computer is standing upright. ~~Sit~~ **Set** the computer on its side before beginning this step.

111 4. Turn on the computer. If the screen is blank**,** call the service specialist at 914-555-5039. If the screen

112 blinks ~~rapid~~ **rapidly** from red to green (or from blue to yellow in model 2W4T), run ~~further~~ **farther** from **113**

114 the screen. ~~This~~ **Blinking** means the worp was installed ~~improper~~ **improperly**; the computer is **115**

altogether unusable. **116**

117 5. You are almost ready to enjoy your new worp**!**! Tap a finger **that is not wearing any rings, including** **118**

wedding rings, on the screen ~~that is not wearing any rings, including wedding rings~~. Depending upon

119 the model number, ~~either~~ press **either** firmly or softly. Some worps can work ~~good~~ **well** no matter **120**

what the pressure.

(91) The contraction *you're* means "you are." In this sentence you want the possessive pronoun *your*.

(92) An introductory verb form (To install the worp wheel) must refer to the subject, but the subject in the original sentence is *a computer*. Reword the sentence so that the subject is the person who is installing — the understood *you*.

(93) The adverb *then* is not capable of uniting two complete sentences on its own. Delete the comma and insert *and*.

(94) The *-est* comparison singles out one extreme from a group of three or more. In this sentence you're talking about a comparison between two things only — model A4019 and the group of everything *newer*. (The group counts as one thing because the items in the group aren't discussed as individuals.)

(95) The verb *send* is in present tense and addresses what the installer must do now, not what the installer must have done previously. The present perfect tense (have sent) implies a connection with the past.

(96) The word *previously* tips you off to the fact that you're talking about past tense, so *had* works better than *has*.

(97) The expression *being that* is not standard; use *because* instead.

(98) The pronoun *it* must have a clear meaning, but the original sentence provides two possible alternatives, *computer* and *manual*. The correction clarifies the meaning of *it*.

(99) Two terms linked by *and* need a similar grammatical identity in order to keep the sentence parallel. The original sentence joins a noun (explosions) with a clause (that software crashed). The correction links two nouns, *explosions* and *crashes*.

(100) A description beginning with *which* is usually set off by a comma from the word it describes.

(101) The tooth belongs to the shark, so you need the possessive *shark's*.

(102) *More flatter* is overkill. The *-er* form creates the comparison, and so does *more*. You can't use both terms in one comparison. The easiest correction is to cross out *more*. You can also keep *more* and change *flatter* to *flat*.

(103) The original sentence is a fragment; it has no complete thought. The correction has a subject (the understood *you*) and a verb (line) and a complete thought.

(104) The expression *a lot* is always written as two words.

(105) A sentence always begins with a capital letter.

(106) *Tightly* is an adverb, needed to describe the verb *clenched*.

(107) *A person* is a new expression in this piece, which has been addressing *you* either directly or by implication. For consistency, change *a person* to the understood *you*.

(108) The original is a fragment, not a complete sentence. The reworded version has a complete thought.

(109) The pronoun *neither* is singular and takes the singular verb *is*.

(110) *Sit* is what the subject does by bending knees and plopping onto a chair. *Set* means that you're placing something else into some position.

(111) An introductory expression with a verb is usually set off by a comma from the main idea of the sentence. Insert a comma after *blank*.

(112) The adverb *rapidly* is needed to describe the action *blink*.

(113) *Farther* is for distance, and *further* is for time or intensity. Here you need the distance word.

(114) The pronoun *this* is too vague. Go for the specific term, *blinking*.

(115) The adverb *improperly* is needed to describe the action *installed*.

(116) A comma isn't strong enough to link two complete sentences. Dump the comma and insert a semicolon.

(117) Don't double up on endmarks. One per sentence does the job.

(118) The description is in the wrong place in the original sentence. Place it after *hands*, the word being described.

(119) The duo *either/or* should link words or expressions with the same grammatical identity. In the original sentence, a verb-description combo is linked to a description. Move *either* so that two descriptions are linked.

(120) The adverb *well* is needed to describe the verb *can work*.

Answers to Exercise Five

If this were a real standardized test, by now you'd be sleeping and a machine the size of a small country would be scanning your answers and tallying your score. Sadly, here you have to check your own work. The payoff is that the explanations reinforce some important points about writing.

(121) **C.** The original sentence contains a description attached to the wrong word. The introductory verb form (*Being a teenager*) must describe the subject, but in the original it's attached to *a large part of my life*. Choice (C) fixes the problem by changing the subject. Did I catch you with (D)? Grammatically it's fine, but because the rest of the paragraph is in first person (the *I* form), the first sentence should be also.

(122) **D.** The switch from active voice (*I love*) to passive (*is frowned upon*) isn't justified. Choices (C) and (D) stay active, but (C) misuses a word. *Accept* is "to receive freely." The word that rules something out is *except*. Therefore, Choice (D) is the best answer.

(123) **C.** The original sentence isn't parallel because *explaining* is paired with *having relaxed*. Choice (C) corrects the parallelism error and keeps the correct tense — present — because the author is discussing an ongoing, current situation.

(124) **D.** Sentence 7 is a general statement that explains why tests are a pain and socializing is fun. You may use it in the first paragraph (not an option in the answer list) or in the third paragraph, which is where Choice (D) places it, because the introduction and the conclusion discuss the same ideas.

(125) **B.** The description *only* should precede the comparison. Here the writer is talking about *one scene*, not *many scenes* or the whole movie, so *only* belongs in front of *one*. The tense change in Choice (D) isn't justified by the meaning of the sentence.

(126) **A.** Surprised? The last paragraph of this essay is the conclusion, explaining the author's point of view. You don't need to label it as opinion — Choice (D), because the reader already knows. Why else would the writer make these statements? Nor do you need additional examples or a different order. The conclusion could be expanded by adding a statement reinforcing the ideas in the essay (Sentence 7, for example), but the answer choices don't include that option.

Answers to Exercise Six

Last but not least, here are the answers that belong to this lovely essay on the virtues of being oneself. Take a look at the answers and explanations to see whether you found all the errors — grammatical errors, that is. I'll let you figure out what else this writer is doing wrong. Buying votes is just a start!

(127) **B.** When you introduce a quotation with a speaker tag (*A wise man once said*), the tag is followed by a comma and the first word in the quotation is capitalized. A quotation introduced by *that* has no comma and no capital letter, unless of course the first word is a name. In this case, dropping *that* solves both the capital letter and the comma problem.

(128) **A.** The first paragraph is short, but it does the job of introducing the ideas in the essay. The other choices are off-topic.

(129) **D.** Context tells you that the time period of this sentence is the present. Therefore, you need the present-tense verb *live*, not the past-tense verb *lived*.

(130) **B.** By the time you get to *cafeteria*, you already know that the writer is enrolled (and presumably *studying*) in that school. Why add extra words?

(131) **C.** You can't promise *voting*, only *to vote* or *a vote*. Therefore, the original doesn't work. Choice (B) falls apart because the first verb, *gave*, is in past tense. It doesn't pair well with the second, future perfect verb, *will have promised*. Choice (D) fails because the introductory verb form (*Giving*) must describe the subject, and *everyone* isn't giving pizza. Choice (C) is the answer you seek.

(132) **D.** Essays should be focused, so adding examples at random to paragraph one doesn't work. Nor does deleting the first paragraph, as it serves a purpose: to set the stage for the anecdote in the second paragraph. What's missing is a true conclusion. The closest thing this essay has to a conclusion is the last two sentences. Give them their own paragraph and expand on the ideas to create a stronger ending.

Index

About the Author

Geraldine Woods has taught every level of English from 5th grade through AP. She's the author of more than 50 books, including *English Grammar For Dummies*, 3rd Edition; *Basic English Grammar For Dummies*; *1001 Grammar Practice Questions For Dummies*; *SAT For Dummies*, 8th Edition; *AP English Language and Composition*; and *AP English Literature and Composition* (all published by Wiley). She's also the author of *Webster's New World Punctuation: Simplified and Applied* (Webster's New World) and a number of nonfiction children's books. She blogs at www.grammarianinthecity.com about current trends in language and ridiculous signs she encounters on her walks around New York City. Her current favorite sign reads, "Help Wanted: Grilled and Deli Man."

Author's Acknowledgements

I owe thanks to my elementary school teachers — nuns who taught me how to diagram every conceivable sentence and, despite that fact, also taught me to love language and literature. I appreciate the efforts of Tim Gallan, a project editor second to none; Lindsay Lefevere, Wiley's acquisitions editor; Cindy Kaplan, the technical reviewer; and Sophia Seidner, my supportive and attentive agent.

Dedication

For Elizabeth and Lucette, whom I love more than words can express. And for Harry, who will always live in my heart.

Publisher's Acknowledgments

Executive Editor: Lindsay Sandman Lefevere

Project Editor: Tim Gallan

Technical Reviewer: Cindy Kaplan

Production Editor: G. Vasanth Koilraj

Cover Image: © Veronica Lara/Shutterstock